Growth in the Spirit

Growth in the Spirit

FRANÇOIS ROUSTANG, S.J.

translated by Kathleen Pond

SHEED AND WARD : NEW YORK

Originally published as Une initiation à la vie spirituelle,

Library of Congress Catalog Number 65–12204

Imprimi potest:
Ph. Durand-Viel, S.J.
Praep. Provinc. Paris.

Nihil obstat:
Thomas J. Beary
Censor Librorum

Imprimatur:
✠*Robert F. Joyce*
Bishop of Burlington
March 14, 1966

The Nihil Obstat and Imprimatur are official declarations that a book or pamphlet is free of doctrinal or moral error. No implication is contained therein that those who have granted the Nihil Obstat and Imprimatur agree with the contents, opinions, or statements expressed.

Manufactured in the United States of America

CONTENTS

Growth in the Spirit

INTRODUCTION

To try to initiate people into the spiritual life by means of a book is an uncertain venture. Personal contact alone can enable one to demonstrate a truth and to put over an experience, but it is precisely such contact that is here lacking. How otherwise than in conversations can one sense the intercourse that can be established between the Spirit of God and our spirit? On this point tradition speaks in no uncertain terms: the disciple in search of God must set himself to listen to a spiritual master who will speak, not in technical terms, but as a witness who has seen and touched the Word of Life. To enable people to penetrate into this world of the Spirit, neither exact demonstration, logical sequence of deduction nor forceful thinking, however useful they may be, can replace the living evidence of interior knowledge—that knowledge which, through the resonance of the very words, makes the listener long to taste this life which to him is a closed book.

Again, no study can adapt its message to the particular needs of the person who is feeling his way towards God. This is especially true of the beginnings of such effort. The spiritual universe is like an unknown land, whose language, although grasped in a physical way, still remains impossible of interpretation. The complete absence of points of comparison robs the most striking evidence of its significance. Dialogue alone is then capable of making us gradually familiar with the speech of this distant country. Later on, however, when our first stammerings have been forgotten, what stagnation we experience and how far we wander from the right path, because we are incapable of grasping the meaning of the words that God utters in our lives, words that would enable us to understand his will.

If such be the case, what justification is there for this book? Are not the following pages perhaps merely an initiation for those already initiated, a key to open a door the threshold of which has already been crossed? It should be possible, however, for what is written here to be used as an invitation to those who have neither time nor opportunity to converse about the things of God, to give greater attention to the utterances of the Spirit.

In any event, an analysis of the spiritual life and an attempt to trace its main lines are justified if they prove capable of inspiring the reader with the desire to understand a world that has up to now remained closed to him, although he has really been living in it for a long time past. At first he will perceive nothing but gratuitous and vague assertions. Then, in the expressions he finds, he will begin to sense the faint echo of what is happening in him. He may perhaps be encouraged to go patiently on his way and to discover the track along which the search for God must pass. The Christians who consider their baptism as a permanent invitation to draw near to the Lord who is waiting for them, are still all too few. It would thus seem desirable that something should be written on the subject. As to those who spontaneously consider the life of the Spirit that has been transmitted to them as an extraordinary adventure in which they will be swept along sometimes without knowing it, they are few and far between.

There is, moreover, another aspect. If any written initiation into the spiritual life is justifiable, it is because it includes many factors that are universally true. It is no doubt necessary to translate them into our own language, to recognize them in ourselves as personal and incommunicable elements, to understand them in so far as this is possible. In this sense the effects of the Spirit in each one of us are unique and cannot be expressed in a general study. The divine action, however, whose model is Jesus Christ, remains at bottom identical for all. The human-divine laws of the Redemption are permanent and are not modified by the vicissitudes of subjectivity. They are universal. We must therefore endeavor to express them for the use of the greater number of men. Under different forms, they preside over each man's destiny, demand the consent of all, and make possible among Christians marked with the sign of the Trinity, the understanding that makes the gifts received bear fruit.

These pages are, moreover, the result of numerous conversations in which, despite the obvious variety of graces and paths, similar obstacles, identical stages and the renewed insistence of a God and Saviour who makes use of the simplest and most constant means, were revealed. Contact with souls has enabled us to discover the different ways in which the Master calls men to a growing intimacy with him. It is sufficient, however, to go beyond the fortuitous circumstances of God's intervention and the formulas in which personal aims have too large a place, to arrive at the certainty that the ways of God always offer the same characteristic features. For in his images he always acts according to the nature of his love.

No claim is made, however, of having reached absolute universality in this book, or of putting forward teaching in which every Christian could find the means of facilitating his spiritual progress. Consciously, although seldom explicitly, the developments advocated refer to the tradition emanating from St. Ignatius, who suggests an itinerary corresponding to the vocation for which God had prepared him. In the Church, however, he stands side by side with saints whose counsels are equally valid. What is linked with a particular spiritual family and depends on a certain form of apostolic life, clearly could not be imposed universally. On the other hand, those who seek God in the active life in the heart of the modern world will certainly be able to draw deeply from this rich stream.

Honesty obliges us to add that it is never possible to understand or express perfectly the way in which a saint has lived out the Gospel, both as a whole and in the harmonious blending of its elements. That is why we are anxious to stress that this work is *one* initiation among others. Inevitably each presentation is limited and contracts or falsifies the message which it believes it is transmitting with respect. If it did not run this risk, however, it would only provide the reader with a series of abstract propositions without any living cohesion. It is thus essential, taking our reflections and experience as a basis, to attempt a new synthesis, which others in view of their particular lights or greater understanding will be able to adjust, correct and perfect. The essential thing is surely to set out on our way and to let God show us what we are neglecting—aspects of the Gospel that are as yet unknown to us and which we shall gradually have to assume in peace and courage.

It is with a view to preventing deviations, always possible in a work of this nature, and to break down any narrowness in it, that it is essential to retain this link with a particular system of spirituality. A saint, privileged by nature and grace, has linked together the fundamental aspects of the teaching of the Gospel in view of the needs of his time and the task assigned to him by God, to the extent of becoming by his life and thought a model whose value the Church guarantees for us. If we take him as a guide, we do so knowing how difficult it is to accept the Gospel in its entirety and depth, and to respect its unity, when we want to adapt it to new historical circumstances. Unless we are endowed with genius and are also receiving exceptional graces, we are in considerable danger of going off the right track as soon as we leave the paths of mediocrity. Among our Lord's words we are tempted to choose those we find to our liking or which seem more important in our eyes, without realizing that this process of selection destroys the harmony of the Christian life. To take our place in the school of a master will not dispense us from the effort necessary for the personal response we have to make, here and now, to God's voice. For us such a master is like a touchstone, all the more valuable when the contact is made through the intermediary of a living tradition that prolongs his action in the Church.

As the plan of the book indicates, the spiritual life such as St. Ignatius conceives it gravitates wholly around the decision to accomplish the present will of God. That is why he insists on the preliminary analysis of the forces which are moving us to action. It is essential to know of the spirit whose impulses we are to be able to accept or reject. Such an analysis, however, presupposes the rejection of sin and an attachment to Jesus Christ. It is only when these conditions are fulfilled that the choice can be made correctly. It is then followed by a period of trial, inseparable from any carrying of a project into effect and necessary for attaining to true joy, the first-fruits of the Resurrection. In thus characterizing the two facets of the spiritual life, St. Ignatius is merely expressing in his own way the pure teaching of the Gospel.

It is indeed to acceptance of the Father's will that Christ Jesus invites us. He wants us to imitate him to the point of identifying ourselves with him by seeking our sole nourishment in the injunctions of the Creator. If Christ's message is summed up by love, he means this love as a continual acceptance of the commands of him who loves us. The loving exchange to which we are gradually led by the Holy Spirit is identified with the re-casting of our existence by the new commands that God imposes upon us. Outside of this perspective, the spiritual life, which is essentially dialogue between the Spirit of God and the spirit of man, would be limited to crying "Lord, Lord" and not, as Christ asks, to realizing the designs of the Father through the accomplishment of his will. When the rivers of living water flow from the open side, it is to conform the creature in all circumstances to the desires of the Creator; it is to enable human liberty to recognize God's inspirations and to restore it to the obedience of the day of creation.

It is, however, difficult in practice not to give the father of lies the opportunity of leading us astray. That is why Christ recommends us to be cunning like the serpent that we may thus frustrate his plans. We often dream of a spontaneous spirituality that would attune us to God and make us tend towards him as instinct attracts us to the things of this world. If the Spirit can one day become as a second nature in our souls, he will never dispense us from correcting the two-sidedness of our interior movements, of which we are in danger of being the victims. Christ wishes to see his faithful followers as wise as the children of darkness, and reproaches them for abandoning themselves to spiritual idleness and for being thus taken in by pharisaical hyprocrisy. If we are to recognize the presence of the Spirit and patiently to discover the characteristic traits of his action, it is essential for us to become increasingly intelligent. We go to considerable trouble to decipher the face of the heavens and the earth, to foresee the moment when rain or torrid heat will come. Why not learn to distinguish the signs that announce the visit of the Word? In order to receive him in the truth of the Spirit and follow him where he may wish to lead us, we must ceaselessly discern his ways.

But if we are not already purified, it is impossible to discern in the Spirit the coming of the Son. Before calling upon the apostles to walk with him to Jerusalem, Christ had driven out the impure spirits and cleansed from sin the threshing-floor of this world in order to winnow the good grain at his pleasure. Thus the Gospel is full of this paradox: he who has come to deliver us from evil is the occasion of its recrudescence. As soon as Christ appears the demons come out of their lair and the struggle with them becomes ever more violent and more painful. The enemies of Christ too are forced to reveal themselves and to bring out into the full light of day the designs they preferred to keep hidden. This is necessary, for the Spirit cannot gush forth freely so long as the source is not freed from sand, so long as the stains of this world, once revealed, are not borne by Jesus Christ and changed by him into love. It is when he has cast the demons into the sea that he can cure the sick and make them hear the breathing of the Spirit.

Such, then, according to the Gospel, is the first facet of the spiritual life. The conditions are filial obedience and lucid decision which submits to God's will. But the spiritual choice, which makes both purification of the heart and clear-sightedness necessary, is yet merely the time of courtship. We could not espouse the Word and share with him the bread of consolation if he did not empty us of ourselves in the trial of the agony and the cross. Night is more favorable to union than the light of day, for it allows the old creation to disappear from our eyes and no longer to disturb us with its mirage. To discover the nearness of God who is hidden from the gaze of men, it is good to lose sight of our certainties and even of the promises he has made us—that of restoring the kingdom of Israel, that of sitting with him to judge the twelve tribes. In seeking him in vain in the tomb where he was placed, we shall allow the Spirit, and him alone, to bring us the true faith that is beyond all hope. Perfect love is capable of seeing the beloved go away without taking anything back, either of love or of the total gift which handed over the very substance of one's being. In the darkness the exchange is consummated. At the center of nothingness the Spirit rises alone so that everything may be filled.

In so far as the cloud of the Spirit covers the world, the Word can there espouse mankind and manifest himself, both from without and within. When it is no longer man who lives but Christ who lives in him, all reality becomes transparent in the love of the Father for his Son. To accomplish the work of God in this universe or to converse with him in secret are now but the two facets of a single uninterrupted search. Christ can indeed come to us when all the doors are closed or he can be taken up to heaven. Nothing can disappoint us for both his presence and his absence are equally clear signs of an action to which we must simply surrender. It matters little whether this assumes the appearance of suffering or of joy, whether the Spirit invades or disconcerts us, the refusal to belong to ourselves and the will to respect God's plans are asserted with an energy that is always peaceful. The universe will become a wood of trees of life and the leaves of the trees will serve to cure the nations in despair.

Thus, summed up in the filial acceptance of the Father's will under the impulse of the Spirit, the spiritual life nonetheless includes successive phases whose order of appearance is unchangeable. There is a preparation indispensable to the spiritual choice—and the latter must be lived out to its ultimate consequences. But as we still have to renew each day our decision to respond to the Trinity, the source of our life, to radiate God's glory and his grace, we have to go through the same stages continually. These stages are so many factors necessary to the equilibrium and permanence of union with God in our day-to-day existence. Such factors will increasingly appear to us as linked to each other from within. Beneath their diversity the unique and multiform action of the Spirit will manifest itself with a growing clarity in proportion as we see in him more and more the reciprocal gift of the Father and the Son.

It is scarcely possible to give an exhaustive definition of the spiritual life at this stage. The developments of this book will endeavor to indicate the elements of it. But, from the outset, there will be no difficulty in agreeing as to what the word evokes spontaneously. In the ordinary speech of our times the spiritual life is distinguished from the Christian life not by its content, which is the common faith put forward by the Church, or again by its origin, baptism, which already transmits to us the fullness of union in the life of the Trinity, but by the awareness we take of it, by the experience we can acquire of it, by the will to make progress in it. The passage from the Christian life to the spiritual life implies a personal grasp of truths that we no longer merely hear formulated, but about which we are absolutely certain because we see them as such. A particular affirmation has been repeated to us over and over again; it appears to us new when we recognize it of ourselves and it seems to us evident independently, in some sense, of the teaching received.

Moreover it would seem essential to distinguish the spiritual from the mystical life. It would thus be necessary to define the latter, yet one knows the difficulties of such a task. Let us content ourselves with saying that the spiritual life is that part of the mystical life to which every Christian can have access by the appropriate pedagogy, by intelligent and continuous search, as well as by virtuous patience. The mystical life, the essence of which is the immediacy of God's presence, presupposes an exceptional grace and lights to which no one may lay claim. On the other hand, it is normal that the Christian life should expand into the spiritual life if it opens out to the divine and human riches offered to all. To harden these distinctions would, however, be a mistake. For everything in the faith is extraordinary, just as everything can equally be considered as ordinary, if it is true that we are made by God, redeemed by him and that he constantly seeks to communicate himself to us in a way that is increasingly clear and more and more complete. What we wish to emphasize is that the very logic of the faith leads to an awareness of it and to an experimental perception of the dogmas it puts forward. Now even if we cannot all hope to become mystics, we all have to enter into this movement of the faith.

Certain readers will perhaps be disappointed by our manner of procedure. What they expect of an initiation into the spiritual life is that it should analyze the ways of approach at length—that it should tell them, for instance, how liturgical prayer, the reading of the Holy Scripture, the sacraments, action in the Church and so on can lead to contact with God. That is certainly one possible method which has, moreover, been followed by others; it is not the one we have chosen. We have judged it preferable not to linger in the outer court, but to penetrate into the Holy of Holies, to go straight to the root of the experience of God, to reach the very center of it and try to describe it. To initiate people into the spiritual life, one must show something of the relationship to God considered in itself, and not only through the manifold spheres in which it is manifested. Our eyes must thus be trained to focus on the very foundations of the existence of the redeemed creature. This does not mean that the elements of the Christian life are abandoned. They are all present but transposed under the features they assume in the personal relationship to God. Hardly anything is said, for instance, of the sacraments, but mention is continually made of life and death in Jesus Christ, the sole source of all the sacraments. Very little is said of the significance of the Church, but the transformation of mankind as a whole here appears inseparable from personal conversion. Nothing is said of the problems which our contemporaries have to face through their apostolic engagements, but the whole book revolves around the search for and accomplishment of the will of God. The spiritual life is a new reading of realities already known on another level. It is thus normal that they should be found in these pages under a form which at first may perhaps disconcert us. It would be a mistake to conclude from this, however, that they are not present.

Under these perspectives it should cause no surprise that the book should be developed on an "interior" register and that before all else it should deal with problems of the soul. If our contemporaries are justified in their distrust of excessive psychology, it is perhaps desirable to remind them that the experience of God is an inward experience. It was surely not by chance that St. Paul, in speaking of the spiritual man, used an expression equivalent to interior man. Christ himself teaches us to seek the Father in secret and asks us to turn aside from those who can destroy the soul. It is he who teaches the discernment of thoughts: "A good man out of the good treasure of his heart bringeth forth that which is good: and an evil man out of the evil treasure bringeth forth that which is evil. For out of the abundance of the heart the mouth speaketh" (Lk. 6, 45). The Spirit who gives meaning and value to all external courses of action and to all religious or secular acts must be experienced in the most remote solitudes. No one can escape this law. In their use of the words "heart," "soul," "deepest strata of the soul" or simply "depth," spiritual writers are not making a concession to pious jargon. They are trying to say in human language, following Christ, what eye cannot see and ear cannot hear. It is only when they have gone down to the depth of themselves, to the point where God gives them being, that they can find the Word of life externally, that they can hear his voice resound in the multiplicity of the things of this world.

1 THE MEETING WITH GOD

THE STRONG DESIRE to know God, no longer through books or sermons but in oneself, lies at the root of every spiritual life. We burn with a longing to reach directly, to see, touch, feel, him who has come among us, whose memory has been preserved for us. He must present himself to our eyes as someone living and in action, so that the certainty of his existence no longer rests on proof and commentary, but on the experience of a personal meeting which is sufficient in itself and, to be recognized and accepted, no longer needs a guarantee outside itself.

In order, however, that this union with God, which is the beginning and end of the spiritual life, may be established in truth and come to fulfillment, it is necessary to avoid two temptations: that of reducing our relationship with God to submission to an external law, and that of seeking in this relationship a refuge for ourselves and of claiming to be guided by our personal convictions alone. Neither of these temptations, doubtless, is found among Christians in its absolute state, for the first temptation would take us back to Judaism under the form of a crushing legalism and the second to paganism, unwilling to admit any other judge but its own experience. These two erroneous ways of understanding Christianity are of interest at least in emphasizing the two tendencies which have to be reconciled, for genuine spiritual life must spring from the uttermost depths of the spirit and impregnate every human activity.

"*God Is the Law*"

In actual fact, many Christians, particularly among men, merely envisage their religious life under the form of a system of morality. The Church has issued a series of laws which have been transmitted to them from their childhood upwards and they have learned to put them into practice together with the social habits inherited from their particular level of society. These laws they do not try to justify. Such an endeavor, they think, would lead them to doubt their faith rather than confirm it, so that it is preferable to leave the task of explanation to those responsible. Moreover, for them the Christian dogmas are often a catalogue of enunciations, praiseworthy indeed, but involving no interior compulsion and which certainly do not provide a source of life. All that matters to such Christians is to know what they have to accomplish. The more we make clear to them in detail what has to be done, without supplying them with various arguments, the more satisfied they will be. Such men have the faith and a faith that is active, but they refuse to enter into what they consider subtleties, which may very well disturb their singleness of aim and, finally, inhibit them, whereas it is urgent for them to pass to acts.

In spite of its defects, this way of living out Christianity already embraces a genuine religious attitude. Obedience to laws that we have not chosen for ourselves and from which it would be relatively easy to work free presupposes the recognition, through them, of a presence which goes beyond man and which is alone capable of imposing an obligation on us. It is possible that the fear of judgment or of some force which must not be estranged, enters for a considerable part into the acceptance of rules which demand of us considerable and almost constant sacrifices. Yet, even if we do not know it, it is by this means that we are trained in the first rudiments of respect for God. Those who claim to have freed themselves from such things are in danger of falling into a religious sentimentality which the claim of having already overcome the fear of Another greater than we are, cannot conceal.

Beneath the refusal to penetrate into the labyrinth of the arguments in justification of Christian morals, it is possible to see something other than idleness of spirit. It is possible to see the conviction that God is God and that he has the right to impose upon us, through his Church, laws that we cannot understand, since he never ceases to be the master of life and death for us. The explanations will never catch up with the force and value of the obligation; if we came to the point of submitting because we understood, the divine injunctions would be reduced to comfortable prescriptions. There is, then, in these Christians the vague feeling that their religion infinitely surpasses the power of man; that the system of morals to which they submit, will always assume an aspect that is incomprehensible and will thus include some portion of constraint which must be attributed to the transcendence of God and the absolute gratuitousness of Revelation. Between what the Church lays down as to the duties of every Christian and the explanations she gives, is there not a certain distance, so that she takes care not to pledge her authority in the same way in both? Just as it is neither desirable nor beneficial for a father or mother always to explain his or her orders, and it would be dangerous to wait until the child was able to understand and take responsibility for an action before making him accomplish it, so it is unreasonable to accept only those obligations of Christian morality whose meaning is clear to us.

This conception, indeed, has obvious limitations—there is the danger of its leading to a kind of estrangement which, far from putting us in relation with God's transcendence, keeps us, as it were, on the outside of ourselves. Considered as a first stage, however, it is a means of educating the conscience, and provides a training that is indispensable to the development of spiritual powers. This is the case, moreover, in every sphere, for without a certain measure of constraint, man does not move beyond the spontaneity of the animal, which follows the attractions and whims of its instincts. He does not attain to the self-mastery which the development of conscience requires.

The moral life, to which so many Christians limit themselves, presents a second aspect. For them it is their way of enrolling themselves as members of a society and of preserving their relationship with others. This was already so in the case of the Jewish people who regarded the observance of the Law as the safeguard of the community and the secret of its permanence. There is a good deal of criticism nowadays of what is called sociological faith, i.e., that which is founded primarily and before all else on belonging to a certain milieu, to a particular land or nation. Clearly the weaknesses of a belief that may disappear by the mere fact of transplantation do not need to be stressed. But in so widespread a fact, we must surely see one of those undeniable human truths which the deepest and most solitary union with God could never abolish. It is our belief that we are never alone and that the communion of the faith is always prior to the acts that we can posit personally. Just as awareness of oneself presupposes the discovery of our awareness of others, so the respect for God which governs our destinies implies the respect for a Church that is more than ourselves and that exists in one sense independently of us. To despise a faith which is chiefly expressed in practices is thus to be in danger of making any more personal assertion inconsistent and impossible. It is perhaps also to cut off religion from one of its indispensable orientations.

Christians who confine themselves to the defense of moral values even if they are unaware of the developments which such values prepare the way for, are nonetheless the nameless auxiliaries of those who are called to a Christian life that is more transparent in its foundations and in its ends. Through the application of the law transmitted by revelation, it is God, in fact, who everywhere penetrates the community and diffuses his love through it. The rules of conduct which are a bond for the people of God prepare and train them to receive the Lord whose will it is to transform his own into himself. Without the persistence of this collective aspect, the spiritual life would be in danger of dissolving into an individual effort which would no longer have anything Christian about it except the name. On the other hand, the respect for objective laws valid for all men, reminds us that, if faith comes through the intermediary of the community and can only grow in it, it is essential to serve the community in order to become a new leaven in it. That is why those who confine themselves to morals have the right to say to so many spurious spiritual persons who shut themselves away in their solitude, that the social effectiveness of the law is worth more than the barrenness of a belief that is alleged to be something above the common. The spiritual life cannot be lived without a relationship to others; indeed, it alone gives us the means of communicating with mankind as a whole. The objective rules are a guarantee of its authentic nature and prevent us from ever putting our confidence in our own judgment without having previously confronted that judgment which comes from God.

A third characteristic of this moral life which prepares us for the life of the spirit consists in its perpetual requirement of self-denial. Without going beyond the awareness that they are giving obedience to rules, many Christians attain to a certain form of self-resignation. They have not thought much about the different forms which the action of God might assume in their lives, but they do not deviate from the truth they know. They will most probably have a tendency towards pharisaism, for, in accepting the principles of existence they have given themselves, they become more concerned with being true to themselves than to the will of God. The heroism of submission to the law then becomes a caricature of death to their own will. They will likewise be tempted to leave aside certain aspects of Christian morality to which they are particularly sensitive, so much so that often we see them enclosing themselves within an inflexible barrier which excludes any re-examination of their position in any real sense. Yet even when these dangers are taken into account, it remains abundantly clear that Christian morality will be able to obtain from such people sacrifices which, although not spectacular, will gradually lead them towards the detachment of the Gospel.

But these characteristics of every Christian life—the sense of divine transcendence, the union of men in obedience to God's will and the necessary passing through self-renunciation—can neither be achieved nor linked together so long as we remain on the level of morality alone. Doubtless, unity already exists in a certain manner, through faith in Christ, and in baptism, but it does not yet appear as such in the eyes of him who is the subject of it. By reason of the general and abstract character of the law, the observance of it does not really enable us to reach God. So true is this that after having seen him reveal himself in the law in order to enable us to have access to him, we have to abandon the law to find him. God is in the law, which is why it can educate me, and I must accept it from his hand, but he is not the law; when I am practicing morality, the desire of finding God himself must pervade my whole being and make me feel how remote fidelity to the commandments is from that concrete meeting which alone is able to quench my thirst for God.

To cease to rely on morality and on our own works is perhaps one of the most difficult of renouncements, but it alone is capable of making us share in the Cross of Christ; and this death to ourselves is the condition of the renewal of our life. Christian mortification, i.e., burial with Christ, is not to be confused with the heroism which accepts the accomplishment of what goes against our tastes and our desires. It is essentially, for man, the refusal to trust in his own strength.

Finally, if morality can show us that laws are necessary to give a particular society its structure and gather its members together, it is incapable of conceiving the union of all men in Christ. Confining itself, in fact, to what it sees, it takes note of the variety of customs and religions, but it does not show how this variety could one day be surpassed. The Spirit alone is powerful enough to reunite mankind in a single body. The law, on the other hand, brings with it the rejection of those who refuse to submit to it; and for absolute disobedience it will never be able to find any other remedy than death. It is beyond the multitude of morals and practices and even through their apparent opposition that the Spirit, speaking to the heart, will be able to cause the walls of separation to fall.

In a word, to confine oneself to the moral life such as the Church can formulate and define it clearly century by century, is to go back to the revelation of the Old Testament and renounce in practice the finding of the God who is Trinity. If we wish to go beyond the frontiers of the law we must learn to observe the injunction of the Father to die in Christ Jesus, in order that the Spirit may establish on earth, by delivering us from evil, the universal Kingdom of God.

"*God Is My Conscience*"

At the opposite pole from those for whom Christianity is nothing more than a system of morality can be found others, perhaps chiefly among women, who reduce it to a secret life, the sole domain of which is the soul's intimacy. The God whom we adore is not only, in fact, he who enumerates our duties but the "God perceptible to the heart."

The essential part of religion is lived within in that place hidden from all eyes, in that interior universe whose riches and variety are in no sense less than those of the landscapes of this earth. Those who are "actives," desperately anxious about the organization of this world and turned towards what is external, do not suspect the existence of another side of things and even have a tendency to despise those who cling to it. Yet, if God is immanent to the world and to each human being, it is essential to seek him beyond appearances and to set out to discover the lost continent where, if we succeed in penetrating, we shall always be alone.

More often than not it is at the time of adolescence that new eyes are given us to perceive this world of thoughts and feelings hitherto unsuspected. Then we no longer want a Christianity imposed from without, but a religion in accordance with the deepest part of ourselves that can be justified in its smallest details and that is of such a nature that it can be understood. External practices interest us only to the extent that we feel their truth and significance, so that we reject the constraints which cannot be integrated into our conceptions of man and the world.

Taken up with the difficult discovery of our ego, we are unwilling to go out of ourselves to find others. It thus seems more important, in view of the progress of our Christian life, to cling firmly to our own being in so far as that being is unique. God, who is beyond the universe, is also in the world to give it life and stability. In this perspective it is thus legitimate to consider Christianity as a doctrine bringing to each one his own good and not as a law of bronze, prone to merge together the variety of men under the same impersonal yoke.

However justified it may be, the assertion of the immanence of God in the world, while it rejects a Jewish-inspired way of envisaging our religion, leads inevitably towards a disguised form of paganism. Morality, for instance, will lose its character as a concrete entity to dissolve into a dust of rules which each one, according to his sentiments and within the limits of his intelligence or his possibilities, will apply to himself in view of the particular circumstances. Under the pretext of adapting ourselves to the complexity of situations and persons, and certain that Jesus Christ has come not to crush but to set free, we carve out for ourselves from the forest of intangible principles those standards of behavior that are most flexible. All this ill conceals a confusion between God's presence in all things, respectful of each one, and the emergence of a spontaneity inebriated with its own autonomy. We are then at the antipodes of the severe training given by the moral law which ran contrary to our instincts but protected us from spiritual retarded development.

Every Christian today is more or less contaminated by the frenzy of man's self-assertion, dazzled as he is by the powers put into his hands. He claims to carry the truth of the Incarnation of Christ forward to its uttermost consequences. Since God has become man and has gone so far as to make us understand our likeness to him, it is from us alone that the conduct and enterprises of each day must come. We must never agree to submit ourselves to the crushing orders which come to us from outside. We want to set ourselves up as free, sentient beings, capable of forging our own destiny, because God is no longer the distant person reigning in heaven, but is among us and is remaking the universe in us and through us. Beneath these pretentious ways which claim to be adult, it is the adolescence of our Christianity which is revealed in its need of opposing the father of the family in order to assert a personality which is still uncertain of itself. Even if it is not an attribute of women, this attitude derives from the feminism of our world seized with panic as it is before confrontations that are inevitable. It continually seems to escape from the harsh countenance of reality. There is no question here of putting our age on trial, but of showing that the discovery of the inner self in which we think we shall find God, goes hand in hand with man's claim to make himself the judge of his own actions.

Yet in order that our faith may be able to grow and expand, it is necessary to pass through this stage. If faith has nothing in common with a narcissism in which conscience seeks to justify itself in the mirror which reflects but its own image, it cannot do without a return within itself to realize that God really wishes to come into us and himself become, as Spirit, the source of our being, thoughts and actions. It is likewise good to reject the figure of a God of constraint who takes pleasure in denying our desires and tastes, so that we may thereby discover in him the goodness which is deeply concerned with our own personal good.

In these circumstances it is normal that the discovery of the interior life and the need for development should lead to the calling in question of the ideas received and principles accepted by our milieu. At this level it is certain that we do not reject such notions in order to attain to a deeper contact with God, but because they kill us with their letter. However lacking in purity this revolt may be, it can serve as a touchstone for the spiritual life, for, to entrust ourselves to the Spirit of God, we must have felt the strength and weakness hidden in the human heart. Submission to social precepts can, in fact, make us inaccessible to the breath from on high and serve as an obstacle to the coming of God. When these protecting walls have fallen under our blows, for a moment we think ourselves freer, but in the instant that follows we taste the bitterness of a solitude incapable of fending for itself.

Because there is an infinite distance between the feeling of our wretchedness and the recognition of the Saviour who could deliver us from it, we shall be tempted to follow, in one way or another, the way taken by the pagan mystics. Instead of facing suffering, man will seek to withdraw himself from it and progressively to deny it by establishing in himself that impassive retreat where the eternal half-smile of the Buddha holds sway. To assume pain, suffering and death, to give them meaning, the daring of God himself was necessary. Human wisdom seeks to provide against this by flight into an interior world where nothing happens any more and where our unawareness of drama is the only means of not seeing it arise. Often in our interior life we are in quest of that blessed invulnerability or insensitivity, in which so many of mankind, ignorant of Christ, have sought to see the supreme virtue. Many a time religion has been denounced as a lying refuge. How can we deny that, instead of turning towards God in our religion, we all find in it primarily our rest and expect from it more a balm to heal our wounds than a light constraining us to become changed men?

When our own awareness becomes the touchstone, the denial of suffering goes hand in hand with the denial of the suffering of others and of the world. In comparison with interior calm and richness, the events and the course of history can only be illusions destined to vanish as they have appeared. If the Christian does not formulate the motives which govern him precisely in this way, he yet links himself in practice to those sterilizing, fixed metaphysics which dream, not of arresting the movement of the universe, but of forgetting it for ever. All that matters, in fact, is the increasingly total absorption of the ego in an absolute, without form or figure, very similar to nothingness.

Christians who accord an exclusive value to the immanence of God in the world, to the autonomy of the human person and to man's development are not mistaken in seeing therein characteristic elements of their religion. They are wrong, however, in not asserting at the same time the complementary truths. They do not realize that thereby they come upon results that man is incapable of attaining by his own means. Forgetting that we have to look to Jesus Christ for salvation and that no one is capable of saving himself, they want to reach immediately the term of the unitive life in which all will be in us, because God will be our only good. Such an attitude comes to confuse the Holy Spirit with the vague omnipresence of an ego, co-extensive with the universe through its desires and perhaps above all through its dreams, unless it claims to carry all things forward to their completion by making itself absent from all, as if it were sufficient to blind oneself in order to abolish trouble and suffering.

Reintegrated, however, into Christian truth as a whole, these statements remain valid. There is no spiritual life possible, in fact, without the conviction that the wealth of the whole universe is contained in each one of us, that the God who has come among us can be sought in this world, and that in short he wills nothing other than our greatest happiness. Yet all these truths are nothing more than mirages when we are guided by them alone. Just as the divine transcendency, which links men by means of the Cross, becomes a Jewish caricature of Christianity when it claims to account for the whole of reality, so the immanence of God which is the basis of the autonomy of the human person and leads it to its fullness, becomes perverted into a self-complacency which denies God in precisely the measure in which it neglects the opposite truths.

Only an authentic dialogue with God is capable of giving meaning and value to the characteristics of the interior life, i.e., of founding the knowledge of self on that of the Lord, of seeking not stoical indifference but the peace born of death to self, in a word of obeying the interior Master who alone will be able to set us free and make us understand that the rules laid down by the Church are a figure of the Spirit. Thus we must now try to grasp more clearly in what our relationship with God consists in all its depths.

God Is Spirit

What is first and last in existence is the initiative of God, for in him is found the origin and absolute beginning of all things. It is thus understandable that the spiritual life, in which we see the expansion of human and even more of Christian life, has no other end but to grasp, weigh and measure this primordial fact. But it is one thing to understand this truth at the term of a well constructed and seemingly decisive chain of reasoning, and quite another to discover that, for me myself, today and for ever, such is actually the case.

When we venture to affirm that some Christians have come into close contact with God and that others who are yet striving to be faithful, still remain on the threshold, we easily lay ourselves open to the charge of spiritual snobbery, or else we even find ourselves accused of again falling into the old gnostic error of separating Christians into two categories that the Church does not recognize. Yet St. Paul, before many other witnesses of God, was already warning the Corinthians that, despite the fact of their baptism, they were not behaving as "unto spiritual, but as unto carnal . . . little ones in Christ," and that one could not "speak to them as unto spiritual" (I Cor. 3, 1), as to those who have abandoned the wisdom of this world because it is "foolishness with God" (I Cor. 3, 19). Whatever may be the complexity of the vocabulary and thought of St. Paul, it is clear that he is inviting Christians to a radical conversion in their manner of judging and understanding, by agreeing to receive "the Spirit that is of God, that we may know the things that are given us from God," this "Spirit comparing spiritual things with spiritual" (I Cor. 2, 12–13).

It is no doubt true that no one can claim to have already reached such a fullness, but surely the essential point is to start out along the road and to seek God and God alone with all our strength, so that we realize more deeply what the word *Christian* means.

The distance between the Christian who has come into contact with God and one who has not yet had that experience is like that which separates two men, only one of whom has had the experience of a great love. Both may have had the same upbringing, are impregnated with the same culture, have perhaps turned over the pages of the same books and travelled through the same countrysides. In other respects, however, they have nothing in common. If both were asked to speak of love and explain their sentiments in this respect, the difference in their views would strike us immediately. The one could appeal only to things learned from the outside, the beginning and possibility of which he perhaps senses in himself, whereas the other would express what he knows because he has lived it. Besides the resonance and tone of the voice, the latter would soon show a certain inner understanding, a comprehension capable of linking together elements at first disparate, for he sees in himself the unity of all the complementary or contradictory aspects of love which then cease to form a number of separate phases to present the manifold richness of a single reality.

What is true of love is equally true of all fundamental human experiences capable of severing a destiny in two, as if the periods prior to and following this decisive event were separated by an almost complete rupture, generally visible only to him in whom it occurred. Thus it is with some great suffering which, when it has broken our spirit, leaves us as it were absent from ourselves without support of any sort. In such cases, even with the clearest of explanations, no one talking to us can have any idea what has taken place unless he himself has passed through similar depths of suffering and, beneath the words of the other person, recognizes a moment in his own history. Are we to say to those who have thus loved or suffered that nothing new has come into their lives, and that after a short interruption things are following the same course as before? Everything in them protests to the contrary. Their eyes have been opened, their past has been abruptly torn from its roots and the future appears in a light hitherto unsuspected.

The meeting with God is an experience as real and as incommunicable as that just referred to. It is characterized by the certainty of an intervention which comes to shatter our existence or re-orientate it. It is not we who turn towards God—at least that is secondary—but it is God who first comes towards us and forces us to turn our attention to him. It is the discovery that Another whose hands and face we do not know, is imposing himself on us in an ineluctable fashion and that we are constrained, in spite of and against everything, to take account of his presence. Before he revealed himself we had, so to speak, suspected nothing. Perhaps he came to walk with us, as with the disciples of Emmaus, but we knew it not, when suddenly he was there. It is he, and already we have to say "It was he," for almost before we have recognized him he has gone. After this transient meeting we can no longer continue as if nothing had happened, for at least once (and once is enough never to forget it) heaven has been opened, at least once the glory of God has shown itself.

This experience we must not fear to call commonplace if at least we advert to what our God is—a Father who holds everything in his hands and who directs the history of men at his good pleasure, yet who continually intervenes to bring us back to him. There is nothing astonishing in the fact that from time to time in our own case we become aware of these sovereign acts which change the development of things and of human beings, transform our ways into his ways and turn us aside from our own paths. If God is the Master, why should he not manifest himself when it seems good to him? In a word, this encounter is nothing more than the definition of God in his relationship with the world, but a definition perceived, grasped, recognized, and experienced with such strength and simplicity that we can never afterwards doubt the evidence for it.

This encounter always occurs in function of some precise, actual circumstance of our existence. God never reveals himself without enjoining upon us the fulfillment of his will or without transforming us so that we become capable of serving him in some particular way. It was a young peasant of twenty-five, already engaged to be married, who amid all the noise of a village fête suddenly heard the words: "I want you to love me like Xavier." He understood at once that he must leave his land and his family behind, although it had never occurred to him before that he could become a priest. On the pier of an American port, a girl remembered a phrase which had been said to her recently, the meaning of which had escaped her at first. Realizing that she must leave everything for God, she rebelled. Years of self-torture passed, at the end of which she surrendered to him who had called her and from whom she had sought to turn aside. Examples not solely concerned, moreover, with the vocation to the priesthood or the religious life, could be multiplied. Emmanuel Mounier wrote in one of his letters:

> On very rare occasions in my life I have had this intense feeling, this spiritual quasi-certitude concerning some important orientation of my life—the first time, shatteringly, during a retreat when I became aware of an interior command (now I am talking heresy!) to drop medicine for philosophy. A second time over our marriage . . . and a third time for *Esprit* and its publishing house. . . . Like young Descartes in his mystical dream, I feel that I—I feel that we are moved forward by a mighty hand . . . along the path we have begun to trace out.*

Thus we should completely falsify the meaning of these divine interventions if we only saw in them demonstrations of God's power or magnificent but purposeless revelations concerning the depths of the Godhead. We do not know the Lord except through his injunctions and his desires, through the intermediary of his love which wills to guide us and to fashion for us, as for all men, new heavens and a new earth. This means that such an encounter can take place in many different ways, and will make use of the most unexpected opportunities. For some it will take place with a violent suddenness, for others it will appear as something quite natural at the end of a long road, as happens with those subterranean sheets of water which fertilize the soil for years, but whose presence seems to be discovered only by accident—"He was there and I knew it not; no, he was always there and I knew it. Now, however, and that changes almost everything, now I know his face." The process is

* *Mounier et sa génération* (Paris, Ed. du Seuil, 1956), p. 219.

similar to the discovery of a man whom we have met several times and whom one day we see, almost without emotion, without surprise, under the features of a true friend. In a life of real submission to the will of God, it would be astonishing if there did not emerge from time to time some form of the divine presence which gives a meaning to all that has gone before, like the light which in the morning reveals to our gaze the path travelled during the night.

Whether God's coming assumes the aspect of a blinding and almost brutal light which throws us to the ground and crushes us, or whether it enters our existence without our even having become aware of it, matters little. The essential point is the coming of our Lord into our hearts when it seems good to him, and that he should be able at his good pleasure and in accordance with his intentions which we do not at first grasp, to come and shape our destinies so that we may return to him. There is no doubt that many Christians have had this experience of God's intervention, similar to that of so many men mentioned in the Bible, from the patriarchs down to the prophets and apostles, but they have lacked the power to interpret it, because they were not prepared for it or because their attention had not been drawn to it.

It is thus now necessary to discuss the attitude which must precede or follow the divine action, unpredictable in its gratuitousness, in order that we may correspond to it fully and recognize it when it comes to us. It is the acceptance of the divine presence.

Between the gift which is given us and its acceptance, there is an infinite distance. God speaks, but it is possible to refuse to hear him; just as when our Lord gives us a command we can delay in carrying it out. To suppose that it is necessary to listen for his word to make itself heard and to obey for the order to assume consistency, would be to reverse the roles and to fail to understand that the divine decisions are without repentance—they have no need of our consent for their formulation.

The gift, however, is, just as much, independent of us because in any case it produces an effect; the advances of God cannot pass unperceived. Even through the lack of submission of some, the Master of all things will accomplish his design: "My word . . . which shall go forth from my mouth . . . shall not return to me void, but it shall do whatsoever I please and shall prosper in the things for which I sent it" (Isa. 55, 11). In the case of an obstinate refusal, the divine intervention will be followed by our fall and our ruin unless at the sight of our misdeeds, we consent to become converted.

Acceptance begins in the desire for the meeting which God gradually awakens in us before increasing it to the point of subordinating every other desire to it. So that the place which our Lord will come and fill may be hollowed out, it is necessary to deepen day by day and year by year the expectation of his coming. Otherwise our hearts would be too cluttered up to be able to recognize him easily and let him act in us according to his good pleasure. Like hunger, the desire for the Other, for the completely Other, sets us free from the slavery of the food to which we were accustomed and makes us relish that for which, in other circumstances, we should not even have wanted to stretch forth our hands. The Gospel often returns to the theme of this state of watchfulness in which Christ must find us when he comes. Now such texts not only make allusion to his return at the end of time, but to his coming day by day. How many times does it happen to us to fall asleep, wearied by this patience which nevertheless had lasted only a short time and which alone was capable of giving life to our interior senses! We indeed wish to find God, but it must be at once and he must come before us almost before he is announced. If we cannot bear to wait longer, it is because through our desire we wish to persuade God to satisfy us. On the other hand, the interminable marking time of our unfulfilled wishes constrains us to abandon the pretense of enslaving the divine power, and we surrender ourselves to it unconditionally.

The characteristic of the desire and the expectation is, in fact, to make us always ready. We know neither the day nor the hour, but that is necessary, for, if God is God, he can only come to us unexpectedly. The unpredictable nature of the encounter expresses the gratuitousness of the gift, the sovereign liberty of him who has no account to render to anyone. God does not amuse himself with us, he is not playing with us with a view to making us seek for him. If we were capable of entering into his designs, we should perceive that he always comes at the right moment, at the exact moment when it was best for us and for everyone else. The future is hidden from us and must be hidden from us, in order that we may not be tempted to construct our lives according to our own views and thereby fail to prepare ourselves for God's approach.

To be flexible will lead us gradually to want to be vulnerable. If we install ourselves in our Christian lives as proprietors, it is not that we consciously will to make use of the gifts received and put the Creator to our service, it is rather that we are afraid of him. We withdraw into a shell of habits, of generous or even heroic acts, to protect ourselves against incursions which might very well call us to account and shake the very foundations of our conceptions and our actions. There is nothing more unpleasant than perpetually surrendering ourselves to an initiative when we cannot imagine where it is going to lead us. This divine Other whose thoughts and will elude us—spontaneously we cannot help but protect ourselves from him. Otherwise, it seems that the way would be open for every wound and every upheaval. We thus prefer to give much, after our own manner, to fight and even to suffer, rather than to surrender ourselves to what always appears to us more or less as the caprice of God. It is a serious but ever-recurring temptation to wish to enjoy the good things of God and even the great graces he may have given us, as if they belonged to us. We must, then, continually learn afresh to expose ourselves to the danger of the encounter with God. The blows he inflicts are the only means he has at his disposal for opening our hearts to his action. Moreover, "he will strike, and he will cure us" (cf. Osee 6, 2).

To welcome God, to desire him, to expect him, to make ourselves flexible or vulnerable, all these words express one single reality—to accept that God's love should be renewed each day in our regard. If he seems to come on the spur of the moment, it is because his love is ever new. Charity, which is the epitome of Christianity, derives from the superabundant goodness of the Father, but his eternity has not grown old, it is always in process of being born. Our eyes cannot become accustomed to this meeting and each time, in one sense, it will be as if we had never seen or heard him before. Because he is the wholly Other, impossible to understand, to grasp and to contain. Not only is it essential that he remain outside our grasp, but we shall only be able to recognize him in the depths of our astonishment as a stranger who comes to dwell in us in a lasting manner. In the meantime, when this Other, already known but always still to be discovered, takes it upon himself to love us, our surprise turns to wonder. This God afar off, who makes himself so close and to whom, nevertheless, our gaze cannot become accustomed, makes us suspect that today life and everything is beginning, that it is the hour of our first meeting, that it is useless and pointless to know if there will be another, if there will even be a day which will be called tomorrow. To accept God is to discover in the end that his love for us is always at its beginning and that it will thus never have an end.

By its very essence, however, this love is exclusive of all other. If God were not jealous, absolutely jealous, it would be the proof that his goodness towards us was not divine, that it was incapable of contenting and satisfying us, that its movement did not tend to fill us to overflowing. Willing as he does, on the contrary, to fill us with himself alone, he comes to empty us of all else. Hence the necessity of a radical detachment which can have no other limit but death; a detachment which, in point of fact, comes from love and gradually rejects all that is not love. When St. Paul identifies baptism with going down into the tomb with Christ, when he explains that by it we are plunged into the Lord's death, he is only developing to their logical conclusions the presuppositions of divine charity. How could anything subsist outside him who is everything and how could what is apparently the rest not be inevitably brought to disappear? The cry which Isaias has transmitted to us, "I am the Lord; and there is no other" (Isa. 45, 18), is not a formula of vengeance but the assertion of a fact and the simple definition of what is evident: if I am God, there is only I and everything through me and in me. It is sufficient to have once caught a glimpse of what the divine charity could be in our regard to accept the fact that this law of exclusion is the only one to give basis to our hope, the only one to make us realize that the love of God, because it is the love of God, cannot do other than triumph over all obstacles, i.e., not make them pass through death.

Yet he who guides us along this way will often find us stubborn and desirous of eluding him. We do not easily agree to lean no longer on anything but God alone, to deny ourselves to the extent of being nothing but expectation. If we had been commanded to renounce the riches we possess, it is possible that we might find this command bitter to our taste. It is a question, however, of something quite different, of a total abandonment of all we are, or, to use the expression of the Gospel, of the hatred of self (cf. Jn. 12, 25), that is to say of the liberation from every attachment that does not come from God and is not retained for him alone. If, as some think, it was a question of withdrawing from the world, we could find access to this form of perfection by a life of effort, silence and austerity. It is necessary, however, to go further—as far as the rejection of all self-love and all self-sufficiency. What is asked of us is to recognize that of ourselves we can do nothing useful, that we have nothing to give to God and that we could take nothing from him. It remains for us to accept that he should be the giver. Or, better still, since it is through him that we receive, we must allow him to give us the power to accept.

All this is so opposed to our usual way of being and thinking that we willingly admit that it is true in theory, but consider that in practice it would be folly to conform to it. We do not wait for the Lord gradually to teach us the rudiments of this language, the first words and indeed the last words of which were taught us when we were baptized. Under the pretense of generosity we prefer to choose our own solution and we come to confuse self-renouncement with leaving the world, abandonment to God with spiritual idleness. Even if we do not want to admit it to ourselves, what goes against the grain most is to allow ourselves to be led and to change continually our desire to know where we are going into confidence and voluntary blindness on the subject of what God may will to decide tomorrow. We are over-ready to classify this venture as inhuman and dangerous passivity, whereas it is the most magnificent activity that men can undertake, because it is a correspondence with the innovating activity of God. From this effort to go against the spontaneous wish to assert ourselves, we shall only be set free by death. It will thus be necessary for us continually to turn our eyes aside from our own life to lift them to God. He can do all things, but at the same time he wants the whole of us and claims that the only desires that subsist in us shall be the fruit of his desire.

Our adventure does not end with this type of negation. We have seen that God never meets us without this contact with him taking the form of an injunction. The acceptance of his love is always response and obedience to his will. Thus the Lord, when he comes, does not take us out of the world or out of time, he comes to plunge us into them more. What he will not have when he comes is our independence. As often as he sees that attitude in the ground of our hearts, our bodies and our actions, he will come down to root it out. This Master, who wills to find nothing other than himself, does not attempt to abolish but to transform, to establish anew and to change the polluted stream into the crystal clearness of his love alone. The more God makes us enter into the strange solitude of the dialogue with him, the more he makes us go down into the depths of man in order that we may accept that he should reign there alone.

Thus, although we may often feel the temptation to do so, it is in no sense a question of suppressing time or appearances to rediscover the absolute and the real, for tragedy and human suffering would then escape this renewal of all things in Jesus Christ, which is the term of divine charity. History, the course of which the Spirit of God has changed by placing there the first-born Son, submissive and obedient, must pass wholly into Christ through an active acceptance of the will of the Most High. When God comes forth to meet us it is to make a part of ourselves or of others enter through our conversion into him who is by nature wholly turned to the love of his Father.

Our paltry acceptance is thus wholly identified with the redemption which has been accomplished, for the nothingness of total readiness to accept attracts all distant things, so that the Spirit may come and create them anew. The more we empty ourselves of ourselves, the more we are in the world enabling God to work there. Human action that would seek, starting from man, to construct a better or more fraternal society is denuded of sense, just as the attempt to forge a universe free from faults and troubles is vain. Yet we spend a long part of our lives wavering between the desire to reach the limits of humanity by our own enterprises and the dream of a purity that nothing and no one will ever come to trouble. Without the active presence of God, we shall either allow these two forces to struggle in us and crush us or else we shall mutilate ourselves by choosing one of them. The only way of reconciling them is to allow God to penetrate into us so that he may fill us with his light and deliver us from darkness. Thereby we shall here and now reach the confines of the universe, not only because, having God who is all things, we shall possess all things in our turn, but because our meeting with him will communicate to us the demands and jealousy of his love and we shall no longer be able to allow a single thing to exist outside the beloved.

If we seek God and God alone, we have no reason to fear that we shall find ourselves entering into an adulterated repose. It is with the same gesture, in fact, that our Lord disturbs our impassiveness to communicate his peace to us and that he stretches the powers of our being to make them work at the gigantic task of the renewal of the world.

At the end of this first chapter, we can already attempt a more precise definition of the spiritual life. In the first place it comprises the certainty of a presence. I am no longer enclosed within myself, I know that Another intervenes to order me to do what he wills. It is impossible to confuse him with my thoughts and feelings, since he reaches me, beyond passing emotions and desires, in that absolutely free domain of the will where my person is posited in its autonomy. If I am certain that he is there intimately, it cannot be after the manner of those obscure forces which are imposed from without independently of any decision, for when I accept it his presence is sweet. Moreover, far from setting up a disintegration, its fruit is a rich, harmonious creation which kindles the desire for a new meeting whose effects surpass our imagination.

This certainty of a presence introduces us to the possibility of a dialogue. God does not show himself as a vague and formless power desirous of invading us unawares; he speaks to us, he challenges us, he solicits us and he does not cease until he obtains a clear response, a free accord, an unmixed acceptance. He respects us, he waits for us. Infinitely more patient than we are, in no case does he want to drag from us a feigned adherence. But the most extraordinary thing of all is that he communicates his power to us so that we may dispose of it; he makes us stronger, more clear-sighted, and he even wills that we resemble him. That is certainly not a dialogue wanting in substance, forged by our imagination, for a day will come eventually when we shall be able in our turn to call upon him and he will answer, even going so far as to submit to our desires.

At the heart of this solitary dialogue, revealing his secrets to me, he informs me of his plans for the world and he enlarges the narrowness of my horizon to the very limits of the universe. If he comes to me alone because the interest he bears me is unique, I can only return to him with all my fellow men, and the relations he maintains with me and I with him will not be developed to their perfection so long as there are men who do not share in them in the way and to the extent he desires. One is never saved alone and our salvation will not be able to find its fulfillment except in that of the whole of mankind.

The certainty of a presence, the possibility of a dialogue, the solitude which opens to others, these are the three characteristic marks of the spiritual life which form in us an image of the love of the Trinity. Who then could welcome in our hearts the presence of the Father, always unknown to us and always inaccessible, if it were not the well-beloved Son? If the Blessed Trinity in its Source is constrained to descend into us so deeply, to the extent that it seems to destroy us, it is because it must find at the root of us the Word in whom we have been created. It can then burst forth and infiltrate itself everywhere like living water. Identified with Christ, who is at every moment a pure "receiving" from his Father, we can allow ourselves to be borne along by the love that is Spirit. From century to century the whole universe will be on fire with this love to the point of being consumed by it, in order that in all things the Father and the Son may speak to each other in their Spirit and their love. The meeting with God is thus to allow ourselves to be met as a son by the Father, it is to welcome him ever more and more, to give him back what belongs to him, i.e., ourselves, mankind and the world.

2 THE MEANING OF SIN AND THANKSGIVING

IF THE DIALOGUE WITH GOD is often interrupted and in danger of terminating, if earthly and human realities cannot be introduced into it and cannot be changed into lasting love, the reason must be sought not from the side of the Creator, for he communicates and gives the superabundance of his riches without measure, but from the side of man who does not wish to receive, because he wishes neither to obey nor to depend on the divine gratuitousness.

It is thus necessary, to prepare the work of God and make it possible, to give some description of human self-sufficiency which forms the major obstacle to the divinization of man and the universe. As there can be no desire for liberation without an awareness of slavery or imprisonment, so the experience of meeting with God is inseparable from that of sin. If the ways of the spiritual life are closed to numerous Christians, it is because they never get beyond a legalistic conception of sin and do not realize that sin is the refusal of a personal relationship with their Master and Lord.

In other respects Christianity becomes an atrophied individualism so long as the dogma of original sin remains a truth apprehended intellectually, but without any link with actual life. An experimental knowledge of the universal nature of sin, allows us on the contrary to enter gradually into the perspective of a universal redemption—man will not be able to find God fully until the grace of Christ shall be extended to every creature and until there is no longer anything on earth but a single song of thanksgiving.

Personal Sin as Act

For many Christians, the consciousness of having sinned is solely the consequence of infringement of a moral law, and remorse continues to prick them until they have been able to accuse themselves of the fault. Even if it is explained to them (or if they know the fact because they have learned it) that sin is essentially an offense against God,* this formula scarcely corresponds to what they experience, for, more often than not, they live their religion on the social level. An act considered as serious in one particular context, seems trifling in another, because the Christian communities in question have made a choice among the commandments of God and the Church in view of their needs and their past, emphasizing some and leaving the others aside. For the individual conscience, the transgression of the law is not grasped in its relationship to the Creator; it appears rather

* This definition of sin can only be understood after a lengthy process of thought. It only becomes a personal experience in the spiritual combat at the moment when liberty, conscious of its autonomy, is tempted "to do something to displease God" (cf. pp. 81–82). What we are advocating here is an education in the meaning of sin. It is easy for the theologian to assert, and to be satisfied with asserting, that sin is evil through its very opposition to God; the spiritual pedagogue knows that for the beginner this formula is meaningless and that it is thus necessary first of all to consider sin in its consequences. It is only when the experience has been taken seriously and developed on that level, that the refusal to love others will be seen in its source as a refusal to love God.

as a failure to comply with the rules laid down by the group whose upbringing has linked the notion of sin with a certain number of prohibitions. Thus Christians often consider themselves more guilty for not having submitted to some external ordinance than for having committed a misdemeanor, clearly recognizable as such, however, which does not come within the usual rules.

There is no point in describing further a situation known to everyone. Sin here appears, beyond question too exclusively, under the form of a rupture of the social bond in its religious manifestations. We think that we cannot enter again into communion with our brothers in the Church, except by an avowal and pardon. Every Christian has at least a vague consciousness that sin cuts him off from his fellows, loosens his bonds with others and prevents him from being completely at ease with those around him. Let us admit, however, that a good conscience soon reassumes its rights and that the realization of one's isolation is often keener when the religious aspect does not intervene at all—in the case, for instance, of a violation of social custom, of some blunder, or frustration, or of a loss of face. Man then feels himself as it were excluded from his social group, for he has broken its harmony, which was indeed more or less artificial. Hence comes this feeling of injury which lasts as long as the mutual embarrassment and recurs with the memory of it. If it is regrettable that the sense of sin is sometimes reduced to this kind of culpability and to the failure to appreciate what might be called religious good manners, that is already an image, a prefiguration of the experience of sin as a separation and shattering of the bond between person and person.

It suffices, in fact, to develop this perspective to find ourselves at the very heart of the Christian mystery. Sin is an infringement of the social law and it is that alone if it is remembered that Christ has given only one commandment to rule, preserve and increase the new society he founded: "Love one another, as I have loved you" (Jn. 15, 12). For the Christian, to sin is to contravene this order, it is to refuse to love. This amounts to separating oneself from others, to breaking the social bond in one way or another. The suffering of this rupture is an experience, a more or less distant echo of sin. Because it is an offense against God, that is, an injury against love, the only valid definition of sin is that it is the refusal of love. It is the contrary of charity, the antithesis of communion.

All this, which leads, doubtless under a very abstract form, to the assertion of what is abundantly clear (sin, because it is the refusal of God who is love, is essentially separation), can also lead, if we draw from it its full consequence, to the enlargement of our religious experience; at the same time it links that experience more firmly with its center. We ought to train ourselves to see sin in every circumstance in which division is established and above all where it is established by us. Under the manifold aspects of the counsel which she bountifully bestows upon men, the Church merely sets out in detail, on all the levels and in every order in which human activity is manifested, the rules to be followed so that in each individual, in each cell of society, in the most widely extended communities and finally in the whole universe, that peace and unity which sin comes to destroy may reign.

To allow parts of my being and of my existence not to communicate or harmonize with each other, to relegate my interest in God to a few privileged moments of prayer, to refuse to let my daily life be submitted to more searching religious requirements, or to refuse to let my religious acts be impregnated with greater truth and a fuller sense of humanity, all this is sin, because it is the toleration and thus the strengthening of the divisions which already exist in me. It is necessary, however, to focus this lens on the other sectors of reality. When the Church is considering conjugal society, for instance, she does not cease to combat the theories which separate love from its sexual expression and the latter from fecundity; or, on the other hand, those theories which would separate this fecundity from the total unity of man and woman. Similarly, when Christians and all men are invited to understand each other and to meet together, it is not so that they may express approval of the cowardice of certain forms of pacifism, for before it can become gentle the peace advocated by Christianity must be more arduous than any other, but it is because the increase of human divisions makes sin and the powers of death increase.

To have the sense of sin means understanding, not only with the intelligence but with the heart, that I am the author of sin each time that, instead of working for the reciprocal penetration of the elements of this world, I cause their estrangement from each other. To discover that I am a sinner is to perceive how, with more or less awareness, I widen the divisions that are latent in myself and in others; how I separate myself from those who are near to me, or distant, and how I work to thrust them aside in the spiritual, intellectual, cultural or material order.

Sin is thus an act by which we accentuate, at every level at which man expresses himself, our own isolation or that of our fellows. Through this universal bias, we come back to one of the classic definitions of sin: the closing in upon oneself and the will to suffice to oneself. He who behaves thus tends to suppress all relationship with God and with others; instead of a union with others which always comprises a certain measure of submission and dependence, he then seeks a personal unity which would have its source only in himself. In so doing, however, he enters into a fatal contradiction, for if something can spring to life in him, it can only be through his relationship with others. We are absolutely in need of our fellowmen to realize and to develop ourselves, so much so that the man who seeks to isolate himself in order not to have to acquire a unity that is difficult for him, no longer finds in himself the least substance; rather he finds only emptiness and absence. To shut ourselves up within ourselves under the pretext that in order to suppress the divisions it is better to abolish all relationships, is to reintroduce into ourselves those very divisions from which we sought to escape, because we then cut ourselves off from the origin of unity—the love which comes to us from others and from God.

Every Christian, every man perhaps, has undergone this painful experience. The keenness of the suffering kills any desire for a repetition of it. Such a person has tried to free himself from the weight of others, or even of the need of others, by immuring himself within himself. From this path of self-sufficiency, which is indeed that of sin *par excellence,* there is no other issue than that of self-destruction, i.e., suicide, wherein is expressed with terrible accuracy, by the suppression of self, the bankruptcy of one's relations with others. For, if in oneself one comes to ignore the Other and others, there remains nothing, or rather what is left is nothingness, emptiness and death. To experience in oneself the temptation to suicide (and what man is there, unless he were blind, who has not at some time experienced it under some more or less veiled form), is to perceive the ultimate consequences of sin, to discover how the assertion of self, of the man who seeks to isolate himself in consummate egoism, links up with self-destruction and the absolute disregard of others. It is not possible to explore this path further or to grasp more clearly to what extent sin is really the contrary of love. In this sense every sin is a suicide because it has sought to be a homicide, that is, a suppression of the other.

If sin is the contrary of love, it is inseparable from death. Everyone can have some presentiment of this, when, being unwilling to open to others, he becomes incapable of initiating the dialogue and exchange which alone can give him the taste for life. For a moment, we can be satisfied with talking idly to ourselves and thus finding in the sympathetic listener that one is for oneself, that perfect accord of which every man dreams and which is identified with his existence. Soon, however, through the very fact of having failed, in turning one's consciousness upon oneself, to find the "other" and because the absence of real relations with another has not allowed us to be known and recognized, we come to the point of devouring our own selves, believing nevertheless that we are feeding our soul with the substance of someone who loves us and who would give himself to us freely. To break the links which attach us to our fellows is to destroy them and to condemn ourselves to the sterility of death.

These are abstract phrases, perhaps, but close to our experience. This is, indeed, the sort of thing we read in news items where crimes begin by an unsatisfied thirst for attention, solicitude and affection. It is also what happens in those lives which are in appearance the least troubled. An unsuccessful dialogue between two friends will perhaps weaken both for a long time; the lack of comprehension between a man and a woman who are called upon to grow in love atrophies the forces which should give them mutual courage. As to the complete disregard for others cherished by the citizens of one nation or by the inhabitants of different countries to preserve their peace or their property, it will always end by turning, more or less rapidly, into conflicts and violence. All this is sin because it is contrary to charity, the law of which is communion.

There is no question of underestimating the definition that Christian morality gives of personal sin in which our responsibility is engaged and which comprises, in addition to a "matter" more or less grave, a consciousness and a will to do wrong more or less deeply marked. It is indeed in this perspective that we have situated ourselves up to the present and it is this which we want to investigate more deeply. It often happens in fact that, losing sight of the very essence of sin and its sole source, we judge our acts according to the notion that our milieu may form of them or in function of questionnaires in preparation for confession, periodically brought up to date. We forget the infinite multiplicity of the forms of sin and have a tendency to confine ourselves to lists made out in advance which do not always correspond with the concrete situations in which we have to make a decision. What is more serious still, we measure the perversity of our acts by their "material" gravity alone, without taking into account the consciousness and deliberation with which we have plunged into them. This reduces morality to the application of a penal code and deprives it of all religious substance.

On the other hand, if, abstracting from even the most detailed and most satisfactorily formulated lists of sins, we focus our attention on sin as an obstacle to divine charity, we see ourselves in the whole extent of our life both active and passive, as guilty of causing divisions. Instead of stopping at limited external actions and thus becoming hardened, our conscience now becomes alert to the circumstances in which we have provoked or accentuated separation. It will then be capable not of fashioning its own morality, but of realizing that sin is everywhere in our lives and that we must recognize and acknowledge it everywhere. This light on the essence of sin will be reflected in our way of conceiving our responsibility and in the complicity which we entertain in ourselves. The more the "matter" of sin tends to become enlarged and to deepen, the greater the lucidity and consent which we bring to the act of sinning appear. Without falling into a morbid sense of guilt, the conscience in growing more tender discovers new forms of wretchedness, as it will discover the secret consent it gives to their accomplishment. We are astonished that the saints claim to be great sinners. It is because they have travelled far along this road and what they assert is not pious exaggeration, but derives from facts duly established which our torpor and blindness alone conceal from us.

Original Sin as a State

The approach we have just indicated is not yet sufficient, for it often happens to us, without having willed such effects, to act in such a way that the immediate or remote consequences are disastrous. Moreover, when we seek to unite men among themselves on the family, political, economic and other planes, with the best will and intentions, we sometimes arrive at results contrary to what we are aiming at. We may perhaps be guilty of ignorance and clumsiness, but since we have acted for the best in the circumstances involved and with the means at our disposal, we cannot think we have committed a sin, for we had no conscious will to do wrong. If then, in spite of this, our actions have resulted in the breaking of links instead of creating them, it is because the source of our divisions is deeper than our will and judgment, that it is in us at a level at which we do not perceive it, and which in a sense is beyond us.

What is even more serious is that the divisions exist even before man's intervention. They surround him on every side and are spread all over the universe under every possible form. There is even one sector where they reign without liberty seeming to be the origin of them, viz., that of nature and the hostile relations which nature maintains with mankind. In the face of such difficulties it would seem necessary to seek elsewhere than in man the principle of an evil as blind as it is widespread.

The Christian dogma of original sin gives a decisive response to these questions. But the error is perhaps to read it in a different way from that of the Church which transmits it and then not to grasp its link with one's personal existence. When it is accepted, like all the facts of Revelation, the aim of which is to save man by revealing to him the truth of his being, hidden until then, i.e., by unveiling before his eyes what his nature is made of, this explanation of man's sinful origin can enlighten and help him to conquer this evil which is rooted in him. Until he takes account of this dogma in his life, he will not be able to acquire the sense of sin. We must, then, stop for a moment to discover its significance.

"Certainly," wrote Pascal, "nothing hits us harder than this doctrine; and yet without this mystery, the most incomprehensible of all, we are incomprehensible to ourselves. The very nodus of our condition takes its twists and turns from this abyss; so that man is more inconceivable without this mystery than this mystery is inconceivable to man."* The account of the Fall is thus not given to us to afford us a knowledge or an intellectual understanding of Adam's sin, to make us grasp this fault as a remote fact of history without interest at the present time, but in order that this primordial fact may make our existence intelligible. It is, moreover, what is suggested by the exegetes who try to explain how this account has arisen. It resembles, they say, the myths of the other religions which seek to explain human reality and daily experience. Starting from this life that they know by experience, the authors of the myths strive to deduce from them what happened in the beginning to give human destiny a significance and a meaning. In their psychology as writers and in their reflection, the inspired authors have followed no other path. Guided and enlightened by the Spirit, instead of expressing only a part of the truth and interspersing it with errors and aberrations of the imagination, they have grasped the origin of our sinful race with an unparalleled accuracy and soberness, thus bringing the fullness of light to bear on human reality. Animated with the purifying and unifying strength of the Holy Spirit, they have perfectly formulated, in symbolic language, the first historical fact which accounts for the present state of man.†

Under such conditions we have not to ask "Why was there an original sin," for that is an abstract question which comes to us from

* *Pensées,* ed. Brunschvicg, no. 434. Cf. H. F. Stewart, D.D., Pascal's *Pensées* with English translation (London, 1947), no. 258, p. 153.

† The idea of a transmission, generation by generation, of the primitive account of the Fall is scarcely any longer considered today by serious exegetes. Explanations on this point will be found in A. M. Dubarle, *Le péché original dans l'Ecriture* (Paris, Ed. du Cerf, 1958), pp. 39–74. Certain fears of seeing the inspired authors here compared with the authors of the myths would disappear perhaps if one remembered the relations between truth and reality—because the account of original sin is wholly true, it is real. In other words a myth that is totally true ceases to be a myth, and becomes a symbolic description of an historical fact that is itself more historical than human history, for it is its explanation and origin.

our condition as man. To ask such a question would make us judges of our destiny instead of our accepting it as it is, and living it to the best of our capacity. Such a question involves no reply for it would presuppose that man, while remaining within the framework of history, transcends it and dominates the principle of it. The only formula that we should and could lay down is the following: "How does the account of original sin throw light on my present situation?" In doing this we make use of this dogma as a light which has been transmitted to us with a view to our salvation and we place ourselves exactly in the orbit of a Revelation which unveils man to himself to deliver him from the slavery in which he suffers.

Without entering here into a detailed exegesis of the first chapters of Genesis, it can at least be emphasized that original sin appears as the type of all sin. Because Adam and Eve refused to submit to the divine injunction they became afraid and fled before the face of Yahweh. But this separation which was thus consummated between God and man, because of the latter's will to independence, immediately caused the separation of man and woman ("They perceived themselves to be naked. . . . Thou shalt be under thy husband's power, and he shall have dominion over thee") and that of these two beings from nature ("Cursed is the earth in thy work. . . . In the sweat of thy face shalt thou eat bread. . . . In sorrow shalt thou bring forth"). Here again we find the classic definition of personal sin as an offense against God and a will to suffice unto oneself, but at the same time we see linked together the characteristics of the experience of sin—sin, which is a refusal of love, becomes the source of the divisions which lead even to death. Moreover the hostility of nature towards man, of which the individual could not say that he was the cause, is now integrated. Thus when we consider the fault of Adam and Eve, sin assumes its full dimensions and, in the darkness it engenders, it takes on the fullest possible light—Adam, i.e., Man, separating himself from God in full consciousness of the fact, is likewise separated, by the same act, from his fellow man and from the world in which he was placed. The separation of man from God is thus the cause of the separation of man from man and of man from nature. The result of this is to divide man in himself and to prevent him from acting in light and in freedom.

It will be objected that this description can scarcely contribute to a sense of sin, for however much the original fault is the type of all sin, it nonetheless remains external to me. Yet, without considering in the first place that it is very enlightening for me to see the significance and bearing of every rejection of God, which, even though in my case it is slighter and of less consequence, yet retains the same structure, it is not at all evident that I *am* such a stranger to the sin of Adam. Theology distinguishes clearly personal sin, the act posited by the individual, and original sin, attached to human nature in such a way that it is in each one of us a state which both exceeds and embraces particular acts, a state that shares in the sin of Adam. The first man is thus in some sense interior to us and that, even after baptism, by the presence of the propensity to evil that is called "concupiscence." Nevertheless we can always object that we have no share of responsibility in the wrong committed by Adam and no share either in its transmission. In this sense original sin remains outside us and we only suffer it through constraint.

Such an attitude, however, far from freeing us from the ills which weigh upon us, rather aggravates them. Here we enter into a religious perspective which is disconcerting, but which alone can enable us to respect this dogma and make it pass into our lives. To disassociate ourselves from the universal evil which inhabits the world is to enter into the *processus* which leads to sin. On the contrary, to take it upon ourselves is to follow an inverse movement which leads us to the justice of grace. When Aaron was questioned by Moses after he had just committed idolatry by making the golden calf, he threw the blame on to the people: "Thou knowest this people, that they are prone to evil" (Ex. 32, 22). The reaction of Moses was quite the contrary. He was not responsible since it had all happened in his absence and yet he was the one who went up towards Yahweh and tried to obtain forgiveness (Ex. 32, 30). After his sin, Aaron behaved exactly as the first man who accused Eve (Eve in her turn accusing the serpent). The movement characteristic of the sinner is to refuse the responsibility and, to explain his misdeeds, to appeal to some constraint which has come from without. Conversely the just man assumes and takes upon himself the weight of a sin which he has not committed. On the one hand the sinner moves away from his fellows and thus increases the divisions, on the other, the just man seeks to reduce them to the level in which circumstances place him, by accepting the consequences of sin.

To rebel against the existence of an evil which is imposed on us even before we have become aware of it, or to think that we have no responsibility for the general disorder, is to cut ourselves off from others, to keep aloof from the human race, to seek to extricate ourselves from the morass alone, instead of bearing our share of the evil. Finally it is to commit once more and here and now the sin of sufficiency and independence which marked Adam's wrongdoing. Once I begin to ask why original sin happened, why evil exists, and am scandalized that there should be any, I place myself outside sin and evil to make myself the judge of it. Thus not only do I step out of my condition, but I show myself to be a sinner in my turn, refusing to enter into solidarity with others and, under pretext of truth and purity, accentuating the separations and divisions. For us, men of Adam's race, to wish to be freed from evil without first recognizing it in ourselves is to play at innocence and attempt to obtain salvation while ignoring our own condition. It is thus to commit anew the sin of Adam.

When we consider Jesus Christ, the just one *par excellence,* and the way in which he has redeemed us, the paradoxes here recalled become abundantly clear. More than Moses did, he has made himself one with us, he has taken our sins upon himself, he who was without sin, and he allowed himself to be led to the gallows like a criminal. He gave us no theory as to the origins of evil, he gave no explanation as to the fact of original sin and its appearance among us, but he was made sin for us (cf. II Cor. 5, 21). Abstract explanations might satisfy our minds, but they would be of no practical help to us. What we ask for is to be really delivered from evil—ourselves, our fellow men and the world. To this supplication, Christ Jesus brings the sole effective response. He invites us to place ourselves among the sinners who have become his friends, to the exclusion of others who consider themselves just and who seek to distinguish themselves from the base people without faith or law.

Every man who wishes to follow our Lord must again pass through the phases of this movement, knowing that, since he is a sinner, he has infinitely more reason than Christ to comport himself thus. Far from accusing others, he will realize his share of responsibility in the present evil and he will think of his own guilt. Entering deeply into himself he will there discover to what extent the roots of division and death are constantly within him ready to spring into life and he will realize that he is more guilty and responsible than anyone else, because, seeing it in himself, he knows by experience the tyranny of sin, whereas as to others he can never affirm anything but the existence of external actions and not that of perverse intentions.

If we sinners move forward along this path, we shall come progressively to understand that each one of our sins proves not only that we are of Adam's race, but that each of us could have taken his place. Or, rather, that Adam is that sinner, that Adam is myself. Until this identification with the first man is perfect, it is likewise impossible to identify oneself with Jesus Christ, the second Adam. In the measure in which we fail to penetrate into the depths of sin by assimilating ourselves with the sinner par excellence, we cannot receive in his fullness him who did not come for the just but for sinners. If in the least particle of ourselves we think we are just through our own efforts, into this tiny particle Christ cannot bring the gratuitousness of his salvation.

A page from St. Catherine of Siena will show with what intensity God's true faithful are capable of undergoing this crucial experience and of remaining in it with complete naturalness.

When morning was come, and the time for Mass, we read in the *Dialogue,* she took her place in the church wholly filled with painful desire, with self-knowledge, ashamed of her lack of perfection, convinced that she was the sole cause of the evil occurring in the world, thus conceiving hatred and contempt of herself and a holy justice. It was in this knowledge, in this hatred and in this justice that she purified the stains that she thought she could find (they were there in reality) in her sinful soul and that she said—"Father eternal, I appeal from me to thee. Punish my offenses in this finite time, and, since, through my sins, I am the sole cause of all the evils that my neighbor suffers, I beg you sweetly to punish them in me."

These are extraordinary phrases which become comprehensible through the explanations elicited by her director. He notes in fact:

One day I asked her how, under the regard of truth, she could judge herself and say that she was the cause of all the evils in the world. She then maintained the same thing, saying that this was completely the case, and added: "If I were all on fire with divine love should I not pray to my Creator with a heart of flame and would not he who is supremely merciful show mercy to all my brethren and grant to them all to be well alight with the same fire that would be in me? What is the obstacle to so great a good? My sins alone, assuredly. For no imperfection can come from the Creator, who can have nothing imperfect in him. This evil must thus come from me and through me."*

The explanation is clear. If Catherine cannot save the world from its wretchedness it is because she does not love her Creator with all

* Cf. St. Catherine of Siena, *Dialogues* (Paris, Ed. du Seuil, 1953), p. 33, and also A. L. Thorold, *Dialogue of the Seraphic Virgin Catherine of Siena* (London, 1925), p. 3.

her being. Incapable of identifying herself with the prayer of Jesus which invokes God's merciful love for the salvation of all and which obtains forgiveness for all, she must necessarily think that she is the sole barrier to the coming of love; more than that, that she is the origin of all evils. To use an expression of St. Paul, until we view the whole of our life as surrounded with disobedience through our own fault, God cannot show mercy to all men (Rom. 11, 32). A stupendous relationship which ought to be familiar to us, for there is no more reason to be astonished at seeing in each Christian another Christ than to perceive in every man another Adam.

Man is not man because he suffers like all men the condition of his race, but because consciously and willingly he takes this condition upon himself and admits that he is incapable of providing a remedy for it. We readily say that each human person is co-extensive with the universe, the wealth of which he possesses in himself. Christianity in turn asserts that each one of the acts we perform has consequences for the whole of mankind, for good and for evil. The dignity of the human person thus demands that each one of us should feel himself responsible for all the evil, in order to be able to become the source and origin of all the good. It is because Jesus Christ, the perfect man, has taken upon himself all the sin of the world, it is because he was made sin (II Cor. 5, 21), in full awareness of the fact and with divine consent, that he could become the cause of the renewal of the universe. Each Christian must thus imitate him, after his own way, by taking upon himself the responsibility of the human race, in order to spread abroad, through history, the overflowing life of God that he has received. To have the sense of sin is thus no longer merely to realize that in our relations with others and with God we accentuate division, neither is it merely to recognize that original sin, such as Adam knew it, is the principle of all division, past, present and future. It is to acknowledge myself a sinner in Adam, or, rather, a sinner like Adam, disposing in myself of the universal power of death, for, in himself alone, each man is already mankind.

We can now see the new links established between sin, death and love. Sin, which is the reverse of love, is the source of separation and thus finally of death. But to reverse this process of disintegration, Jesus Christ, who is love par excellence, uses death itself. He comes to find us in this state of extreme division and communicates his love to us. On the Cross death and the sharing in agony no longer appear only as consequences of sin but as the sole means of obtaining salvation. From this it follows that the divisions in which we live, which are all marked with the sign of death, but also with the sign of his love, become for us so many steps which will give us access even to communion.

The Act of Thanksgiving

To make the dogma of original sin part of our lives does not lead to despair but to thanksgiving. The more spiritual experience considers how much sin turns us aside from God who is the sole source of all life, the greater the realization that existence, even physical existence and much more intellectual and moral, can only be the fruit of divine mercy and long-suffering. If nothing of creation escaped man in Adam, since God had made him lord and master of it, nothing ought to have remained after he had broken his bond with the Creator. When Yahweh threatened him with death if he touched the forbidden tree, he did not put before him a punishment expressive of a purely external relation with the fault—the sanction was identified with the transgression. For to refuse to obey God is to cut oneself off from life, to move towards death. The Creator did not have to punish Adam, it was the latter who brought death upon himself, who brought it into the world and who normally should have consummated the destruction of the universe created for him.

But since the return to nothingness has not taken place, it must be that God has not willed that sin should reach its ultimate consequences; or rather, to the inexorable logic of sin which must do its work he has added another logic, that of the promise, and he has again communicated his life to us. If then, becoming fully aware of our sin in Adam, of its amplitude, of the universal effect that it ought to have had, we nevertheless find that we are still living, we cannot fail to be astonished or to recognize that if we exist, it is through superabundant grace. The universal corrupter has not succeeded in his enterprise. This means, then, that the second Adam, the universal Redeemer, has already triumphed in all things.

To discover that we are the cause of all evil is thus to understand that we are already pardoned and that the gift which had been made to us has now become multiplied in pardon. If from the evil recognized in our life we have been able to pass to the universal sin which alone can account for it, it is because already, in our Redemption, the cessation of all suffering and all perversity is given. The awareness of sin can sometimes precede that of salvation. In reality the latter alone enables us to subsist despite the destructive force of evil. It leads us gradually to recognize what lies behind this life which continues to persist. If we had the sense of sin we should ask ourselves, with St. Ignatius, how it is that our sin has not provoked chaos and why the stars have not fallen upon us and the earth opened under our feet.* We should then understand that one single cry can rise from our lips, that of thanksgiving in the face of the gift of love, whereas by our self-sufficiency we had sought to destroy everything. But, to speak truly, only the man who deliberately situates himself in Adam can see the link which exists between sin and the universality of division and death and can consequently grasp the absolute gratuitousness of all life. Otherwise, we shall doubtless be able to thank God for his benefits, but we shall with difficulty perceive that our being not only rests on a relationship from creature to Creator but that it is wholly founded on pardon and on merciful grace. It is sometimes said that God has first of all given nature and then grace. But if we place ourselves in the light of the dogma of original sin, it becomes clear that nothing

* Cf. *Spiritual Exercises,* tr. J. Rickaby S.J. (London, 1915), p. 34.

escaped death because of sin and that nothing can remain except by the redoubling of a gift which is grace.

All is grace. We must not even be afraid of adding: sin itself is grace. In fact, although it is evil and the source of evil, it is re-integrated into the movement of redemption and becomes capable of serving it. The liturgy goes so far as to make us sing at the Paschal Vigil, alluding to the transgression committed by Adam: "O happy fault which has merited for us such a Redeemer!" In history such as it is and not such as it might have been, sin has been the occasion for God to manifest his love more completely. That is why St. Paul could write in amazement: "Where sin abounded, grace did more abound" (Rom. 5, 20). As if man's disobedience induced God to extend the means of salvation more. This was already the case in the Old Testament. Yahweh revealed himself to Moses in the burning bush by the words, "I am who am" (Ex. 3, 14), thus enclosing himself within the secret of his power. But, after the idolatry of his people, he showed himself as the "God, merciful and gracious, patient and of much compassion, and true" (Ex. 34, 6).

These facts which concern mankind as a whole must be transposed to throw light on the destiny of each individual. St. Ignatius used to say that the more he sinned and humiliated himself, the more consolations he received.* He also admitted that when he was in a state of aridity he made an effort to remember his past sins and this drew down upon him an abundance of graces.† Our usual reaction is to hide our faults from our own eyes and to forget them right away as soon as they are forgiven. This is because, haunted by the wish to assert ourselves, we desire to need no one to save us. If in past days it has been necessary for us to accept God's mercy, today we hope to be able to act on our own strength. The saints, on

* MHSJ, *Fontes Narr.* II, p. 477.

† MHSJ, *Const., praev.*, p. 133.

the contrary, have lost all hope of saving themselves by themselves and the sins they find in themselves give them the assurance that Christ will make them his friends, for they approach him as needy and sick. To acknowledge that without our Lord we can do nothing and to recognize that his grace alone can give us life, is to move out of ourselves and into the love of the Other. It is to establish ourselves in thanksgiving.

Transporting into her life the conviction that the sin of Adam was a happy fault, St. Teresa of the Child Jesus said that she made use of the discovery of her imperfections, because each one of them hollowed out the abyss towards which merciful love could not but rush like a torrent.* Clearly this does not mean that we must multiply sins in order "that grace may abound" (Rom. 6, 1), but that sin, once it is a fact, should help us to open up the goodness and tenderness of God. As a free creature we can believe that we are something and that we are capable of doing good, but if we remain in the knowledge of our sin we shall be led to gratitude towards a God who loves us not only despite our weakness, but in spite of our denial of him. We shall then be emptied of ourselves, as much by the knowledge of our nothingness as by that of the divine gratuitousness ready to lavish its goodness upon us.

If the acknowledgment of sin alone gives us access to salvation, thanksgiving is in turn necessary to an awareness of sin. It is not because we suffer from a sense of guilt that we know that we are sinners. It is when we perceive that we have failed God and attributed to ourselves what did not belong to us, to enjoy it at our

* "Later, no doubt, the time in which I am now will appear to me still full of imperfections, but now I am no longer astonished at anything. I am not troubled at seeing that I am *weakness* itself. On the contrary it is in that that I glory and each day I expect to discover fresh imperfections in myself. Remembering that Charity covers a multitude of sins, I draw from this rich mine which Jesus has opened before me." *Manuscrits autobiographiques de sainte Thérèse de l'Enfant Jesus* (Paris, Ed. Livre de Vie, 1961), p. 263. Cf. *Autobiography of a Saint* (*Teresa of Lisieux*) [London, 1958], p. 270.

good pleasure, that we realize this. Now for man, to give thanks to God is nothing else but to recognize that he has nothing, that he is nothing and that he owes to Another all that he possesses. From this we can understand why St. Ignatius says that ingratitude is the greatest of all sins and the source of all evils.* Sin should even be defined as the absence of thanksgiving. For to refuse to give thanks is to think that all is due to us, to make ourselves God, like Adam in paradise. The practice of thanksgiving would thus be a privileged means for us to liberate ourselves from the sin *par excellence,* which is the sin of pride. Through it, in fact, we should be brought into constant relationship with God, we should recognize what we owe him in the past and we should expect that he would grant us his rewards.

Between the acknowledgment of sin and thanksgiving is established an exchange in which both are intensified. The more we know who we are and the little we are worth, the more gratitude springs freely from our hearts. But, conversely, through the love which makes possible a new birth, it is the divine light which enlightens our darkness and reveals our disorder in depths hitherto unsuspected. If we enter into this twofold movement, our deep-rooted poverty will be revealed to us ever more and more. Instead of being astonished, we shall enter into it with courage because there truth lies and to recognize it leaves the way open to the intervention of God who fills us with himself alone.

At this stage we shall no longer be able to be scandalized at the presence of evil in the world and we shall take care to refrain from asking God in a more or less aggressive tone the reason for scandal, for henceforth the question is reversed in our eyes. It seems to us incomprehensible not that there should be evil, but that everything should not be absolutely evil. We then question God and ask him to explain to us why there is good in the world, why he has not let everything revert to nothingness, why he wills our

* MHSJ, *Epist. Ign.*, I, p. 192.

happiness and why he loves us. That man can be good, that a single being can still be capable of generosity; much more, that there are on earth beings capable of disinterestedness and love, is henceforward an inexhaustible source of wonder. The scandal does not consist in the fact that evil exists, but in the fact that good exists, and this scandal is that of the Cross and of love. Why did a God embrace death, a thing more contrary to him than water is to fire? Why, from evil, has he willed to make that which is good and the source of all good, of all happiness? This is folly that is indeed a mystery. If we knew our hearts we should have no difficulty in admitting that Adam's sin is the thing we best understand from within. Of that folly we know we are capable and that is why we are so greatly scandalized over it, but ought not the folly of Jesus Christ to become increasingly day by day the subject of an unlimited wonder which would deliver us from all other? No one could then any longer disturb our peace or our serenity, or snatch away from us the interior freedom which always expects new wretchedness through its own fault, yet which sees that the power of God surmounts the most inveterate resistance.

When man sees himself as a creature made in the image of the Most High, he understands that he must obey, but the liberty he has at his disposal makes him hesitate freely to commit himself to this course. The day he recognizes himself under the features of a pardoned sinner, he no longer bargains over his submission, for he knows that of himself he possesses nothing at all but the power of death. However paradoxical this may appear, sin can thus become a valuable help in the search for God. It opens us more completely to divine action and makes us wait humbly until the Saviour deigns to come to meet us.

It must not be forgotten, however, that sin plays this part after it has been committed, after it has become in the world an ineluctable fact which, from being an obstacle, should become a means of salvation. Far from making us adopt a passive attitude, the thanksgiving which is born of the pardon received constrains us to embark upon an unending struggle to efface even the very traces of sin and its innumerable consequences. Gratitude for God's mercy leads the Christian to labor within the framework of history in order to bring it back to God, by making use of sin, but with a view to making sin disappear.

3 THE SPIRITUAL COMBAT

EACH OF US IS ENGAGED IN A STRUGGLE which will last as long as his life on this earth. Speaking in his own name but no less to give expression to the drama which is in all men's hearts, St. Paul used decisive words: "But I see another law in my members, fighting against the law of my mind and captivating me in the law of sin that is in my members. Unhappy man that I am, who shall deliver me from the body of this death? The grace of God, by Jesus Christ our Lord. Therefore, I myself, with the mind, serve the law of God: but with the flesh, the law of sin" (Rom. 7, 23–25). We are thus torn by two contrary forces, that of sin which seeks to enslave us to the powers of death, that of grace trying to lead us to the total and final victory of the Spirit of God over every creature.

In so far as we allow ourselves to be led away by the force of sin, God assumes in our eyes the features of the enemy—he forbids us, in fact, to allow ourselves to go to the evil that attracts us and he puts a barrier across the road by which we think we can attain independence. But when God has won us to himself to the extent of making us obedient as his son was obedient, Satan is revealed as the true adversary who, the better to deceive us, was hiding his seducer's face. Then, with Christ, we can struggle in this world in order that all death may be abolished and the Spirit that gives life may be spread abroad.

The Combat with God

It may appear strange to include the combat with God among the normal stages of spiritual development. Doubtless the manner in which God is opposed to us and we to him has little resemblance with the conflicts in which men engage among themselves, for he remains the Father who never departs from his charity and love in regard to us. But because we only enter into his plans slowly, he cannot but appear to us with a hostile face. Again we must carefully distinguish two forms of spiritual struggle with God, according to whether we are seeking to avoid him or, on the contrary, trying to draw near to him.

The sinner's first reaction is to avoid the conflict with God. We know that the Lord is an exacting master and that we shall not be able to enter into contact with him without suffering the consequences, without an account being demanded of us as to the administration of the wealth which was entrusted to us. To retain our peace of mind we must keep ourselves as far as possible from God, not let a word of his existence or his presence escape from us, in order that we may go on our way along the path to forgetfulness. We maintain that, if God willed that nothing should escape him, he ought not to have set man up as lord of creation and conferred immense powers upon him. Since for the time to come he has remitted all things into our hands, it is doubtless for us to use them at our good pleasure. We did not ask to be born. Let God not seek a quarrel with us if we dispose of his benefits according to our own desires and views. In any case it is best never to raise pointless questions and to confine ourselves to the tasks that are set before us—we shall close our ears to the divine songs, which seem to us foolish.

But it is impossible not to fall under the hand of the living God. For us to find rest, to escape all debate with the Most High, he would have to obliterate the traces of his presence, the imprint of his footsteps in this world. The voice of the creatures who cannot cease to hymn his praises makes it impossible for us to forget him and no wizardry can be successful in expelling him from our lives. He is always there in the sting of remorse; and the sadness which takes possession of our hearts when we have turned aside from him is a reminder of the image he has placed in us. By the folly of turning aside, man seeks to hide from his own eyes his disavowal of the Saviour, but the later it comes, the more bitter is the hour of truth. We cannot for ever ignore him who has formed us by his word and molded us with his hands.

Realizing that this attitude of flight is in danger of leading us into difficult combats we come to the point of giving God a certain place in our lives. We thus hope to preserve at least a part of ourselves and dispose of it at our good pleasure. We think we shall be able to placate God by this kind of underhand bargaining and live peacefully with him as we do with our fellows—if you say nothing about the wrong I am committing, I will keep silent about the wrong which you are planning. To turn aside God's anger we sometimes even submit to burdensome rules of life with the childish thought that God, satisfied with this tribute, will not come to disturb the harmony of the small world that we have carved out for ourselves.

To such mean calculations, however, God replies unequivocally: "I desired mercy and not sacrifice" (Osee 6, 6). He cannot be satisfied with these remote acts of obedience or these few moments of attention, for it is our heart and our whole person that he will have dependent upon him. Because God is our Creator, he cannot but will that we should know him increasingly and that we should recognize in full clarity the act by which we exist. The obstacles to this close contact that we should have with him are doomed to disappear, for it must be that the glory of God shall shine resplendent in the universe. That is why God cannot but enter into conflict with us who refuse to accept his love.

To triumph over man who rises against him or who seeks to shun him, God is faced with the necessity of abolishing what is corrupted by sin and with the impossibility of destroying his work. If Adam and his sons persist in their claim to make themselves the equals of Yahweh, how could we bear them before his face? After driving them out of paradise, the angel who dismissed them must again pass among them. None of them can enter the promised land where no face of man defiled by idols can dwell. But on the other hand, God cannot separate himself from his creature to whom he has communicated his own life and of whom he has made his image. He is attached to him as to himself. When he thinks of avenging himself, his heart is moved like that of a mother and he is incapable of carrying out his designs. A free creature, made in God's likeness, could not return to the nothingness whence it has come. Yet God himself cannot prevent death, introduced by the sin of this free creature, from producing its effects; otherwise it would be proof that man's responsibility in evil was only a mirage. It is through the jealousy of his love that the Lord owes it to himself to allow man to destroy himself; but in the generosity of his love, he cannot do otherwise than wait for his creature to return from his crooked ways.

These two contradictory aspects account for the origin of our spiritual struggle. God cannot bear with man because he is a challenge to his almightiness. On the other hand God cannot but bear with man, for he loves him from all time. As can so often be seen in the Old Testament and even more clearly in the Gospel, the heart of God is as it were divided between anger and patience. Man appears to him as the first and last obstacle to the work begun in love and destined to be continued in love, but this man is already the friend whom the Father loves in his son, the inevitable friend, dearer than his own life. Right from the very first day, on the threshold of the Garden of Eden, began a long dialogue, continually interrupted and resumed. An interminable adventure during which the catastrophes are already triumphs and where the defeats are sharper to the victor than the surrender of a brother. God is thus forced to enter into a struggle with man, since he must seek and obtain man's submission through the slow, tactful work of a pedagogue.

Herein lies the explanation of this interplay of love, the interplay of gift and the iron hand, of liberation and seduction, which forms the rhythm of the history of Israel, the type of all human history. After lavishing his goodness upon the patriarchs, God brought their descendants to the captivity of Egypt. When he delivered the Hebrews from the hand of Pharaoh he made them cross the desert, and the nation which reached the promised land was one day to depart from it in exile. Throughout centuries the tremendous effort of Yahweh to educate his people, to make them more pliable in his hand, less greedy for the good things of earth, capable of resuming the wandering life of the nomads, of sleeping in tents instead of building houses of stone, is made manifest. The dream which haunted Israel, and which haunts every man who comes after Israel, was to find a support elsewhere than in the gratuitousness of the unforeseeable gift of God, a rampart against the divine incursions, a treasure on which he could in the final resort fix his heart. Now, this hope is always doomed to disappointment. If man is to discover the true countenance of God, this must be so. As the years passed, the visible and temporal signs of God's blessing thinned out and for their satisfaction the Jewish people now received only the promise of future benefits, wholly spiritual. If the Father wills to teach us to put our trust in him, he cannot at the same time not assume the features of an enemy who prevents us from taking pleasure in what we think we possess.

God is not, in fact, our enemy, and he never seeks to snatch away from us what he has deigned to give us already. He is satisfied to give without ceasing. He who is love alone cannot but communicate himself ever more abundantly. It is we who transpose into him our hostility in his regard, when we realize that the things of this world which come from him no longer serve us as we had expected. We refuse to acknowledge that God tears nothing away from us and that our hands have only to touch them for God's gifts to deteriorate. Creation is nothing except in relation to the Creator. How then could it subsist in its splendor when we fail to recognize in it the God from whom it comes? Separated from the flux of the stream the stagnant water becomes polluted and no one can raise his lips to it without disgust. For the work of mankind to become corrupt, God has no need to intervene as a monarch would do to avenge his rights—all that is necessary is for time to reveal the consequences of lack of respect for the Creator in the work accomplished here on earth.

By virtue of the real liberty he enjoys, it is possible for man to make use of the gifts of God without taking God himself into account. But, molded over again in accordance with projects that proceed from pride, the things of this world remain creatures. Immutable laws which relate to the Creator are inscribed in them and it is not possible to ignore what they are destined for indefinitely without destroying them and without this destruction affecting man, the author of it. We can move about in the world for some time ignoring God, but, one day, when things rebel against us, we shall be obliged to acknowledge him. When we see the hostility of creatures in our regard we consider that the Creator is our enemy, whereas it is we who have been lacking in intelligence and have been wholly unwilling to ask the Giver how his gifts were to be used.

If the contest is inevitable for the man who seeks to avoid God, it is just as much so, although in a different sense, for him who is striving to draw near to his Master and Lord and to be faithful to him. Under the pretext of not venturing to take God to task and entering into conflict with him, because the things he has made crush us, we may be tempted to reduce our conflict with creation to the strict minimum. Incapable of mastering this chaos and discovering the laws which could regenerate it, we think it better to withdraw to the desert and maintain a peaceful dialogue alone with God.

Yet it is good to face the hostility of things and of beings. In claiming to prevent his acts from becoming the occasion of a conflict, man seeks to shun God's glance, in order not to have to renounce the tiny universe which is the scene of his mad frolic. He is unwilling to risk seeing his inconsistent certainties called in question when they are brought face to face with the wretchedness which emerges everywhere. Finally he is afraid to face God, for he senses that he will find himself forced to change his manner of looking at things and his way of acting. To struggle with God, on the other hand, because we are asking him for the reasons for the evil that surrounds us is to place ourselves within the truth, to start out from our true condition and the wounds that afflict it, in order that our Lord may show his power in them and give us the strength to bear them. It is not the comforters who are closest to the heart of God, it is Job himself, persisting in disputing with his Creator because he has placed all his confidence in him.* Often

* St. Thomas explains Job's audacity as follows: "It would appear that it is not seemly for man to argue with God, given the superiority of God over man. It must, however, be taken into account that truth does not change with the variety of persons. Hence, when a man speaks the truth he cannot be vanquished, whomsoever it may be with whom he argues. Job was convinced that he was speaking the truth with which God had inspired him through the gift of faith and of wisdom" (*Expositiones in Job,* c. 13, 1.2).

enough we think that the dialogue with God should take place in some serene harbor, where the backwash of this world, which we expect to cease in our lives or in our souls in order that we may draw near to him, is not felt. In acting in this way, however, we are in danger of placing under the sign of unreality a relationship which should take its point of departure from what we are and the problems that are ours. So that the Lord may cure us, it is essential for us to come to him with our anguish and our questions.

To interrogate God on the subject that is troubling us, not to cast the blame on him for we know that he is without stain, but to be enlightened and strengthened, is indeed to honor the Creator. To be silent because we sense that the tone of our conversation may come to be raised would be to prove that we assent to God's frustration of our desires without wincing, to maintain that creation and our own existence do not interest God or even that they are so damaged that it is impossible to provide a remedy for them. When we question the Most High, even be it with vehemence, we show on the contrary that our hope is intact. We assert that no suffering, even if it appears intolerable, is capable of separating us from God and preventing us from speaking to him. We declare that he possesses the key to the enigma with which we are wrestling and that he has the power to hand it to us when he wills. This combat is that of the believer who seeks to rely on God alone and who desires to obtain from his Lord that he shall come to him to suppress the evil.

One of the most valuable results of this struggle with God is that by means of it the personality gradually becomes unified. If we sought to avoid difficult problems in order to present ourselves in the most favorable light, we should maintain within ourselves the divisions which form an obstacle to progress—in certain sectors God would have the right to intervene, whereas others would be reserved and his action would not be able to penetrate them. But if we accept the struggle, all our living forces will be mobilized, all the elements which constitute the human person will be thrown into the battle. Thus it will be the whole being which, such as it is, without lying or subterfuge, will enter into the dialogue with God. In this way a decisive step will be taken along our Saviour's triumphal way, for he can only deliver us through ourselves, he can only accord his grace to a liberty capable of recognizing him and of committing itself when it perceives the way that is to be followed. If God seems to communicate himself so little, it is because he finds in us interlocutors inclined to disappear and to come and go without any resolution or objective. On the other hand, in so far as we do not cease to wrestle with God we enable him to act freely as it were in advance and to provide solutions for our crucial problems. He then takes the initiative and obtains the submission so long desired in vain.

Without ever becoming weary and, it seems to us, without sparing us, he searches for the secret point from which he will be able to begin to re-create without destroying. Because he cannot master us easily, like Jacob at the crossing of the brook (Gen. 32, 26), he strikes us on the sinew of the thigh while we wrestle with him. He wounds us at the very joint in our being that we wanted to preserve at all cost. We should be willing to sacrifice everything if only this desire of ours did not come up against a prohibition, if such and such an unbearable humiliation were spared us, if only this friendship or that love could remain intact. But it is precisely our acceptance of this happening, this crushing event or that rupture that God seems to demand of us. The light of his love is concentrated precisely on the place where we wanted to avoid his guidance. Because of this insignificant thing that is imposed upon us, or which we lack, our whole destiny capsizes. We were still attached to ourselves by that invisible thread that no human eye could see—and now God has come to break it. To external eyes, perhaps, nothing is changed, but everything takes place now as if our heart had been torn from us and as if the taste for everything in the world were leaving us. We may be filled with everything, but that for which we should have been capable of abandoning everything is lacking to us. Thus at the height of the struggle, almost without touching us, our Lord abolishes the previous universe which can no longer have any solid foundations for us. In one of her poems St. Teresa of Avila suggests this underground work of detachment, which a mysterious adversary undertakes relentlessly, striking and healing with the same gesture, for if God takes something away from us, it is to give himself to us without reserve:

> O loveliness that dost exceed
> All other loveliness we know,
> Thou woundest not, yet painst indeed
> And painlessly the soul is freed
> For love of creatures here below.*

As at this hour we have nothing more to lose, we want to seize hold of God while the struggle still lasts and, before the dawn, constrain him to bless us (Gen. 32, 26). Let him give himself to us at last since he is no longer willing for us to attach ourselves to anything else. But if he has been able to reach to the depths of our being and touch this secret fibre, it is because already, without our knowing it, he was present and acting in us. He thus easily allows us to snatch from him this blessing that his hands, always ready to open, sought to grant us. Thus his victory in us, which consisted in making himself recognized in his gifts and in forbidding us to take pleasure in a single one of them without reference to him, ends in our triumph, since from generosity to generosity we have brought him to give himself to us and, in obliging him by our wretchedness to grant us ever more, we have finally drawn him down himself.

He sought to bring us back in our flight, but it is we who, at the

* E. A. Peers (ed.), *Complete Works of St. Teresa* (New York, Sheed & Ward, 1946), Vol. III, p. 283.

end of his course, have captured him. In this spiritual combat which is here only in its first phase, conqueror and conquered meet. God could not seek to obtain from us the dependence of a slave, he willed to place us in the liberty of his children to make of us, in the image of his Son, true servants striving for the establishment of his Kingdom. For this he was to give man this power that those who no longer seek for anything but God have over God. When the creature exclaims: "I will not let thee go except thou bless me" (Gen. 32, 26), it is not a lack of respect towards his Master and Lord, it is only the expression of the legitimate desire of a son. At the hour when the Word, finding the place purified and free, can at last be born in us, he is heard by his Father in all that he asks for us.

The Combat against Satan

When man has understood that God is not the adversary, but by his triumph is only seeking to discover anew the face of his Son, he feels an immense desire to imitate Christ and enter into his victory. He knows that there is no other way for the blessing of God to be spread abroad in his life and in the world, bringing the peace and joy which are the certain signs of his Kingdom. But two temptations make themselves felt: that of confusing the spiritual victory with perfect self-mastery; that of considering oneself already victorious in Christ and of thinking that total liberty in regard to created things is henceforth possible.

When we contemplate the harmony which dwells in the person of Jesus, even at the height of the combat, we think that a similar success is open to us by taking literally the hatred of self mentioned in the Gospel. Then arises periodically in our life, or in that of Christian communities, the aspiration to a contorted asceticism which seems to be the shortcut to sanctity. We think we can take the initiative towards our perfection ourselves, reducing it to the mastery of our instincts, and we feel, so far as we ourselves are concerned, that it depends primarily and essentially on our will. But to crush the impulse of our vital powers or to whittle down our strength to the point of reaching a kind of insensitivity is a caricature of the spiritual triumph. Christ Jesus did not come to reign over what was destroyed but to order every form of life by leading it to its term. If we take this so-called shortcut, we are in danger of ending up in a pharasaical pride which is in fact the antithesis of union with God. Nor do we take into account that we are thus imposing upon ourselves a burden which in the long run we will be unable to bear, preparing for ourselves awakenings all the more violent and painful the longer this artificial sleep has lasted. Christianity is not the severe doctrine which rises up to combat every display of vitality, and which would seek to shut man up in a sordid prison. To establish his Kingdom, the Father, far from seeking the crushing or death of his creature, only wills that that creature should be converted wholly to the victory of his Son.

It would be a contrary error to consider that it is already possible for us to make use indiscriminately of all the things of this world. It is true that "our wrestling is not against flesh and blood" (Eph. 6, 12) for Christ has come in the flesh which he then strove to cure before resurrecting it in his body. But this radical transformation is a goal that is as yet inaccessible. We shall not be able to reach it except through a long and painful struggle. Like ordinary human life, the life of the spirit always presupposes a share of discipline and austerity, so much so that a frenzied search for expansion in reaction against a merely sentimental religion is in danger of compromising the plenitude desired. St. Paul has already warned us: "For you, brethren, have been called unto liberty. Only make not liberty an occasion to the flesh" (Gal. 5, 13). The greed with which we turn towards the world's riches under the pretext that they are not evil in themselves, is well calculated to wear out our courage, enervate our vigor, and make us incapable of following Christ.

The spiritual victory is not to be sought either in a proud asceticism or in "making liberty a cloak for malice" (I Peter 2, 16). It resides in the person of Christ whose supreme mastery is at the same time submission of his whole being to his Father's will. If, in respect of all things and of all beings, he appears as much the master as the friend, it is that nothing resists him because he respects everything and is perfectly attuned to the laws that govern the creatures who have been made in him. In his words and gestures, there is neither hesitation nor tension, neither impatience nor proud reserve, neither brusqueness nor compromise. With the ease of God "playing in the world" (Prov. 8, 31) he is present wholly and entirely at the uttermost ends of man's universe and, like Wisdom, he "reacheth everywhere" (Wisdom 7, 24). It is indeed from him that we must take our model, but remembering that he is the victor, because everything is subordinated to him and because he ordains all to the glory of his Father.

True asceticism is that which tends to discover anew in each man and in mankind as a whole the divine Order established in the Word, in the heart of creation, and re-established by the Word who died and is risen again. To the extent that each element of this world, or of our person, finds its place and agrees to fulfill the role assigned to it and not which it chooses for itself, harmony is made or remade in the universe. It is not a question of working for an order imagined by man in his need for peace or logic, but of positing desires, feelings, thoughts and affections in obedience to him who is our Lord and Master and who cannot communicate his victory to what is chaotic.

As to authentic liberty, it takes its source from absolute forgetfulness of self, in the exact hatred of self enjoined by the Gospel which prevents us from sufficing unto ourselves and which re-creates the whole man, spirit, soul and flesh, through his relationship to God. Liberty is identified with love which, no longer having anything of its own but utter poverty, can with equal facility take and give, wait or advance fearlessly, be silent, or raise its voice. For Christ, all actions can reach the same fullness of significance—it matters little whether they are public or secret, easy or painful, lowly or grandiose.

But in all this we are speaking of victory and no longer of combat. We are in danger of forgetting that, for us, total harmony and unfettered liberty constitute an achievement that is still remote and to which it is not possible to tend without unmasking the evil which continually prevents us from advancing, without discovering him who is barring our route. Who then is our adversary?

Our Lord defines him in the Gospel in terms of "murderer from the beginning" and "father of lies" (Jn. 8, 44). His aim is to kill, his method to deceive. He leads us astray by making us think we are just and that we have no need of another to practice the justice of the law. He suggests that we are not sick and have no need of a physician. We are victims of Satan each time that we think we are faithful to God and are obeying him as we should, each time that we consider that good is as it were established in us. The same misconception and the same illusion are present throughout our lives and that is why we find it so difficult to understand that the sin *par excellence* is that of the pharisee who, with a good conscience, does the opposite of what he claims to be doing. In seeking to respect God, he ends by putting him to death. Satan's astuteness consists precisely in making sinners of us under the appearance of justice. He makes use of the laws instituted by God. At the same time he induces us to submit to them not because they are God's commands, but of our own will. We cut ourselves off from the source of life, asserting nevertheless that obedience to the commandments and nothing else interests us.

This lie, of which Satan is the father, is very often at work without our knowing it. At every level of our existence, we invest a considerable part of our strength with a view to justifying ourselves in our own eyes, for we do not want to await justification from another. Moreover, when we do this we have no consciousness of reproducing that sin of hypocrisy which is the leaven of the Pharisees. Our imagination easily paints them under the features of Christ's enemies whereas they were good-living men, like ourselves, who submitted to the laws of their ancestors and whom the zeal of God devoured, as it does us perhaps. Saul of Tarsus who persecuted Jesus was a devout follower of the Law, hardly more intransigent than those who treated him who was sent by the Father, as "a Samaritan and having a devil" (Jn. 8, 48).

If, on the other hand, Jesus cured in Galilee those who were suffering from blindness, it was with the purpose of showing that we are all blind by birth and that we have need of him if the scales are to fall from our eyes. The whole drama of the Gospel turns around this double fact: by dint of lying to themselves, those who think they can see are blind; those who admit their blindness perceive the divine light. "If you were blind, you should not have sin: but now you say, We see. Your sin remaineth" (Jn. 9, 41). That is to say, if you were to admit that you are blind and deceived by Satan, there would be some hope of liberating you from the darkness, but since you do not perceive this, since you refuse to perceive it, I cannot manifest the light to you.

The spiritual combat is here summed up in its paradoxical simplicity: the just man is a sinner, God's enemy and soon a murderer, who blinds himself by his good conscience, his good will and even his devotedness to the good cause; the sinner will be justified, for he admits that he is blind and a sinner, he raises his hands towards him who comes and knows that all he has to do is to wait for him with patience and respect. "If we confess our sins, he is faithful and just, to forgive us our sins and to cleanse us from all iniquity. If we say that we have not sinned, we make him a liar and his word is not in us" (I Jn. 1, 9–10). But we must be careful not to think that on the one hand there are those who wrap themselves in their justice and on the other those who acknowledge their sin—these two phases confront each other in every Christian; and the combat consists in the fact that our liberty is incapable of becoming stable and the danger of perversion is ever present. For if recognition of the sin obtains grace for us, we can monopolize it as our own possession and thus find ourselves in the position of the man who thinks that he has attained to sanctity by himself.

From this we can understand the significance of the weapons of poverty and humility recommended in the Gospel. The rich man who will be rejected because his hands are empty is the one whom his own justice fills without saving him. The one who amasses possessions on which he sets his heart, by that very fact establishes himself on a lie. On the other hand, the poor man asks himself in what he is blind, in what he lies to himself, wherein lies the hypocrisy of his thoughts, his will and his gestures. He even goes further (and, instead of remaining in the troubled waters of a bad conscience which turns everything to poison, these judgments on himself bring him sovereign peace) and with a clear-sightedness that is always on the alert, he sees that he is blind, that the lie is in him, that he is an obstacle to God, and that he is the real adversary. To enter into the victory of Christ, it is essential to begin by penetrating, right in the very center of liberty, to the discovery of the Pharasaical pride which is capable of denying God and putting him to death.

In this present phase of the spiritual combat, it is not only a matter of recognizing that we are of the race of Adam and of identifying ourselves with him as cause of all the evil, according to the formula of St. Catherine of Siena, for that is to assume a fact prior to our own existence, prior to our historical nature. It is equally essential to grasp that in our present liberty we are capable of doing harm, of advancing consciously and voluntarily into the darkness, of formulating a lie and of hypocrisy, i.e., of making ourselves like demons.

Adam is not the contrary of Christ, since the Word has willed to take flesh like that of the first man. Similarly, to recognize ourselves as a sharer in original sin is, as we have seen, the means of integrating ourselves into the human race in order to enter into the history of its salvation. There are present as yet only the first-fruits of the true combat, the essence of which lies in the absolute struggle within our own person of the spirit of evil and of the spirit of good. When we understand that we are capable of shutting ourselves away for ever, and absolutely, in a denial of Christ, our liberty finds itself torn between two possible issues and the conflict takes place, so to speak, outside history, beyond the successive situations through which we pass, in a sphere where the spirits confront each other openly. Between the first and the second Adam there is communication, even if, from the one to the other, there is a reversal of perspectives; between God and Mammon, between Christ and Belial, there is no similarity and their opposition when face to face can lead only to exclusion. The death struggle which is set up in our liberties is that between the murderer and him who is the Living One *par excellence,* and this conflict is expressed in us by the confrontation of the demoniacal pride which seeks to kill and the humility of the Gospel which is alone capable of receiving life.

The more our personality grows, in the very communication of the divine riches, the greater is the temptation, in fact, to turn against God. So long as we are children in the spiritual life, we have a constant need of dependence—our revolts could not last long. Urged by this desire of liberty which then finds no other issue but in flight, it is in vain that we try to escape for the panic experienced when we withdraw ourselves forces us to retrace our steps. It is the story of the Prodigal Son, it is that of the women who were sinners, whose heart, even in the sin committed through the heat of passion or through weakness, remained like the soft earth in which the good seed can always grow. But when through slow progress, our life and person have been brought into subjection to our clearness of mind and our will, when we have acquired the mastery over them and can move them according to our desires, what happens is that we are dazzled by the power entrusted to our liberty and that, seized with vertigo, we want to use it to assert ourselves, ourselves alone, without having to depend on anyone. Then sin is no longer accomplished through the deceitful seduction of the forbidden fruit, but becomes, without any intermediary, the satanical rejection of God and his invitation to us. This is the sin against the Spirit that will not be forgiven.

Mary of the Incarnation tells us how one day she experienced this tremendous temptation, when she was already very advanced in the ways of God:

> It seemed to me that I was in Paradise and in possession of intimate enjoyment of God, who held me in his embrace. That, however, soon passed and served to make my cross the greater, for I passed from an abyss of light and love to the depths of obscurity and painful darkness, seeing myself plunged into a hell which bore within it the sadness and bitterness coming from a temptation to despair. This temptation was, as it were, born in this darkness, without my knowing the cause of it, and I should have been lost through it if, by a virtue that was hidden, God's goodness had not supported me. I was sometimes suddenly pulled up short and it seemed to me that I really saw myself on the brink of hell and that, from the mouth of the abyss, flames came out to swallow me up. I felt in myself a disposition which made me strongly inclined to throw myself into them, in order to displease God whom this disposition was tempting me to hate.*

At first sight, such an experience which is found in other saints,† remains incomprehensible. The nearer we approach God, the more

* Cf. Mary of the Incarnation, *Ecrits spirituels et historiques* (Paris, DDB, 1930), II, pp. 377–378.

† We find the following in St. Teresa's *Autobiography of a Saint* (Knox, *op. cit.*, p. 255): "When I want to rest my heart which is weary of the darkness that surrounds it, with the memory of that country of light to which I aspire, my torment is redoubled; it seems to me that the darkness, assuming the voice

the forces of evil ought to become whittled down. Now what happens is the contrary: when our person gives itself to God in submission, the opposing spirits who confront each other show themselves with uncovered face.

Moreover, this is not only true of each individual, but of mankind as a whole. The Father overwhelms us with his gifts, but in proportion as he enriches us, our belief that we can do without him increases. Human enterprises then become more strange, more chimerical. Although they claim to set us free, they lead to slavery. This will be the case right through future centuries. Through the very intervention of God who assembles, enlightens and allows us to accumulate knowledge and strength, the power of man is ever increasing, at the same time as the risk grows of using these benefits we have received for evil. The adage according to which "the corruption of the best is the worst," can be applied not only to each person but to the human race which does not cease to perfect itself and whose revolt against God is in danger of becoming more monstrous, yet at the same time opens the possibility of a more perfect submission. This is indeed a mystery of human liberty which its very grandeur is in danger of wrecking.

The story, related by our Lord, of the unclean spirit driven out of a man who returns to retake his victim with seven others more wicked than he (Matt. 12, 45) retraces the conflict of the man who draws near to God. According to a process that is usual in all combats, when one of the adversaries has won a first battle, the other

---

of sinners, says to me as it mocks me, 'You dream of light, a fatherland embalmed with the sweetest perfumes, you dream of the *everlasting* possession of the Creator of all these marvels, you think you will one day come out from the mists which surround you! Advance, advance, rejoice in the death that will give you not what you hope for, but a night deeper still, the night of nothingness.' " A few lines below she notes: "I don't want to write about it at greater length. I should fear to blaspheme. . . . I am even afraid of having said too much. . . ." It must be added that this experience of Teresa's is really apostolic, for she is living over again in her faith the experience of the unbelievers of her time in order to save them from their unbelief.

redoubles in strength to crush his enemy. Thus was the case with Christ, who, light of the world, confronted darkness in the absolute and had to meet Satan from the beginning of his ministry before seeing him increase his violence and his audacity during his public life. No man who is anxious to follow the Saviour will be able to withdraw himself from the hostility of the prince of this world, ever more relentless and more subtle, for as long as he is a wayfarer the human being remains two-sided and the increased penetration of his gaze unceasingly reveals darker regions which, until then, have been beyond his reach. As the soul becomes more vigorous, how could evil, in the places where it must withdraw, fail to attain to a fresh concentration, daily more dangerous? Innocence, not the sweetness of the child in repose, but the force which goes through the folds of the heart, sees the source of sin rising before it, to the extent of sometimes being crushed by it, and fearing that the powers of the demons will succeed in submerging it. Woe, indeed, to him who, having discovered the purity of God, allows himself to be carried away by degradation—his "last state becomes worse than the first" (Lk. 11, 26).

However strange the fact may appear, the immense blessing of the meeting with Christ is inseparable from the danger of rejecting him. The fault of St. Peter was more serious than that of the rich young man, who thrust the appeal aside from the first glance. Because he had waited for a long time at the side of Jesus, because he had seen him accomplish works which no one else had done, and heard him expound the mysteries of the Kingdom, Peter committed a sin unknown to the man who, in the half-consciousness in which his desires wrapped him, refused a step forward in order not to have to renounce immediate blessings which he could feel and handle and to which his existence was accustomed. The wound of Peter, however, was changed into tenderness and love whereas the devotee of the Law went away from Jesus with his sadness—his hands full, but his heart withered, without a taste for life, nor perhaps even for the enjoyment of his riches. If we seek to withdraw from the peril inherent in the contact with God, we thus find ourselves thrown back into another and greater danger, for in it man compromises his humanity.

Thus the expansion of liberty cannot be effected without a struggle, and this manifests its dual nature. It is precisely this confrontation, this decisive battle of spirit with spirit that Satan seeks to avoid, for he knows that in it he must lose his power. So long as our person is involved in earthly cares and our actions are wrapped in shadow, he can at his ease mingle his poison with the benefits of God. The adversary hides himself under a semblance of life, utilizing what is not his to distill his venom into it, in order to strike and destroy. But when the full light appears and when, converted by the Word made flesh, the just man finds his innocence again, Satan no longer has anything left with which to seduce; it is no longer possible for him to veil his designs. He then reveals his perversity, his identity with evil and with death. Just as he did with Adam, the father of lies can deceive man by the promise of more life and more knowledge, but, at the very moment when he reveals himself in his inconsistency and nothingness, each one turns aside from him. However threatening the vision of evil may be in its origin, the horror it provokes strengthens liberty in the will to be faithful to God.

In order that Satan's downfall may be complete, we must go further still and accept death as the punishment of our sins. We have deserved it by the connivance we have entertained with evil. Moreover it is the supreme means of disarming Satan. Let us listen to Mary of the Incarnation continuing the account of her experience:

Then, in a moment, by his goodness and mercy, by a secret outpouring of his Spirit he roused the higher part of my soul to will in fact to be cast into hell. This was so that the divine Justice might be satisfied by the eternal punishment of my unworthy deeds which had deprived him of my soul, which Jesus Christ by his infinite mercy had redeemed by his Blood, and not with any idea of displeasing him. This act was a simple view of faith which drew me away from this precipice. I saw that I deserved hell and that God's justice would have done me no wrong in casting me into the abyss and I indeed willed this provided I was not deprived of God's friendship.*

Thus, although it is unpredictable to Satan, does the reversal work which turns his victory into a defeat. The superabundant light of God has caused the temptation to hate him and to prevent him from arising in us, but we can see that this temptation was leading us to death and the "night of nothingness." Far from begging God to deliver us from this abyss, we want to go down into it, but for a different motive. We desire hell which we have merited and death which is the fruit of sin. We welcome them, however, not to reject God but to remain in his friendship. At this moment the devil no longer has any power over us, for he has completed the work of death he had begun in Adam. Instead of separating us from God, death unites us to him, because our sinful being has passed through death.

The experience that the saints describe to us is the transposition of the struggle between Christ and Satan. When the latter has succeeded in putting God to death, he has doubtless attained his objective and he has no longer anything either to do or to desire. But, as the death of Christ is only the consequence of the Father's love, so his descent into the tomb is the supreme manifestation of the divine intimacy. The Christian thus enters into the combat of Christ, when Satan reveals himself to him as Sin and as Death, and when he accepts the fact that Sin and Death shall produce their effect in him, not because he loves them, but because it is necessary to pass through the death merited in Adam to have access to salva-

* *Ecrits spirituels et historiques,* II, p. 378.

tion. In each of our lives, the hour of Satan and of the power of darkness must thus one day, as in the earthly existence of Christ, link up with the hour fixed by the Father.

The Combat for the Kingdom

But the combat is not yet over, for it is essential that the victory of Christ should be made manifest. Just as our Lord rose from the dead and sent his followers to travel the earth in order to announce the good news, so it is necessary that upon the crushing and humiliation of the just should follow a new life of expansion. We have borne "in our body the mortification of Jesus, that the life also of Jesus may be made manifest in our bodies. For we who live are always delivered unto death for Jesus' sake: that the life also of Jesus may be made manifest in our mortal flesh" (II Cor. 4, 10–11).

If the coming of Jesus into the center of our person is not followed by our utter openness towards his love, it is because we have not yet completely passed through his life-giving death. We must therefore continually eat the Pasch in order that the old creation may disappear, making way for the new. For each one of us this will last until our own death, and for mankind until the second coming of Christ, i.e., until the moment when, all mankind having been transformed by his Cross, Christ will be able to present to his Father a perfect Kingdom.

In order to move towards this definitive establishment of the Kingdom the first weapon* which we should use and which will

* Faith, charity and hope are in reality the necessary and sufficient weapons of the combat for the Kingdom, for they both symbolize and bring about the presence of God in all our action. If the theological virtues are sufficient, it is because they fill human time and human liberty in accordance with their three dimensions—faith is turned towards the past on which it is based, charity is the eternal presence of God in the present, hope stretches out to-

enable us to save our lives (Lk. 21, 19) is patience. Under the pretext that we are already Christians, we often feel that we have reached the goal and want to see the unity of all things in Christ realized. In the face of the resistance we meet with, we are tempted, like the apostles, to call down upon our adversaries fire from heaven. Here again, to do so would be to return to Judaism and to confuse our manner of conceiving respect for God with the respect itself. With our own hands we shall never be able to make water issue from the rock, unless it is at God's order, to quench the thirst of the multitude. Even if, devoured by zeal, we travel the earth to make proselytes, it is not certain that God's blessing will accompany us. Divine wisdom remains foolishness in the eyes of men; and the strictest collective discipline or the most effective apostolic organization will attain their real objective only at the hour appointed by God.

Through a contrary but parallel impatience, we may even be tempted to judge that the essential thing is to make visible the power of Christ, who went through the world doing good, who cured the sick and who will come to dry the tears of our eyes. No longer under the calm impulse of Christ, but with a restlessness that is pagan, we then try to work frantically for the welfare of men and to measure the Kingdom, and the value of Christianity, by the possibility it offers of increasing temporal well-being. Any slowness is an object of scandal to us, and we ask to see, here and now, what

---

wards the future and towards the realization of the promises. These virtues are necessary, for it is through them and through them alone that our spiritual being is rooted in God through faith in Christ, through charity which comes from the Spirit of love and through hope which awaits the hour fixed by the Father and known to him alone. To be more concrete and to avoid sidetracking, we have preferred to treat here of patience which is, in the apostolate, the expression of faith, then to speak of detachment, considered as the negative counterpart of charity, and lastly of watchfulness, the concrete figure of hope.

are the fruits this message bears, threatening no longer to believe if they are not numerous enough and if they do not ripen quickly enough.

It is, of course, true that it is essential to re-establish in the world the unity of that first day when God, through man, exercised dominion over all things and all beings. It is also true that we must seek to translate into act "the charity of Christ which presseth us" (II Cor. 5, 14) in order to show that we have a mission to men. But Jesus Christ repeats to us: "It is not for you to know the times or moments, which the Father has put in his own power. But you shall receive the power of the Holy Ghost coming upon you, and you shall be witnesses unto me . . ." (Acts 1, 7–8). It is in the water of the spirit which flows from the Cross that we shall obtain the courage of patience. If God keeps us waiting, it is so that we may renounce dreams of domination and the thirst for enjoyment. He asks us to receive his Word "in a good and perfect Heart" and assures us that, on this earth, it "will bring forth fruit in patience" (Lk. 8, 15).

Patience would be a virtue to our own measure if it were not founded on faith in Jesus Christ. "The victory which overcometh the world: Our faith. Who is he that overcometh the world, but he that believeth that Jesus is the Son of God?" (I Jn. 4, 4–5). In order that the Kingdom of God may advance, we must thus base ourselves on the certainty that Christ, by his death, has triumphed and that, in his resurrection, he has already manifested this victory in human flesh. If we are uneasy over the future, disturbed by the obvious effects of the powers of evil, it is because we have not yet allowed to penetrate into the depths of our being the assurance that the universe is already, and as a whole, re-ordered to God in Jesus Christ. By faith we welcome into the world and we show in the light of day this strength of God which has overthrown the ancient serpent in his Son and we give this strength the possibility of expansion. It is, on the other hand, the lack of faith which bars the route to the Son of God and which prevents him from revealing his triumph. Far from leading us to idleness, the conviction that Jesus Christ is truly the Saviour of all is the means of receiving the communication of his energy and vigor.

The constancy of faith, which goes hand in hand with tried virtue (Rom. 5, 4), will enable us to acquire an even more precious weapon for the coming of the Kingdom—detachment in regard to our own works. "When you shall have done all these things that are commanded you, say—We are unprofitable servants; we have done that which we ought to do" (Lk. 17, 10). If we act, it is to obey God and not with the pretension of doing something of ourselves. As to the term of the action, that does not belong to us either. Everything comes from God and it is to him that the glory must revert. This stripping of self, at the beginning as at the end of our enterprises, is difficult. Since we must be good and true servants, how are we to devote ourselves entirely to a task, give ourselves to it with attention, interest and even with passion, use up our strength for the success of what we have begun for God, and at the same time remain entirely disinterested in regard to the result? Nevertheless, until we have succeeded in uniting these opposing terms, we cannot promote the effulgence of the glory of Christ, for it is our own glory that we are still seeking. It is essential that God should be the source of what we undertake, and that we should embark upon nothing unless it is for him and because he wills it. But it is equally necessary that he should be the terminal point and that, in success as in failure, his love alone should be made manifest.

In order that detachment in regard to the work to be undertaken and pursued may not lead to lack of interest, in order that the certainty of having done nothing may not lead to despair, and that, successful or unsuccessful, the issue may find us equally at peace, it is essential for us to act in and through the Spirit, and he alone must be our reward. What our Lord said in regard to alms, must be applied to all our activities, small and great. "And when thou dost alms, let not thy left hand know what thy right hand doth, that thy alms may be in secret; and thy Father who seeth in secret will repay thee" (Matt. 6, 3–4). Not only ought we not to act to be seen by others, but we ought not to accomplish anything that is seen by ourselves. We shall be detached and enthusiastic at the same time when our attention is no longer focused on ourselves, but when, coming from the Spirit who suggests the beginning of such a work to us, it considers only the Lord, who is the term of every enterprise. When obedience to God alone interests us and when he alone can quench our thirst, we can easily spend ourselves so that he is our only reward. When an enterprise has been begun, because the Spirit has come to us to move us, we can carry it to its conclusion without any return upon self, for we can see the Spirit advancing to fill us with himself alone. Our action then becomes transparent—the Spirit joins himself to our spirit to produce the fruits of the Spirit.

So that this wish may be realized in the concrete, we must keep a constant watch. We cannot slumber under the pretext that the Lord is all powerful and that he will easily know how to overcome the difficulties. Doubtless, redemption is already perfect in Jesus Christ, but he has come among us in order to make us enter into his suffering and his labor. Nothing can thus be accomplished if the liberty established by the Saviour does not respond to his invitations and if, by its work, it does not draw the universe into obedience to the Father. For the Christian, history is something real; it is not a book written in heaven once for all, whose words must be left inscribed upon the earth in a fashion that is always identical. If it is essential to watch, it is because something is really happening here on earth, it is because both each man and mankind are truly in danger of being swamped by evil and that creation is still in the labor of childbirth. We know the final outcome, but the route remains dangerous, and those who do not watch with prudence will find the house of the Bridegroom closed when they come to knock at his door. Human action is invested with incomparable seriousness because man is not considered by the Creator as a slave or even only as a servant—he is a friend and an indispensable collaborator. Through their contact with the Master, men have become gods (Jn. 10, 34) who must cooperate in the divine action here on earth. If the talents entrusted to us are not riches which it is optional to increase, it is because they belong to God and because he puts them into our hands so that through their transformation we may share in his power and even in his nature.

Emphasizing the necessity of vigilance, the Gospel marks the absolute price of each one of the moments in which human liberty finds itself engaged. It is in the present alone, by acting in it with all our strength and all our power, that we can find God. Christ appears under the guise of a thief intervening unexpectedly, not because he seeks to baffle us, or would wish to catch us by surprise, but because his coming is actual and because the moment in which he shows himself is sufficient for him, since his presence in it is total. It serves no purpose to have waited for him and found him yesterday, for it is no longer he whom we possess today but only the memory of his passage, which depends on our own resources and is in danger of enclosing us within ourselves; we must begin to keep watch all over again, so that he may approach at this very hour. Our past can have a meaning since it facilitates that attitude of complete opening of ourselves to God that has earned for us the reward of seeing God. It could not be a guarantee, as if the previous gifts could serve us as hostages and constrain the Lord to give himself.

Vigilance sets us free from what is passive to make of the human being and of all the realities to which he is linked, a pure spark of energy and of eternal youth. In this way, it is the forces of evil that are vanquished, those forces that strive to lull human liberty to sleep and enervate our courage. To turn towards the future which will see the full realization of the Kingdom is thus not to forget the present to dream of the coming day. It is rather to plunge into the actuality of the world, to allow God to raise it up even to him, to go down into the heart of the world in order to set free its energies, to free the universe from its leaden weight in order that grace may appear in it in its purity. Thus Christian hope is not a flight towards a distant future, it sends us back to present action, at the heart of which God pronounces the word of salvation and of meeting.

We can see in what sense it is possible to speak of a spiritual combat. It is not a question of crushing the enemy, still less of killing him as in the battles of men, but of allowing God to manifest his glory in the world, in letting the divine seed bear its fruits. To resist the enemy by not putting our confidence in ourselves, but by leaning on the rock which is Christ; to recoil before the enemy, to accept the sufferings or humiliations by which he strikes us, in order that we may be emptied of ourselves and that the Spirit of love may fill us; to work in this world while humbly waiting for the Father to put a term to his work, such are, in the spiritual combat, the means of conquering.

The marvel of the coming of Jesus Christ is that he has transmitted to men, his creatures, the weapons of God. Formerly Yahweh was seen to fight and triumph with his fidelity, the jealousy of his love, salvation and zeal (Isa. 59, 17). Henceforward it is we who fight in his place and who establish in the Spirit the Kingdom of his Son, by a faith as lasting as the fidelity of God, by a charity as jealous as his love, and by a hope of salvation which will increase our fervor.

4 THE DISCERNMENT OF SPIRITS

IN THE STRUGGLE AGAINST SATAN, liberty finds itself at grips with opposing forces that seek to entice it to evil. It must welcome the light and reject the darkness. But, as our enemy makes use of a lie to cause us to desire evil under the appearance of good, some work of discernment is necessary. The Gospel counsels us to join the wisdom of the serpent with the simplicity of the dove (Matt. 10, 16), for we are in danger of being led astray not only by the attraction of the things of this world, but even by our own good will and our very generosity. It was not courage that the Pharisees lacked, but perspicacity. "They have a zeal of God," says St. Paul, "but not according to knowledge" (Rom. 10, 2).

If we are to make progress in the discovery of God, spiritual intelligence is just as necessary as abnegation and the gift of self. As he concluded the parable of the Unjust Steward, our Lord even then deplored that "the children of this world are wiser in their generation than the children of light" (Lk. 16, 8). By what signs, then, shall we be able to recognize the spirit of Jesus and the spirit of Satan?

The criteria are of two kinds: subjective, i.e., concerning the affective situation and its trend; objective when such criteria consist of values which can be verified by others. These two courses of light, internal and external, will clearly have to be set in relation with and corroboration of each other.*

Subjective Criteria

When we open the Gospels, that of St. Luke in particular, we are surprised to see that the good news includes, together with the sending of the Spirit, the gift of joy. As the angel announced to Zachary, "Thy wife Elizabeth shall bear thee a son. And thou shalt call his name John. And thou shalt have joy and gladness and many shall rejoice in his nativity . . . and he shall be filled with the Holy Ghost even from his mother's womb" (Lk. 1, 13–15). Our Lady sang her joy after seeing Elizabeth (filled with the Holy Spirit) whose child leaped for joy (Lk. 1, 41–47). Then step by step joy

* Although we have not followed the rule adopted by St. Ignatius in his exposition of the different aspects of consolation, the present chapter can be considered as a short commentary on the third rule for the discernment of spirits, of which the following is the text: "When there is produced in the soul an interior movement by which it comes to be on fire with the love of its Creator and Lord and in which it can then no longer love for its own sake any created thing on the face of the earth but can only do so in the Creator of all things, I call that state consolation, as I do when the soul sheds tears which lead it to the love of our Lord through sorrow for its sins, or of the Passion of Christ our Lord or of other things directly ordained to his service and his praise. Finally I call consolation all increase of faith, hope and charity and all interior joy that calls and attracts us to heavenly things and to the real good of the soul by resting it and giving it peace in its Creator and Lord." *Spiritual Exercises,* no 316 (Rickaby, *op. cit.,* p. 68). The last lines will first be commented on and then the first, with emphasis on the love of the Creator as brotherly love and adding to the confession of Christ submission to the Church; lastly the relationship between consolation and the theological virtues will be explained.

spreads because the "consolation of Israel" (Lk. 2, 25) has at last come among us. Later, on the occasion of that going up to Jerusalem which was to prove decisive, St. Luke again makes the same connection between the two: "Jesus rejoiced in the Holy Ghost and said, I confess to thee, O Father" (Lk. 10, 21).

Joy is the principal sign of the presence of Jesus in us, because the Spirit is the overflow of love come down to us. Dwelling in our hearts, divine charity shows itself as a flood that wants to spread over our whole being to spiritualize it, to remove from it the weight of evil and suffering, to lighten it, that is, to communicate joy to it, that lightness that makes it possible for it to rise up to its source. Within this joy the ascending and descending movements are inseparable, for the God who stoops down towards us wills that we should rise up to him. That is why many spiritual writers have chosen the term "elevation of spirit" to express this dynamism of the joy that tends to bring us back to our origin.

On the prolonged joy of the ascent towards the Most High, follows a third sign of the Spirit, for the result of this ascent is not forgetfulness of things and of the world, it is the peace and rest of those who have at last found the object of their seeking, the God who fills them to overflowing. Spiritual tranquillity is thus in no sense comparable to idleness, it is, on the contrary, the ordering of our living forces, our facilities, our powers to divine Love. It is, in the welcoming of the Spirit, the supreme harmonizing, the complete response of all that we are. Thus it is integral activity. It is from harmony rediscovered that peace comes, it is from the reconciliation of the various elements of our being and at the same time from their differentiation that this equilibrium of the whole of our affective life, which gives us full awareness of ourselves and the strength to dispose of ourselves, can arise. In a formula charged with meaning, in which he takes these three signs of the Spirit of God and shows how each produces the other, St. Ignatius thus defines spiritual consolation: "All interior joy that calls and attracts us to heavenly things and to the real good of the soul by resting it and giving it peace in its Creator and Lord."* The love which comes down from on high immediately makes us rise up toward God, but the latter bends down towards us anew to fill us with his love and give us peace.

From this point it is easy to discover the characteristics of the spirit of Satan and the effects he seeks to produce. To joy he opposes sadness, to loftiness of soul, attraction towards what is base, and to peace, anxiety. But it is not in following this order that one can best define the method used by Satan in his will to enslave us. If he were to begin by sadness we should not move towards him, for no one can actually seek sadness unless he is already perverted.

The end eagerly pursued by each one of us is our own expansion; the spirit of evil will thus present a shortcut for attaining this by suggesting pleasures that give the appearance of happiness, but not its reality, the shadow and not the truth. Here we once more find the devil, the father of lies who, not being able to offer fruit of substance, weaves before our eyes a tapestry of illusions. By chaining us to the realities of the objects of sense, willed for themselves alone, he increases the creature's powerlessness to rise above things earthly. He tries to make us believe that our kingdom is in the visible and the tangible, and that there is nothing beyond. To prevent us from desiring and relishing the things from on high, he invites us to focus our attention on what is earthly, in order that we may seek to nourish and satisfy ourselves with it. The things and beings that are in the world do not belong to him; even through our sin they remain creatures of God, but what Satan suggests is that we should love them for themselves and he veils from our eyes the principle from which they emanate. Because he knows that our gaze should rise from this universe to the Creator, he draws us down towards flesh and blood to assimilate us to them.

* *Spiritual Exercises,* no. 316 (Rickaby, *op. cit.,* p. 68).

If we allow ourselves to be taken in by this artifice, a state of trouble and anxiety ensues, emanating from the disorder in which we are—we then find ourselves in a topsy-turvy state. It is in fact this attraction towards lower things that gives our person its orientation, whereas we were created for the subjection of the flesh to the spirit, the subordination of the powers of sense to those of reason. The universe is reversed for us and the only consequence of this is to prevent the elements of our personality from setting themselves in their rightful place. Along this road there can be no other outcome than destruction, failure and death, i.e., the dislocation of all the powers with which the creature had been provided. When man no longer admits that obedience is due to the Spirit of God, he separates himself from his Creator and, by that very fact, from the source of all unity and becomes incapable of avoiding the process of division that separates him from himself.

The normal consequence of this on the affective plane is sadness. It is the sadness of the rich young man who could not abandon his possessions to follow Jesus. Even more, it is the sadness of Judas, in whom we can grasp in all its brutality the final sign by which Satan can be recognized. Whereas joy leads us to supreme activity, which is a responsiveness to God in this world, the disturbance provoked by "the enemy of human nature," as St. Ignatius often calls him, throws us into distress and not only renders this radical abandoning of effort by which we think we can find the solution of the distension that is crushing us half-hearted and savourless, but brings it to the utter sloth of despair and soon to suicide. The unity sought for and desired is then attained under a contradictory form, for we disappear at the very moment when we think we have access to repose.

The effects produced by the spirit of good and the spirit of evil (effects which can be called *consolation* and *desolation*) each follow their own movement, through which they can easily be recognized. Nevertheless, these indications are still too fragmentary and do not account for the complexity of the problem under discussion, for Satan can cause false joy in a soul, disguising himself, as St. Paul says, as "an angel of light" (II Cor. 11, 14). Moreover, there exists a sadness which those who are willing to experience the Cross of Christ must inevitably experience. If that is the case, the problem of discernment is raised anew: how are we to know if our actual sense of feeling utterly crushed means that we are drawing near to our Lord and thus to his Passion, or that we are submitting to the domination of Satan; and, conversely, may our tranquillity of soul allow us to think that God is acting in us to direct us to him or should we conclude that tepidity and mediocrity have taken possession of us?

In the first place, no criterion enables us to recognize with certainty, at a given moment, the origin of a particular sentiment. To judge of the value of the tree we have to wait until the present consolation or desolation have borne their fruit. In other words, we can know of what spirit we at present are only by our spiritual orientation. Now any trend reveals itself only over a period of time. The light is all the easier to focus on the principle that moves us in proportion as the time at our disposal is greater. A man who read the Gospel for the first time would at first with difficulty distinguish the significance of the struggle which brought the Pharisees into opposition with Jesus. When he witnessed the zeal they manifested for God he could well foresee their conversion; he might on the other hand be worried at the prolonged lack of intelligence of the apostles. It is only gradually that the aim and intentions of each one will appear to him clearly. Similarly, at the moment of the Passion, would the denial of Peter of itself alone, allow us to foresee a contrary outcome for the treason of Judas?

Thus it would indeed be a mistake to think that we can establish ourselves in consolation once and for all even if we are fundamentally and constantly submitted to the Spirit of God. In the second epistle to the Corinthians St. Paul gives a typical example of this alternation of sadness and joy. The interest of this passage is to set forth the sentiments of the apostle in his dialogue with the faithful of whom he has charge; their reactions are inseparable from his. Paul's reproaches have saddened the Christians, but this suffering was good because it resulted in their conversion:

For although I made you sorrowful by my epistle, I do not repent. And if I did repent, seeing that the same epistle (although but for a time) did make you sorrowful, now I am glad: not because you were made sorrowful, but because you were made sorrowful unto penance. For you were made sorrowful according to God, that you might suffer damage by us in nothing. For the sorrow that is according to God worketh penance, steadfast unto salvation: but the sorrow of the world worketh death (II Cor. 7, 8–11).

The desolation wrought by the just reprimands of St. Paul might have provoked among his correspondents a refusal to recognize their fault, might have enclosed them within themselves and resulted in their spiritual death. On the contrary, in the case under discussion, the Corinthians have acknowledged their sin, have repented and have been flooded with a joy that has reflected back on the apostle.

If, however, we are really attuned to the Spirit of God, the sadness thus remains transitory and everything terminates in Joy. The term of God's action is always and without exception consolation, for the Lord can never will anything else in our hearts but the upsurging of his love. Yet, so long as our resistance lasts, the very brightness of the joy reveals our disorder and the darkness in which we live, so much so that the sight of it makes us suffer. The expression "sadness according to God" must thus be correctly interpreted. It is not God who causes this sadness, but our own incapacity to receive him. His coming is the occasion of suffering, but the latter has no other cause and origin but Satan. Of sadness, as of the Cross of Christ, it can be said that it is a good, because it is a passage towards joy and towards the fullness of the Resurrection in us. In itself, however, it is an evil. It is even the revelation of evil *par excellence* and in no case can it be the end of God's action. The twofold aspect at any given instant of consolation and desolation thus does not signify that they are in any sense equivalent.

Again, however, it will be objected that so long as we are on this earth there is no term that is not a passage to something else. If, then, we admit theoretically that the special attribute of God is to give joy and that of Satan to give sadness, how am I to know from a practical point of view if this sadness that I feel comes from the Saviour entering into and purifying me, or if I am plunging into sin under the impulse of the spirit of evil? Conversely, how am I to know, in the case of an alternation of joy and sadness, whether the joy is not perhaps a false consolation coming from the "sadness of the world," or whether it is the consolation of God? We shall only be able to answer this question by examining the objective criteria of discernment, but even at this stage valuable indications can be given.

If we review a fairly long period of our existence, we can easily perceive a general trend which shows us whether we are moving towards an increase of joy and of the liberty which is inseparable from joy. If, indeed, the sadness, far from weakening us, is always an occasion of our progressing in the understanding and practice of the things of God, this will then be the proof that the Spirit of God dwells in us and that he is guiding us towards an increasing responsiveness towards his action.

When setting forth the causes of desolation in one of the rules for the discernment of spirits,* St. Ignatius suggests the three prin-

* The following is the text: "There are three principal reasons for which we find ourselves sad. The first—because we are tepid, lazy or negligent in our spiritual exercises; then it is on account of our faults that spiritual consolation

cipal stages we shall have to go through to find consolation. In the first place we must recognize that God's action in us encounters sin as an obstacle. As St. Paul counselled the Corinthians, we shall have to repent before the sadness experienced by our own faults can be changed into joy. In order to penetrate more deeply, the Spirit of Jesus will then have to purify the alloy we form and change us into gold. This transformation, however, cannot take place unless we pass through the fire of trial. The love of God is a flame that is not consumed because in it there is no admixture and no impurity. If we have the impression that it is devouring us it is because it must consume whatever in us escapes it or still refuses to abandon itself to it. Hence our present desolation. If, however, instead of seeing in it only the negative aspect, we realize its significance, far from being crushed by it, we are awakened to progress and become capable of crossing the desert with a peace and a strength that do not come from ourselves. It then remains for us, in order to taste consolation in itself, that is, the gratuitous gift, to discover in a third form of desolation that we are powerless to give ourselves love and joy. In this final stage, desolation is identified with humility. It can even assume the appearance of sadness and yet be indistinguishable from consolation, for its sole source is to be sought in the open side of Christ. Through the Spirit who is given to us, all sufferings become joy.

We can see how consolation and desolation in turn provide the

---

is withheld from us. The second—to test what we are worth and how far we can go on his [God's] service and praise, without such a salary of consolations and immense graces. The third—to make us learn and know in truth, so that we may feel it interiorly, that it does not depend upon us to produce or preserve very great devotion, an intense love, tears, or any other spiritual consolation, but that all is the gift and grace of God our Lord; and in order that we may not go to make our nest elsewhere and puff up our mind to pride or vainglory, by attributing to ourselves devotion or the other effects of spiritual consolation." *Spiritual Exercises,* no. 322 (Rickaby, *op. cit.,* pp. 70–71).

rhythm for important periods of our lives. Yet this alternation is not repetition. It has a meaning and it assumes, in proportion to the rhythm of our life, new aspects which allow us to glimpse the goal. Thus it is not a vicious circle into which we enter, in which in the course of each alternation, joy and sorrow are again found identical with themselves. Very much to the contrary, the increasingly purified forms which consolation assumes, correspond to the figures under which desolation appears, so that the certainty of our growth in the Spirit of God may be conveyed just as much by our consolation as by our desolation. Their succession during a definite period informs us about our situation as a whole. To perceive that we are sad because of our sin, and then sad because we can serve our God only so little and so badly, in short that we are sad because we see ourselves radically incapable of responding to love, this will have as much significance as to see ourselves at first freed from conscious faults, then brave during times of aridity and finally radiant with humility. When the soul grows in God, the nature of the desolations by which Satan seeks to disturb us reveals the significance of our present state with as much clearness as the consolation transmitted by the Spirit. The conjunction of these opposing sentiments thus increases both the possibility and the correctness of our discernment. If the forms assumed by consolation and desolation followed each other in inverse order to that just described, it would then be clear that Satan's hold upon us was in process of growing.

It is easier to understand why there is no discernment possible at a given moment. A succession which points to a definite significance is necessary, for the forms assumed by joy and sadness are reciprocal. The more the spirit of Jesus reigns in us, the more energy Satan puts into his attack. Certainly the two terms difficult to distinguish at the starting-point, become increasingly differentiated until they confront one another clearly. But as the spirit of evil is capable, during a period of desolation, of imitating the appearances of consolation, it is impossible to discern their true nature here and now, particularly as the maximum of light at which we arrive is equally a maximum of obscurity. For the believer who today listens to the account of the Crucifixion, it is clear that Christ overcame Satan on Golgotha; at the actual time, however, all appearances were to the contrary, since the primitive design of the devil was accomplished. Even in our own days, if it were possible to stop the course of history in the evenings of our Good Fridays, would it be so easy to grasp immediately the difference between the atheist who proclaims the death of God as a triumph for his cause and the Christian who rejoices in it for a different reason? The action of the spirit which is made manifest through our affective nature must thus be interpreted in relation to the time and transformations which are effected in it.

Of themselves alone, however, these subjective criteria are not sufficient to enlighten us, for existence must manifest its truth externally as well as interiorly. We must thus look to objective criteria so that, the tree being judged by the fruits it bears, all ambiguity as to the direction and value of our thoughts and sentiments may be removed.

Objective Criteria

What joy did in our hearts to make known the presence of the Spirit of God, fraternal charity effects in a visible fashion. In both cases it is indeed a question of the upsurging of divine love, always unpredictable and always awaited, which but lately regenerated our persons and which now seeks to show itself in works and construct the Kingdom which men will have to recognize. This movement which carries away in its train the Christian dwelt in by the Spirit, is not to be confused with the need of giving ourselves to others such as a happy temperament may feel. It is the quiver of never-failing divine youth which tends to communicate itself. When it fills a human being, the true joy that is love cannot be contained in him. It must show itself, utter itself, find expression in word or song, change into gestures and acts, since, for the love of God, the soul is only the temporary resting-place of a force that is self-diffusing. On the countenance of Moses who, in order not to dazzle the children of Israel, had to veil his face, the reflection of glory is the image of this charity of the Spirit who, after having illumined our hearts, cannot but diffuse himself.

In his first Epistle which is a veritable treatise on the discernment of spirits, St. John on several occasions returns to the importance of the love of our neighbor as a criterion of our belonging to God.

> He that saith he is in the light and hateth his brother is in darkness even until now. He that loveth his brother abideth in the light; and there is no scandal in him. But he that hateth his brother is in darkness and walketh in darkness and knoweth not whither he goeth: because the darkness hath blinded his eyes (I Jn. 2, 9–11).

The justification of this principle is simple: "He that loveth not knoweth not God, for God is charity" (I Jn. 4, 8). If it is to dwell in us, this love must be continually related to the act by which God first loves us. It must always subsist in the state of inception and reveal the gratuitousness from which it has sprung. To love one's brother is in fact to enter into communion with him not once for all but in such a way that each day it is as though we were meeting him for the first time.

We have considerable difficulty in accepting the fact that our charity is precarious, that it depends, in truth, on the actual outpouring of the Spirit of God. To stop where we are, to make our relations with others flow within fixed channels, or simply to put our confidence in the past to establish the union which should exist today, is to leave room for the spirit of death and lying which makes us repeat acts devoid of meaning and gestures that are incoherent.

Charity is a daily finding of the Spirit who renews himself in us so that the obstacles may be surmounted, the fetters broken and an understanding created that we could neither suspect nor even imagine. More than this—just as in sadness the Spirit enables us to expect liberating joy against all the evidence, so fraternal love considers in its generosity that nothing is definitively lost, that no situation is irremediable and that sooner or later union will triumph. For the light brought by the Spirit enables us to go further and deeper and to find again that secret point where, even in the very eyes of the blind, there still exists the possibility of sight.

The love of others is a criterion of the presence of the Spirit only in so far as it is creative, as it builds up better relations, clearer, more solid, more fruitful. It can only be a visible sign if we see it in process of causing growth and if we can perceive it in the building of the fraternal dwelling, all the stones of which will be perfectly joined together. Joy was tending to become elevation of spirit and attraction towards the things from on high, for it had to revert to its origin. Similarly the love of our neighbor that is spread abroad is extended into an ascending movement which bears the new temple formed by the faithful towards the keystone who is Christ our Lord. Divine charity which has come down towards us in Christ ascends again with him towards the Father after having united together those who claim the same faith and the same baptism. If Christ gives us a new commandment whose execution will enable his true disciples to be recognized, it is to group us together under his shepherd's crook and make us all return to the one and only sheepfold.

From now onwards we shall understand why, after counselling us to "believe not every spirit," St. John gives this second principle of discernment: "By this is the Spirit of God known. Every spirit which confesseth that Jesus Christ is come in the flesh is of God; and every spirit that dissolveth Jesus is not of God" (I Jn. 4, 2–3). In appearance this principle is insufficient if we do not understand it deeply enough, for every Christian confesses Jesus Christ or at least claims to confess him, without thereby acquiring the certainty that he is absolutely on the right path here and now. Spiritual tradition supplies us with a first indication when it invites us to meditate continually on the Word of God, especially on the Gospel, and to contemplate Jesus Christ in his different mysteries. In thus making contact with the Lord who is ever living among us, and who manifests himself to us in the narratives of the New Testament, we shall be compelled to respond and to allow the secret desires that dwell in our hearts to appear in the full light of day. We are still the hearers of Jesus. Even today he accomplishes miracles before our eyes and he explains his doctrine so that we cannot avoid taking sides and placing ourselves either among the sinners who call upon him or among the Pharisees who reject him. The reading of the Gospel is thus not only a practice to be commended, capable of rejoicing our hearts, it is also the privileged means of bringing to light the deep trends of our lives. Christ who has come to lead his people to his Father is still the one who is training us, he is "the sign which shall be contradicted . . . that, out of many hearts thoughts may be revealed" (Lk. 2, 35).

But just as consolation is impossible to interpret at a given moment, so we cannot know what spirit moves us if we content ourselves with choosing one scene or a few episodes in the Gospel. It is by going through all the mysteries of the Word Incarnate that we shall be able to discern the meaning which actually informs our existence. It may happen that with Peter we are scandalized at the announcement of the Passion; yet the way still remains open and, tomorrow, we shall be able to follow the Christ who walks before us. On the other hand it may happen that we are in admiration before the miracles that Jesus accomplished, that we are even filled with enthusiasm by the force of his words and the power of his actions, though this will not prevent us from abandoning him with the crowd or even from betraying him. Only the Blessed Virgin, because she was totally receptive, has been able to live the Gospel while growing continually in the Spirit of her Son. All others have passed through alternating phases of doubt and hope, of failure to understand and comprehension.

To choose and retain only some particular aspect of the Gospel is to let rejection seep into us, for it is to break the unity of Christ and by this fact to bar the route to the Spirit who gathers all things together. On the other hand to go over the whole of Revelation repeatedly is to enlarge our soul to the dimensions of the Spirit. Like the joy that finds in us a certain resistance, the totality of Revelation will find considerable difficulty in assimilating us, in making of our history and each moment of our history, the perfect reproduction of our Lord's own history. The obstacles that we shall see arising will then be for us so many signs of refusal more or less hidden. To neglect some particular scene in the Gospel, to pass over it in silence or not be able to contemplate it, shows that it is charged with a truth that we have not yet understood, and that on this point we are under the dominion of the evil spirit. On the other hand, if we make sufficient effort to get out of ourselves and to meditate on all the mysteries of the life, death and resurrection of Christ, like his hearers we shall receive light from him as to our person and we shall gradually enter wholly into the truth.

To confess Jesus Christ is thus to conform ourselves to him, to strive to follow him in order to imitate and love him better. We can doubtless be mistaken as to our sentiments and intentions if we are satisfied with professing our faith in Jesus Christ with our lips; but if we strive to raise towards him all the powers of our mind, if we allow ourselves constantly to be drawn by him towards what is on high, it is impossible that our sluggishness of mind and the malformations that, perhaps unconsciously, we keep secret, should not be unmasked. It is in this perspective that St. Ignatius in the course of the *Spiritual Exercises* proposes the contemplation of the

Gospel. He thinks he can thus see arising the reactions that enable us to discern the will of God in our regard: "Meditating on the life of Christ our Lord, let the retreatant consider, when he finds himself in consolation, in what direction God is urging him and similarly when he is in desolation."* The objective criterion that the confession of Jesus Christ constitutes thus sends us back to certain subjective criteria. Through the gaze we bring to bear on Jesus Christ, a judgment is effected and we have to recognize the conformity or non-conformity of our sentiments with the Word made flesh. To acquire spiritual intelligence, it is thus not sufficient to follow the course of our own thoughts, we must refer ourselves to the fullness of light given to us in Jesus Christ, which more adequately than our effort at lucidity, will separate the chaff from the good grain.

The upsurging of love that raises our spirit towards him who will submit all things to himself does not merely order our desires. It builds up the Church into an harmonious dwelling. The third objective criterion of our subordination to the Spirit thus resides in our obedience to the Spouse of Christ, in the correspondence of our thoughts and sentiments with what she asserts as true. That is why St. John writes: "They are of the world. Therefore of the world they speak, and the world heareth them. We are of God: He that knoweth God heareth us. He that is not of God heareth us not. By this we know the spirit of truth and the spirit of error" (I Jn. 4, 5–6). The Church is the new humanity that restores things and beings by situating them in the place willed by God and by making each one play the part assigned to it for the good of all. The consolation of the Spirit of God should thus lead us to respect better the laws of nature and grace established by the Creator and Redeemer, of which the Church is the sole guarantor here below.

* MHSJ, *Directoria,* p. 76.

Conversely, the desolation corresponds, in one way or another, to a resistance, in us and outside us, to that force of the Spirit that seeks to establish the universe anew in the Bride without spot or wrinkle. "For the creature serving thee, the Creator, is made fierce against the unjust for their punishment; and abateth its strength for the benefit of them that trust in thee" (Wisdom 16, 24). In this sphere, however, as in the interior world, disorder and harmony can be interpreted in contrary ways at a given moment. That is why it is essential to pay great attention to their alternation. Sin can produce a malformation of the real, but this difformity which causes suffering can lead to conversion.

The judgment of Solomon is a typical example of this discernment of spirits, wrought with the help of objective criteria (III Kings 3, 16–28). To bring to light the thoughts hidden in men's hearts, the wise judge inspired by God makes use of the most natural, the most primitive reactions, and he elicits them by proposing to kill the child that has survived. It is then clear that the woman who agrees to this proposed murder is in the wrong, for this proposal shows the term towards which the spirit that animates her is tending. On the other hand, manifesting her rejection of this supreme disorder, the mother of the child shows that she has not begun to spread division by what would be a theft. This biblical episode illustrates the way in which the different spirits, the spirit of good and that of evil, are at work in the most natural forces and how we can distinguish them.

The enlargement of this perspective enables us to apply the same principles to everything which touches the ordering of our personality. In regard to penance St. Ignatius explains on the one hand that we can be tempted not to do enough "through love of what is of the senses and through the erroneous judgment that human strength could not bear penance without becoming seriously ill."* But else-

* *Spiritual Exercises,* no. 89 (Rickaby, *op. cit.,* pp. 49–50).

where he says that we shall see on the other hand that we have exceeded the measure if "in this abstinence we have less physical strength or are less disposed for spiritual exercises."* The spirit of evil is thus the master in us if we are incapable of submitting our body to penance, but this spirit is equally in us if we disturb an equilibrium that we should respect because it is necessary for action. Thus when our body resists the suffering that we want to make it undergo, we can ask ourselves if this comes from the fact that we are demanding too much of it, or, perhaps, not enough, but in both cases its reactions show us that we are not in submission to the laws that govern it. The lasting harmony it will experience which will make us freer and more active will thus mean that we are in the hands of the Creator.

The passage from the natural to the personal plane gives rise to similar remarks. When the Church, for instance, pronounces the rules which are to govern conjugal, family, national or international society, she is merely uttering for our minds which are always more or less blind the laws which underlie the order and cohesion of these communities. She invents nothing, she adds nothing, she merely unmasks what the spirit of evil keeps hidden to prevent us from attaining peace and to multiply disorders.

It is the same in the religious sphere. If the Church demands submission of us, it is because she is already mankind totally ordered to God, and because, since the Spirit of God dwells in her, she already finds herself raised by him in harmony even to heaven. Obedience to the Church is thus the way in which we enter into the life of the Spirit which renews man, whereas insubordination puts us into disharmony not only with that universal institution but with mankind as a whole and thus, finally, with ourselves. When we declare that obedience to the Church is the sign of the Spirit of God in us, we are translating into objective terms what is true of

* *Ibid.*, no. 213 (Rickaby, *op. cit.*, pp. 189–90).

affective life—the joy that raises our spirit gives it the peace that is "the tranquillity of order"; whatever contradicts this peace can only come, in the last resort, from the spirit of evil. To disobey the Church is thus to refuse to submit to the laws established by God in renewed humanity. It is to do Satan's work.

It remains true that the suffering caused in the Church by resistance to our views or desires can have a twofold significance. In as much as the Church is already the perfect Bride, all suffering that we bring to her proves that the spirit of evil has spoken in us and is seeking to destroy man or something of man. In this sense the Church can say to us in truth: "You, you are of the world; I am of God." But in so far as she is not yet identified with the new humanity and remains a particular kind of society, her sadness comes to her from the fact that she is not totally submitted to the Spirit and the latter finds resistances in her.

In reality we cannot absolutely compare the situation of the Church and that of our liberty. United to her Lord, the Bride grows and develops according to the Spirit. She is always correctly orientated and all the sufferings she experiences will turn to her good. The Christian can never affirm that he is always in a state of spiritual growth and that he will not finally become, one day, the enemy of God. This means that his sadness can be a "sadness according to God," but it can just as easily cover "the sadness of the world that leads to death." On the other hand the suffering of the Bride who rises ineluctably towards Christ, her Head, is always a passage to a greater consolation. He who enters into conflict with the Church can thus be certain that, if he is not heard, it is because he himself does not sufficiently listen to the Spirit and that he does not show sufficiently that he is the bearer of the Spirit. If he agrees to be purified in the midst of the suffering he finds and causes, there will follow a more striking manifestation of God in him and the Bride of Christ will no longer have any reason not to submit to his desires. If she continues to oppose him, as, in her, darkness can only be passing and salutary, it is for him to think that he is wrong.

It would be contradictory for the Church, who is ever in process of growing in the Spirit, to be able to resist the Spirit who speaks in a Christian. If she does so for a time it is because the voice of the Beloved is still too intermingled in us with human words and intentions. So long as the Church does not admit our point of view, it is she who is right and we must thus obey her. For him who dwells in the Body of Christ, "all chastisement for the present indeed seemeth not to bring with it joy but sorrow: but afterwards it will yield to them that are exercised by it the most peaceable fruit of justice" (Heb. 12, 11).

Spiritual Experience

The presentation of the criteria of discernment has merely described certain aspects of the theological virtues*—brotherly love which manifests charity, the confession of Christ in whom faith is expressed, finally submission to the Church, which already realizes the promises and thereby establishes our hope. These facts are in danger of remaining formal if we do not consider in them the unfolding of the activity of the Spirit in the world and if all the signs of the presence of the Spirit, in us and outside us, do not

* The weapons of the struggle for the Kingdom (cf. pp. 87–88, note) already sent us back under particular modalities to the theological virtues. There is nothing surprising in this, since they are in us the fruits of the presence of the Spirit. Their order of appearance is not the same here, for, in the combat, patience, detachment and vigilance followed each other in accordance with the appearance of the virtues in time: faith, linked to the past, precedes charity, active in the present, and hope which leads us along towards the end. In speaking of the criteria of discernment, we adopt on the other hand an essential point of view; that is why charity at first appears as the source of faith, for it is the Spirit of love who enables us to believe in Jesus Christ and who tends to fill the universe at the heart of the Church, the place of hope.

lead to an experience and a dialogue with God, in accordance with a depth and an extension that are new. To say that the Spirit of love engenders brotherhood, that in him alone we are capable of seeing the Word and of submitting to his Bride, this could easily express merely abstractions, useless for helping us to live more in communion with God.

At a time when technology has desacralized the universe and when man no longer sees in it more than his own image or that of his power, religious consciousness could not, in order to find itself, adopt any other ways but those of interior experience. For the scholar, such, at least, as many imagine him, all can be explained, all can be transformed, in accordance with his desires. Losing its mystery and in some way its transcendence, the visible world becomes incapable of giving us access to God. Thus an appeal to the resources of subjectivity is inevitable. The psychologist, that other wizard of modern times, doubtless tries in his own way to link up his domain with pure science, but he knows that his endeavor is more delicate, for the laws of man and of what is human elude our investigation much more than those of nature. However this may be, experience proves that the interior life can be progressively trained for the meeting with God, whereas the research made to reveal the divine action in the universe clashes with mental habits so deeply anchored that the bold men who venture therein are not unreasonably taxed with poetry and illuminism.

We must thus first teach discernment by the interpretation of interior sentiments. Through them is made clear at the root of liberty the intervention of the Spirit who transforms our existences, slowly opens broader horizons and awakens us to a more receptive understanding. Many are the Christians whom the knowledge of the will of God leads to unexpected changes, to a deliverance from miseries which they thought they would have to retain till death, to a peace which nothing could disturb any more. By the evidence of this progress such people come to discover that the dialogue with

God is effective. The existence of the Spirit is no longer merely asserted by them in blind faith; it is grasped as a reality, more certain than the things and the beings that we can feel and touch.

If, however, spiritual experience, made possible by discernment, remained at this stage, it would sink into subjectivism and would never link up with total human experience. If it is to see that the presence of God is active in history and in the universe, it must go out from itself. Moreover it is the dynamism proper to the interior grasping of the Spirit which moves such experience to turn towards visible things for, when indeed it is real and not imagined, the result of God's intervention is to transform our vision and give it a keener penetration and a wider field. If it were the result of pure introspection, the analysis of thoughts and sentiments would inevitably tend to make us forget the world but since it puts us into relationship with God, the human subject from his very source is projected outside himself, so much so that he can no longer content himself with discerning a God "who can be felt by the heart" and he finds himself sent back to creative interest in others and to the objectivity of the divine work. From the very center of the person in his secret relationship with God, the world rises up no longer like an image spread out before our eyes but as an operation that reveals uncreated wisdom. Well guided spiritual progress is not achieved only in enterprises carried out here on earth, but in a new knowledge of the cosmos, in which God makes himself manifest, and of history, in which he reveals his designs to mankind.

The exchange which is established with God by the certainty of his interior action is thus inseparable from a link at the source with what is created and what is human. For thousands of years men have affirmed the presence of God in the heart of the visible world. A religious experience would be neither complete nor true if it did not integrate afresh this element which touches the very essence of all religion and all culture. Neither would such experience be Christian, since the confession of Jesus Christ in the flesh can never be separated from faith in a redemption of the whole universe by the same Word and Lord.

For the man of today, the recognition of the action of the Spirit, in the totality of human history and of nature, will come more often than not through the understanding of the mystery of the Church, as the body of the mystical and total Christ, an understanding which will grasp this action through a hierarchized human society, inscribed in time and subject to the vicissitudes of time. We can no longer, like our ancestors, enjoy the immediate evidence of the unity of all things in God, for our civilization has produced manifold divisions at all levels and in every order. We must thus patiently fashion, under the guidance of the Spirit, an experience that excludes nothing and that is equally at ease in the search for God's ways in the most intimate heart of the human person and in the grasp of his work throughout the unfolding of the generations or the progressive development of life under all the forms it may assume. All visible manifestations, from the elementary figures of the inanimate down to the complex juridical structures of societies, those of the Church in particular, must gradually become realities within the Spirit, realities in which he wants to be loved and contemplated. In turn, the mysteries of the Godhead must appear, as it were, diffused at every moment and given to men each day in order that they may be impregnated with them in this world which strives to be profane but which nevertheless everywhere breathes forth the true and unique Spirit.

Explaining what the coming of the Bridegroom, the word, means, St. Bernard shows us in a sublime passage how consolation is both joy, warmth, awakening of the soul within, and, without, the transformation of our lives, whereas desolation produces, both within and without, contrary effects. Spiritual joy is a force which renews our existence and this renewal amplifies and deepens our dialogue with God.

Since his ways are forbidden to our investigations, you will ask me how I have been able to know his presence. It is because he is living and active—scarcely was he in me than he drew my drowsy soul from its sleep. My heart was hard as stone and sick; he has roused it from its lethargy, softened and wounded it. He also began to weed, to pull up, to build, to plant, to water the arid earth, to light up the dark places and open the closed cells, to make the frozen parts glow with warmth; better still, he made straight the crooked ways and smoothed the rough ground to such an extent and so well that my soul blessed the Lord and the whole of myself began to sing the praises of his holy name. You can see clearly that the Word, the Bridegroom, who has entered into me more than once has never given me any sign of his coming whether by voice, by visual image, or by any other approach perceptible to the senses. No movement on his part indicated his coming to me, no feeling has ever warned me that he had crept silently into my interior retreat. As I have just said, I have understood that he was there by certain movements of my own heart—the disappearance of vices and the repression of my carnal appetites have made me know the power of his virtue. The calling in question or testing of my hidden sentiments has brought me to admire the depth of his wisdom. The amendment, however slight, of my way of living, has given me the experience of his sweet goodness. On seeing my spirit, I mean the interior man in me, renewed and reformed, I have caught sight of something of his beauty and, finally, the excess of his grandeur, when I consider all that together, has thrown me into amazement.

On the other hand, as soon as the Word has withdrawn from me, all this falls back immediately into its former torpor and begins to grow cold as if the fire were removed from beneath a boiling cauldron. Here then is the sign given me of his departure. My soul is irresistibly caught up in sadness until he comes back and, as on each occasion, warms my heart, which is the mark of his return. Thus having this experience of the Word, do not be astonished that I dare to borrow, in order to call him back when he is gone, the very voice of the Bride. My desire, if it is not equal to hers, is not without resemblance to it. As long as I live, to recall the Word, I shall use familiarly this same word—Come Back. I shall not cease in some way to cry after him, to proclaim the desire my heart has of him, begging him to come back and restore to me the joy of his salvation by giving himself to me again. I admit to you, my children, I no longer take pleasure in anything so long as what makes my only pleasure is not within my reach. I thus beg him to come not with empty hands, but all full of grace and truth, that is, in his usual way, as he did yesterday and the day before.*

* St. Bernard, *Oeuvres Mystiques* (Paris, Ed. du Seuil, 1953), pp. 766–768.

5 THE SPIRITUAL CHOICE

When the nature of discernment has been understood, it would seem easy to define the spiritual choice as rejection of the spirit of evil and acceptance of the spirit of good. But in order to understand the significance of such terms, it is necessary to focus our attention on the other trends of human liberty. Human liberty goes far beyond deliberation, which is linked with discernment, eventually appearing as a pure relationship with God; but it goes equally far in the earthly sphere showing itself, in the results it achieves, as a force capable of transforming the world into the image of Jesus Christ.

The taking of any decision thus links us with the human person on three levels. First of all at the center, where the origin of our being is revealed in that relationship of love which is creating us at every moment, a relationship which we must recognize and ratify; then at the point of awakening of our faculties in that domain in which the affective nature of the person is an expression of the general state of harmony or division of those faculties; finally at the exercise of our different faculties of memory, understanding and will, which posit acts to make us effective in the world.

Though it is total and complete when it expresses itself according to these three dimensions, liberty can, however, be grasped by our consciousness only through one of them. We then judge of the rightness of a particular choice by the true light in which it places one or other of these sectors of the personality. To estimate the worth of a spiritual decision, we thus have three criteria at our disposal: the authenticity of our union with God, the unity of the different elements of our being, the cohesion which our action assumes in relation to ourselves, to others and to the world.*

Union with God

Every decision engages our destiny. We can indeed spend the greater part of our lives behaving like automata or like superior animals who allow themselves to be guided by their desires and remain the playthings of the forces imposed upon them. But a

* The development of the present chapter is an attempt at an explanation of the three times or occasions of election mentioned in the *Spiritual Exercises,* no. 175–177 (Rickaby, *op. cit.,* pp. 152–153). It seems to us that these times are situated, as has just been said, on the three levels of human existence in its relation to God, to self and to the world. It is clear that these three aspects are found in the three ways of choosing the will of God, but in each of them one element is privileged and it is from that one element that the others are envisaged. The spiritual choice is perfect when it covers all these aspects of human reality and when, from the center of the person, it descends to the source of the faculties of the soul and guides them in their exercise.

Here we again find the three trends of liberty, such as the sin of Adam found them under a negative mode. Instead of separation from God, the spiritual choice should lead to union with God; instead of engendering separation with man, it should accomplish the reconciliation of man with himself; finally, instead of provoking the hostility of nature, it should work for the progress of the cohesion of the world.

conscious and voluntary act cannot remain entirely profane. Since nothing escapes him who is the sole Creator of all things and our sole Redeemer, we are compelled to take position for or against him as soon as we go beyond our instincts and seek by a movement of reflection either to curb them or on the contrary to satisfy them. To wish to occupy ourselves solely with what is earthly, in a fashion that is earthly, without appealing to any transcendental values, is tantamount to refusing to allow such values to penetrate our lives—thus it is to reject them. Such is the burden which weighs upon man, of whom Pascal said that he has "set sail" and cannot bring it about that this should not be so. To refuse to turn our eyes towards other things than the preoccupations of this world or even to separate our religious from our temporal life leads in the practical order to denying that our existence can have a meaning. For us there is no natural destiny that would be sufficient unto itself and from time to time would come in contact with a supernatural destiny. There is only one concrete and existing man, condemned to choose between plenitude, both natural and supernatural, given in Christ, and the total destruction of self in Satan. That is why our Lord put this dilemma clearly: "He that is not with me is against me" (Matt. 12, 30) and "he that is not against you is for you" (Mark 9, 39).

If every free act is a religious act, it follows that it cannot be the invention of the one who chooses. It is obedience or disobedience to the will of God. To free oneself is not to pass from the enchainment of self to licence, it is to be "freed from sin to be made the servant of justice" (Rom. 6, 18). St. Paul points out clearly that there are only two possibilities for man: to be the slave of sin and free in regard to God in order to journey to death, or to be the slave of God and free in regard to sin, to find eternal life.

As you have yielded your members to serve uncleanness and iniquity, unto iniquity: so now yield your members to serve justice, unto sanctification. When you were the servants of sin, you were free men to justice. What fruit therefore had you then in those things of which you are now ashamed? For the end of them is death. But now being made free from sin and become servants to God, you have your fruit unto sanctification, and the end is life everlasting (Rom. 6, 19–22).

In any case, then, as creatures we are subjected to a force that is beyond us and our liberty is never self-creating. If it becomes a living thing, it is in so far as it enters into the creative and redeeming act and welcomes the divine life within itself. "Present yourselves to God, as those that are alive from the dead; and your members as instruments of justice unto God" (Rom. 6, 13).

The true spiritual choice is thus that which leads us to the acceptance of the will of God in our regard and to the refusal to follow our own solitary desire, which is always that of evil. But it is necessary to go further, for not only can our liberty not give itself its laws, not only is it obliged to live in obedience to another, but of its own strength this submission is impossible to it. God has first to put his will unto us, then he must make us recognize it and enable us to accomplish it. In fact, only Christ can respond in us to the injunction of the Father; and so long as he is not in possession of our hearts, so long as we do not act with him, through him and in him, our daily conduct can only be inspired by the spirit of death. It may come about that we consider this life in Christ of which St. Paul speaks as something extraordinary and remote. The formula, "I live, now not I: but Christ liveth in me" (Gal. 2, 20), seems to us true indeed, but unrelated to our experience. Yet it sums up the whole of Christianity. In so far as we do not know that our liberty consists in ratifying the action of God and that, despite our helplessness, it is for him to show us the way and make us walk in it, we have not yet entered upon the spiritual life and cannot speak in the Spirit the language that is spiritual.

Moreover, all we usually perceive is our acts, our feelings and our thoughts, although we know by faith that God alone in us can respond to God and that only Christ, with whom we have been crucified, can accept the will of his Father in the Spirit. To use an expression of St. Ignatius whose aim, though in quite another context from that of St. Paul, was the same reality and the same definition of our liberty as his: "The love which moves me and makes me choose a particular object must come down from on high, from the love of God. In this way he who chooses must first feel within himself that the greater or lesser love conferred upon the object of his choice is solely for his Creator and Lord."* Although apparently unbelievable this language of the saints is yet the only one which exactly defines the essence of our lives as men and as Christians. So long as the love of God is not recognized and grasped as a primordial truth, our human experience lacks depth. It knows nothing of its principle and foundation. Yet this love of God is, in its entirety, in Christ who has been given to us. We do not have to seek it elsewhere in some esoteric discovery or other which would put us in contact with it by subtle methods. It is integral in this Jesus Christ whom the Gospel puts before us, in these sacraments in which he continues his acts as Redeemer and his miracles. As he delivered himself once, so he delivers himself for us still each day and at every moment. Our mistake is that we continue to know him "according to the flesh: but now we know him so no longer. If then any be in Christ a new creature, the old things are passed away. Behold all things are made new" (II Cor. 5, 16–17).

To know Jesus according to the Spirit, that is, to realize that he has identified himself with us on the Cross, we have to re-learn that expectation of the Bridegroom, of which Christ speaks to us. Just as he came once for all on the occasion of his Incarnation, in order to come to mankind, so he comes for each one of us in the eternal

* *Spiritual Exercises,* no. 84 (Rickaby, *op. cit.,* p. 155).

present. In the middle of the night of a faith which is not yet developed, a cry is raised: "Behold the Bridegroom cometh—Go ye forth to meet him" (Matt. 25, 6). But to hear these words, we must have waited patiently, we must have kept watch and must without ceasing be ready to walk before him. We must have turned towards him with an attention which remains ever awake, never wearying at finding that he tarries in coming, and knowing, as St. Bernard says, that if he always comes too late for our desires, he always arrives in time for our deserts.*

This experience of the love of God which seeks to descend into us to become one with us and enable us to accomplish the will of the Father as a divine will which will assume the whole of our humanity in itself, is not only a difficult thing—for us it is absolutely impossible. Yet it is on this very impossibility that our faith must peacefully rest. No more than it depends on us to add one cubit to our stature, is it in our power to accomplish, according to the Spirit and in Christ, the acts which are suggested to us. Where we are wrong, however, is in not making up our minds about this fundamental absence of strength and in seeking another way of liberty through ourselves alone. For, outside Christ, no other way is open but that of death by submission to Satan. To remain in a bearable or less uncomfortable no man's land is already to give way to that mediocrity and tepidity that God vomits out of his mouth (Apoc. 3, 16). We must, then, believe in love or else abandon ourselves to destruction.

In suggesting to the Christians of Corinth the mystery of the nuptial union of God with mankind, St. Paul is aware that he is no longer speaking the language of human wisdom: "Would to God you could bear with some little of my folly! But do bear with me. For I am jealous of you with the jealousy of God. For I have espoused you to one husband, that I may present you as a chaste

* Cf. *Oeuvres Mystiques,* p. 765.

virgin to Christ" (II Cor. 11, 1–2). Pursuing the trend of his thought and sensing the scepticism of his readers, the Apostle evokes the example of Eve, "who was seduced by the astuteness of the serpent." Either the Christian will agree to become in his daily life with all its details, the spouse of the Word made flesh, or he will again accomplish in his own way the sin that is the source of all other sins. There is no other outcome for our liberty.

It was foolishness on the part of those who approached Christ to think that he was going to be able to deliver them from their evils, it is folly to expect the love of the Father to descend into us, "to move our wills and put into our souls what we have to do."* Yet this amazing thing is more certain than the evidence of our senses, for the Lord has come to accomplish it in each one of us and there will be no cessation of his bringing us to receive his love and allowing it to well up in us. But for this it is necessary for the faith that cries out to God, as to the one and only Saviour, to arise in its purity, to leave aside all other support and abandon every other possibility except what is impossible to man, which is what is possible to God. So long as we have not reached absolute denial of self which means that we place our confidence in God alone, and so long as we have not entered upon that road of poverty which is without return, there is no chance of meeting him, for he does not come to us unless he can occupy the whole of our hearts.

At the approach of the Bridegroom, it is of no use for his friends to mourn (Matt. 9, 15) any more than it is to purify their hands or wear themselves out with zeal to accomplish the works of the law (Gal. 2, 16). We must then only await him, desire him, listen to and receive him, allow his love to enter into us, that is, to reveal to us what we are, and how he wills to make us live in him and through him, established in his love, so that we may accomplish his work and his glory may be made manifest to all with the

* *Spiritual Exercises,* no. 180 (Rickaby, *op. cit.,* p. 153).

diffusive radiance of his grace and beauty. This experience is at the same time unpredictable and commonplace, for if "I live now in the flesh: I live in the faith of the Son of God, who loved me and delivered himself for me" (Gal. 2, 20). Whatever he has done that I do not yet realize, it is thus sufficient that I should allow it to appear in me and that I should recognize it as authentic.

To respond to his will and obey him is thus first to allow him to love me freely and as he understands it, without setting before him as an objection my limitations and helplessness. If he loves me it means that he chooses me although he knows me, that he prefers me such as I am and not such as I might be. Consequently, to accept the divine will which offers itself to me today amounts to allowing myself to be chosen by him and to letting him choose in me what he wants me to effect. I should thus decide nothing that he has not himself previously decided in me. I shall do his work in truth when I content myself with allowing his love to indicate to me the direction to be taken and to give me the strength to go forward. This is the utter passivity of the soul who is the bride. It is also the supreme activity, because the greatest effort that can be demanded of man is to renounce all initiative, in order no longer to accept any but that which comes from Christ our Lord. In this abandonment, there is more strength, more passion, more courage and determination than in heroism, in which pride stretches itself forward to obtain salvation by its own efforts.

The Son only chooses me in the eternal present to make me choose here and now such and such a particular thing that I must accomplish so that his Kingdom may come. In calling me to him he does not take me out of the world, he rather brings me into it so that I may serve him in it; and my acceptance of his love remains inconsistent if I do not immediately undertake that which he destines me for. What an astonishing paradox is this divine preference which springs forth in me to raise me to God, in order that I may approach him with what I am and what I must do, but a paradox that becomes transparent when I have come to understand that love is only revealing itself to me in order to manifest itself in every place and in every creature, as it has unveiled itself in the whole of mankind and all creation through the Incarnate Word in whom the universe has been created and redeemed.

The essential criterion of the rightness of a particular choice is thus now defined. If in the act by which he clasps me in his love, God indicates his will to me, I shall know that I cannot evade the call I have heard except by turning away from the tide of love that is invading me. To soften my resistance the Father has no need to mingle with the goodness with which he favors me the severity of a threat, for he shows me that his love is identified with the return of all things in his Son, and asks me to share in it in my own way, that it may be hastened. If I acquiesce without further deliberation it is that the order given both fills all my desires and raises me above myself, bringing the universe with me. The sentiment with which the injunction received is accompanied is the affective resonance of this fullness of the Kingdom, beyond which nothing can be wished for and which my decision already brings about and realizes. Thus we recognize the will of God in unmistakable fashion, when there are found together, at the moment at which he unites himself to us, the act of his redeeming charity, our unhesitating acceptance of, and unshakable determination to accomplish, his work. That is why the most perfect sign of a "good and healthy" spiritual choice is given "when God our Lord moves and attracts the will in such a way that without doubting or being able to doubt, the faithful soul follows what is shown to it."* To look for an external criterion for this perfect act would be to allow the possibility of judging God from a point of view that would be situated outside God.†

* *Spiritual Exercises,* no. 175 (Rickaby, *op. cit.,* p. 152).

† The first "time" or occasion of the election according to St. Ignatius can be considered as the definition of the essence of liberty. For its perfection in fact does not reside either in the power of choice or in the deliberation, but

Reconciliation with Ourselves

The divine intervention of which we have just outlined certain traits takes place at such a depth that we will never perhaps be able to realize it except in its consequences. It is, moreover, wholly gratuitous; and, if we can ask for and desire it, we could in no case demand it. It is thus necessary to seek by other ways the present will of God in our regard.

The union that is born of the pure response of love to this present love of God cannot be grasped by our vision of things, but it is possible to discern the presence of its action through the fruits of unity that we see growing in ourselves. Although the root of our being remains hidden, we shall understand that we are in the truth in relation to God, if the elements that make up our personality are established in harmony and peace, for the one and only God is likewise he who unifies what he touches.

When consolation and desolation follow each other, they are accompanied by thoughts which suggest to us actions to be undertaken or abandoned. In a general way, if we look back to what has been said of the subjective criteria of the discernment of spirits, we can conclude that the thoughts that are accompanied with joy come from the spirit of good and, conversely, that those linked to sadness come from the spirit of evil, "for in consolation, it is chiefly the spirit of good which guides and advises us, and in desolation it is the spirit of evil whose advice cannot make us take a road which leads to a right resolve."* But, as has already been seen above, it is impossible to give a definite interpretation to such signs at any

---

in pure correspondence with the creative act in a moment coextensive with eternity. If we need time to welcome God and to carry out the order he gives us, that is a sign of our weakness. This factor which depends on the historicity of the human person, is not constitutive of its essence.

* *Spiritual Exercises,* no. 318 (Rickaby, *op. cit.,* p. 69).

particular moment. A certain length of time is necessary to discern the origins of the suggestions that arise within us.

The new element constituted by the thought of action to be undertaken seems to complicate the exercise of discernment, but, in fact, it makes it easier and more sure. If the enemy of human nature is, in fact, capable of causing an apparent joy to arise in us, it is to bring us through it to his "perverse intentions."* It is sufficient to follow the course of our thoughts to perceive that, from the good, we have passed to the less good and then to evil.† The positive climate of our affectivity matters little. Since God cannot will that we should accomplish an evil action, it is necessary to declare that we have been mistaken in considering as coming from the Holy Spirit this repose of the soul or this joy. Conversely, if the desire comes to us to do some good or very good action which because it is good seems as if it must be inspired by God, but if in other respects this project is soon accompanied by sadness, we can conclude that it is Satan who is endeavoring to make us accomplish what God is not asking of us, what he is not calling us to. Thus on the one hand, what I desire with joy can be objectively bad, and, on the other, what is best in itself, may be bad for me.

The spirit of evil no longer reveals itself only by the unfavorable affective climate in which it places us, but by the absence of harmony between some particular intention of acting and the sentiment which goes with it. Thus in the exercise of discernment we have at our disposal a double criterion, so that we should never decide before having seen united in us the good and our own happiness. So long as we remain torn, and the different parts of which we are made up are not in harmony when they would have become strengthened and enlightened, we can be certain that the spirit of division is still

* *Spiritual Exercises,* no. 332 (Rickaby, *op. cit.,* pp. 143–144).
† *Ibid.,* no. 333, 334 (Rickaby, *op. cit.,* pp. 144–145).

at work in us and that he is mingling his venom with the decision we are seeking to take for God alone.

It may be objected that a particular project, suggested by God, casts us into sadness because it makes us afraid and because it constrains us to the stripping of self, whereas the refusal to submit ourselves may bring us a certain satisfaction. This can occur for a time but since Satan has at his disposal only "apparent pleasures"* and not "true joy,"† he could not maintain in us a lasting happiness accompanied by determination and courage. But let us suppose that our joy is caused by an evil desire and the sadness by an intention of acting which would be good for us. It then remains for us to pass from the project to its accomplishment by the decision to act accordingly. If this choice in fact presupposes submission to the spirit of evil, nothing good can come out of it. After a certain time the anxiety and trouble in regard to the engagement which has been taken will be seen to reappear. The soul will not be satisfied, and will hesitate to follow this path with no outlet. If we then take the reverse decision, we shall soon perceive its fruits and, despite an initial repugnance and a sadness caused by a lack of renunciation, we shall find true joy and the strength to continue.

We sometimes wonder how it is that certain men, after an authentic religious experience, have been able to stray far from God. It is probably because, as happens to us in the smallest things, they have sought to entrust themselves exclusively to the feelings that led them to act. A violent passion can give the illusion of joy for some time. It enables man to go beyond his own limits, to undertake and bring to a satisfactory conclusion grandiose actions. Yet, in the course of time it blinds us and makes us abandon not only the customs of the Church, which would be of slight consequence, but her rules of morality and her ordinances. The mind then loses

* *Spiritual Exercises,* no. 314 (Rickaby, *op. cit.,* pp. 67–68).
† *Ibid.,* no. 329 (Rickaby, *op. cit.,* p. 143).

sight of the rules it should never transgress, and our sentiments are forged from new principles thus uniting the elements of the personality in their own way. Such a false harmony can remain for a long time before receiving the challenge of reality. This shows how necessary it is never to put our confidence in personal enthusiasm alone and to confront it relentlessly with what is recognized objectively as good and valid. "It is essential that all the matters on which we wish to make an election be in themselves indifferent or good and that they are connected with the warfare that our holy mother the hierarchical Church wages, being neither evil nor in opposition to her."*

Conversely the desire for the best and the most perfect can invade the human person to the extent of silencing the need for happiness and expansion. That is another sort of passion which sacrifices everything to the realization of a generous ideal which crushes all obstacles. Considerations of kindness and humanity are rejected as so many weaknesses and exhibitions of softness, and we see a withered perfection appearing which destroys what it touches instead of transmitting life. It may happen to us to act in this way, with the best of intentions, whenever, instead of allowing ourselves to judge by the authentic spiritual joy received from on high, we prefer, to the gentleness of God, the inflexibility of some project put into operation without waiting for it to have matured. If we wish to choose according to God, it is thus necessary to view the matter as a whole, seeing if our intention is good in itself and if it is confirmed by the spiritual element.

In the course of our deliberation the affective factor can be the first to enter into operation, the Spirit causing in us trouble or peace, in order to place some new proposition before us. When these various impressions follow each other, we may think first of all that they are due to fortuitous causes and that we should not dwell

* *Spiritual Exercises,* no. 170 (Rickaby, *op. cit.,* pp. 150–151).

on them. They follow courses the laws of which are unknown to us and their appearance or disappearance seems to depend on chance. Gradually, however, if we look carefully, we shall begin to perceive links between some project which returns to our mind repeatedly and a particular affective climate. Then, as we gradually become more attentive, a series of links will appear and it will become evident that God is expecting something from us—a change of life, a new trend to give to a former undertaking, etc.

We shall hesitate, perhaps, for a long time, but the hours that pass outline the contours of the divine will, and the lights, positive and negative, in which it is bathed make us understand that God is moving us in a certain direction, whereas Satan is seeking to draw us towards the opposite goal. A certain tearing apart then becomes inevitable, for the stronger the joy and the more clearly defined the thought attached to it, the more painful, too, is the sadness which would lead us to the contrary decision. At this time we experience what was described in regard to the spiritual combat, namely, that the increase of light, which is at the same time warmth and brightness, intensifies the darkness. But the more violent the conflict becomes, the more the opposing forces show themselves as they really are, so much so that it becomes increasingly easier to discern the origin of the thoughts that seek to move us to action. The prolonged struggle does not only show us the direction to be followed, it purifies us from any connivance we might entertain with evil, it strengthens our power of choice by detachment in regard to ourselves and by the desire of submitting ourselves to the Lord who speaks within us.

The affective context in which a decision should be taken is that of joy; but the latter is inseparable from interior liberty. Because we wish to begin, pursue and successfully accomplish the order of our Creator and Lord, we are attached to it only in so far as God himself is attached to it and wishes to see it realized. If he should come to change or even to reverse the sense of his command, we should have no difficulty in passing from one extreme to the other. Often we fail to modify the direction of our enterprises because we cling to them for our own sake and not for the profit of the Other whose love can move us at his good pleasure towards a certain end or its contrary. Hence in the man who chooses according to God is found this paradoxical union of passion and liberty, of determination and detachment, of tenacity and flexibility. The clearer it is that the Lord expects such and such an action from us, the less we are tempted to see in it a personal affair. Those who see a Christian undertake or abandon something with equal ease can cry out that it is indifference and that he is inhuman. From the outside they cannot grasp that this man is drawn not by a taste for domination or the need of building up a work with his own hands, but by the love of God alone, the God whom he seeks to listen to and the slightest tones of whose voice he tries to follow. The slavery of justice, of which St. Paul was speaking, brings with it the genuine liberty of sons. Because it matters to my Lord to see me accomplish such and such a task here and now, I have attached myself to it more than to anything else. But if he should come to turn aside from it, his holding aloof passes into me and I no longer then find any reason to spend further time over it.

At the end of this second way of finding the will of God, we again come into contact with a situation comparable with that defined above. When we have passed the stage of hesitation and patient search, when we have decided to submit to the divine injunction, the whole person is unified and, without doubting or being able to doubt, it follows what is shown to it,* allowing itself to be moved by the divine attraction. The preparations for the choice may be long and various, the result is always the same—the

* *Spiritual Exercises,* no. 175 (Rickaby, *op. cit.,* p. 152).

soul who is at the same time the bride listens to the voice of the Bridegroom and, joining herself to him, she obeys without tarrying.

In the course of this process, the intervention of the different spirits has set our affective nature in movement, and we have seen contrary projects arise, in accordance with our successive states. The initiative did not come from us; we gradually realized that, to find peace again and make the alternation of desires cease, it was essential to prefer the will of God to the suggestions of Satan. But it can happen that the necessity of choice is imposed in an imperative way, because circumstances claim our intervention without anything happening in us inwardly. In this case, without waiting further, we can elicit the reactions of our affective nature by alternately fixing our will in the direction of the two possibilities that are offered to us. This is what St. Ignatius recommends in his own way, in the directory of the *Exercises:* "We shall be able to present to God one day one side and another the other, for instance one day the counsels and another day the precepts; we shall then observe where God our Lord gives most sign of his divine will—after the example of him who presents various dishes to a prince and observes which of them pleases him."*

In this there is nothing which should cause us surprise. From the moment we have taken a decision, either the latter opens towards the future that the Son of God has willed for us and which he is preparing for us in his glory, or else it encloses us within our own limitations because it does not form part of God's plan and does not enter into his designs. In the first case, our person soon finds light and joy along this divine path, for the God who is calling us can indeed make us pass through suffering, but that is only the narrow gate of a vaster happiness and a more intense love. In the second case, on the contrary, we are cut off from God so that this separation produces fruits of division which overthrow and

* MHSJ, *Directoria,* p. 76.

rend us. If a choice turns us towards God, we are placed, so to speak, in the prolongation of his creative act, our hearts directed towards the open spaces, whence comes the breath of his Spirit. Filled with his strength and his light, we do not feel the difficulties, fatigue or danger. It is true that these struggles towards the rectitude of a free act will occur increasingly in the very course of the realization of our project, but if we are sensitive to the action of God, the simple fact of situating our will in the direction of his or, on the other hand, of maintaining it in the blindness of self-will will suffice to inform us as to the goodness or perversity of our intention.

More active than the preceding method, this way of procedure does not respect the divine initiative any the less. This initiative is manifested by the reaction of our affective nature which the different spirits seek to dominate. In addition, it has the advantage of exercising our liberty which, under the pretext of waiting for God's intervention, is in danger of remaining self-willed. If the Spirit reveals himself to us so little, it is because we are incapable of responding to him with determination by saying yes or no. We remain in a certain tepidity of will which is at the same time a negation of will, so much so that we never see the effects of an authentic acceptance or genuine refusal come to light. To choose one side and when this decision is formed and is capable of engaging the future, to choose the alternative, gradually forges our liberty, reveals to it that it is inevitably linked with a single objective and that preference is thus impossible. Negligence in putting such methods into practice is often a mask for our lack of comprehension of the ways of God. He can only communicate himself to men who are free and capable of a firm response, so much so that to train our power of choice by exercises of this kind is to prepare ourselves to receive our Lord and already to allow him to act in us according to his good pleasure.

At the conclusion of this effort, the same truth is again brought into light. We may think for a moment that we have taken the initiative, whereas by God's grace we have merely turned to him and given him the possibility of communicating to us this divine will of his which was in us before we took the trouble to seek it. Then, without the possibility of doubt, we follow it by the strength that God has placed in our hearts.

The Harmony of the World

At this stage, however, spiritual liberty has not yet shown itself as capable of reconciling man with the world. In fact the union with God in the love which gives itself at the moment of choice could not be separated from the actuality of our work nor would the interior unity of the human powers be conceivable unless throughout the length of the search action to be undertaken in the visible universe was aimed at. But the relations of man with things and beings were not the actual milieu in which the discovery of the divine will was operating. It is thus desirable to see now how the decision can be made manifest at this level.

When we have to take an engagement in some determined direction we find ourselves faced with a multiplicity of facts and currents which tend to impose themselves even before we have had the time to judge them. We must thus use the objective criteria of the discernment of spirits to perceive the imperative trends which must be favored or those whose sphere of action we must, on the contrary, curb. As we saw in regard to sin, each of our acts is capable either of accentuating the divisions that exist in the world, or, on the other hand, of building, in charity and peace, the Kingdom of Christ, who is Creator and Lord.

Placing ourselves in the heart of the world and letting its aspirations re-echo in us, it is thus important to examine whether the act we have the intention of positing here and now will lead to separation or to cohesion, whether it will make mankind grow in submission to the Redeemer or whether, on the contrary, it will for its part contribute to the destruction of man. Not to respect the laws of things and beings, not to listen to those whom the Lord has charged with lighting up our route or with revealing to man who is blind the paths with no outlet, not, above all, to welcome him who has come to show us who we are and to what our destinies should lead, is equivalent to retarding his second coming and lending ourselves to the designs of Satan who is a murderer from the beginning.

In practice, it is true, we must be carefully on our guard, for an act may assume an appearance contrary to its true significance. Christ himself has pointed out to us that the way to his peace is through struggle: "Do not think that I came to send peace upon earth; I came not to send peace but the sword. For I came to set a man at variance against his father . . ." (Matt. 10, 34). In the same way he has explained to us that to keep our life we must first of all lose it and vow hatred to it in this world (Jn. 12, 25). Thus, no more than in the case of interior discernment should we trust in the appearances of what is proposed to us immediately and which may serve as a veil for Satan's malice.

"The enemy of human nature" seeks primarily to urge us to an action without our having had time to sit back and judge the influence or consequences of our enterprise.* He is afraid that our

* We would refer here to the rules given by St. Ignatius for making election according to the third occasion: "Imagine a man whom I have never seen and whom I do not know. Being desirous of total perfection for him, to consider what I should tell him to do or to choose for the greater glory of God our Lord and the greater perfection of his soul. Then to do the same thing myself and observe the rule that I should propose for someone else.

To consider, as if I were at the point of death, the attitude and standard that I should then wish to have observed in the making of the present election. And wholly to establish my determination in accordance with that rule.

reflection may lead us to penetrate his mark and to grasp his "perverse intentions."† He wants us to build a tower without allowing ourselves to "first sit down and reckon the charges that are necessary, whether we have wherewithal to finish it" (Lk. 14, 28). On the other hand Christ who moves swiftly but calmly precipitates nothing; he enlightens, explains, counsels and helps us to judge in all its depth the value of the enterprise and the possibility of its accomplishment. More often than not, if we refuse to stop to consider the problem that our existence posits today, it is that we have already settled the solution so far as we are concerned. Our prejudices and our bias then blind us to such an extent that the suggestions God might have to transmit to us cannot get through to us. We have not the courage to call ourselves in question and sharpen our gaze so that it will cease to focus on a passing illusion but will reach to the lasting truth.

This sitting back and considering of ourselves must lead to a genuine going out from self, an image of the charity of Christ, and must mean that in our choice we must not be more easily dupes of ourselves than of a stranger whose case we should judge objectively. When Christ wanted to make his hearers enter into themselves, he repeated the tactics of Nathan (II Sam. 12, 1–4) in regard to David: "A certain creditor had two debtors; the one owed five hundred pence and the other fifty . . ." (Lk. 7, 41). In the case of a situation in which the man who has to choose is not involved with his passions, the response is clear and salutary. It is easy for him then to apply the solution to his own particular case and to acquire towards himself a similar rectitude of judgment. For our personal

---

To regard and consider the state in which I shall find myself at the day of judgment. To think of the way in which I should then wish to have decided about the present matter. To adopt now the rule I should then wish to have followed in order that I may taste happiness and full joy." *Spiritual Exercises,* no. 185–187 (Rickaby, *op. cit.,* p. 155–156).

† *Ibid.* no. 332 (Rickaby, *op. cit.,* pp. 143–144).

disorders prevent us from letting things live in our presence, from appreciating them for what they are. They prevent us, moreover, from refusing to paint them with the color of our own desires.

The spiritual judgment which must precede the choice is thus not an escape from the world into a sphere that we claim is superior. It is, on the contrary, a descent into the world, respect for what exists and for that in which God is at work. The effect of a long search to know what we ought to do is, more often than not, to lead us to recognize evidence which our habits, our folly or our wretchedness prevented us from noticing. The Pharisees who were acting under the impulse of Satan were incapable of opening their eyes to clear facts and of drawing the consequences from them. When we want to discover God's will, our first care must be to let things and beings assume their own value and their own weight, to thrust aside previous impressions and to welcome as a living reality this world in which God is at work. Under the well-known appearance are hidden deeper, more lasting forces which only the eyes of the poor in spirit can discover. To become, day by day, as a traveller who awakens to landscapes he had not even imagined or a stranger who journeys through an unknown land for the first time, is to make ourselves capable of understanding the order of the universe and of situating our own action within the work of God.

Yet this natural evidence should not lead us to limit our view to earth. This would be to return to that clinging to self which is the contrary of objectivity. We can, however, content ourselves with looking at the world as something that we have to leave—in the light of our death. Our Lord blamed the fool who wanted to build a lasting dwelling and store what he owned in barns, to give rest to his soul. It was an apparent wisdom which made him foresee the future, but as he had laid up treasure for himself instead of becoming rich in regard to God (Lk. 12, 21), what he was able to accumulate had no more consistency than an illusion and would disappear with his earthly existence. In reminding ourselves that we are doomed to death, we do not go out of this world of which death forms a part, but we do go out of ourselves, radically, and we accept as a fact capable of throwing light on our existences the total vanity of a universe which can find its foundations neither in us nor in itself. To find our right place here on earth, we must consider human history as doomed to disappear. It is not sufficient, then, as it was just now, to open our eyes to the action of God in the world, it is essential to consider that all that exists must pass through death and that only that which is founded upon God and lives in him will subsist.

But to discover the vanity of the world cannot be an end, for the very reason that death, which reveals it to us, leads us to this judgment. In it we find ourselves face to face with the Master whose appreciation of us depends on the way in which we have recognized him here on earth. Whatever gestures we have made on this earth in regard to men, we shall understand at this moment that we have made them to him himself, for God has espoused mankind, and identified himself "with the least of these little ones" (Matt. 25, 45). In the light of this final discernment of the value of our acts, it is the importance of human enterprises that is revealed. Because the verdict of the Creator, to which we must adhere, assumes the most ordinary traits, we deduce from it the infinite religious significance of our most ordinary choices. To decide in the Spirit, it is thus sufficient to ask ourselves if Christ will consider our project as a confession of his presence, so that he can defend it before his Father. "Everyone therefore that shall confess me before men, I will also confess him before my Father" (Matt. 10, 32).

A free act which has thus been objectively considered in the light of the facts of our lives; which has then sought to show, by confrontation with death, the vanity of our decisions; which finally through the very humility of them has rediscovered the absolute value they can receive from the divine presence diffused through the universe and hidden in a special way under the human countenance, is capable of reassembling in all their truth the forces at work in the world, because it situates them in their exact place. The peace of Christ thus passes through the sword of our earthly end but it is founded on the meeting with the merciful countenance of the Lord of glory. The history of men, which should be destroyed, becomes a new creation when our eyes recognize Christ here on earth in the least of our brethren. We can then behave among them as if we had already returned to Paradise and were back with the Father. "It is necessary first," writes St. Gregory, "to regulate morals, then to consider all present things as if they were not, and, in the third place, to contemplate the supreme interior realities with the fine point of the heart. . . . When one has acted well in this world, one should then despise even the honorable things of this world and contemplate finally the secrets of God."*

There is here a movement essential to the soul, at the center of which each one of our choices should be formed with a view to its gradual adaptation to the divine will. In order that the world may receive its cohesion from our liberty, it is essential to respect the laws which are proper to it and, through a calm wisdom, to allow the trends of living force which our tendency would be to overlook, to show. But the clear-sightedness of the prudent man comes even more from his will to practice evangelical poverty than from his

* Gregory the Great, *Super Cantica Canticorum expositio,* PL. 79, col. 477. In this passage St. Gregory the Great, after Origen (P.G. 13, col. 73–76) and Cassian (PL. 49, col. 566), explains the place of the Canticle of Canticles in relation to what he calls the other two books of Solomon—Proverbs and Ecclesiastes. At first it is Proverbs which teaches wisdom. Then comes Ecclesiastes which aserts the vanity of all things. Lastly the Canticle of Canticles opens the way to contemplation. This succession does not seem to us unconnected with the three rules of St. Ignatius cited above, which invite us to consider things by putting ourselves in the place of another man to judge with wisdom, then to regard them from the point of view of death and finally to contemplate them in the light of the divine judgment.

effort to attain objectivity. If the light of God's judgments enables us to discern his intentions, it is because we have recognized beforehand that we had nothing and even that we were nothing; for by his ever present intervention, God alone sustains our being and our possessions. Thus we here find once more, although under another form, the three fundamental elements which served to define the essence of liberty—to follow in this world the paths that have an outlet and to avoid those that are blocked, the faithful soul must be formed to detachment from all things by him who, in attracting us to him, judges our acts and communicates to them the force of his love.

The three modes of choice that have just been described have so universal a character that it is possible to give them a multitude of meanings. It is not unreasonable to note their relationships with the three elements that tradition recognizes as constituting our spiritual being. "The first occasion of the election," according to St. Ignatius, seems comparable to the Christian life led under the impulse of the gifts of the Holy Spirit. In fact, those who have access to these lights constantly recognize the action of their Master and Lord and allow themselves to be guided by them, without having, so to speak, to deliberate. They have found access to the higher spontaneity of God's love found in its fullness. That "the second occasion of election" is linked to the theological virtues has been sufficiently marked in showing that the latter contained in themselves the principal characteristics of the discernment of spirits. Lastly, "the third occasion" can be linked with the moral virtues in light of which every Christian must conduct himself in the world.

If the Christian conscience acts more particularly on one of these levels, all must enter into play, in one way or another. The gifts of the Holy Spirit are inseparable from the theological and moral virtues, just as the divine motion which urges us to action does not dispense us from trying the spirits and from taking account of visible realities. One of the advantages of the Ignatian perspective consists in the liaison it establishes between these various stages of our being. It shows how the gifts and virtues are interdependent and strengthen each other. If our spiritual life ordinarily moves within one of these terms, it must strive to know and experience the two others.

6 TRIAL AND SUFFERING

ONCE THE SPIRITUAL CHOICE has been accomplished it might seem to us that our history has come to an end, since in uniting ourselves to God we have reconciled man with himself and with the world. But, on the one hand, the union which began at the center of our person must be realized in deeds. Moreover, if each of our choices binds us in every respect, it does so in function of particular facts and thus cannot transform the universe. Identifying himself with mankind, only Christ at the Last Supper could decide to put to death, by the supreme suffering of his Cross, his flesh, "like to that of Sin" (Rom. 8, 3), and passing through death could then rise again with all men in the transparency of his spiritual body. Always partial throughout our existence, our sufferings and the death to sin will have to be continually repeated until the day comes when we can disappear to be born again perfect with Christ. Moreover, to reach this goal it would be necessary to accept the sufferings of this present time as God requires of us and that we should never, by our sin, go backwards, increasing those sufferings and retarding the moment of our deliverance. Sufferings and trials have a meaning which is to be discovered, an orientation to which we must submit, if we want to take them upon ourselves to abolish them. They must be undergone in the first place because of sin, then accepted through liberty and finally desired in love.

Undergone Because of Sin

The first reason why trials are imposed on man is his sin. But in making such a statement we must be careful of the significance that is to be given to it—it would seem if God punished after the manner of a judge, inflicting a penalty proportionate to the sin. In actual fact it is man who, by separating himself from God, creates divisions each one more crushing than the other. The Creator has no need to invent punishment, for the latter results immediately from the wrongdoing. By breaking his relationship with his principle and his origin, the sinner destroys himself and injures his relations with his fellows or with the world. The type of all the transgressions committed by men, that of Adam, throws full light on ours and shows us that it is we ourselves who impose sufferings and evils on ourselves.

It is no doubt true that our own personal sins are not the cause of all the trials we undergo. Yet the only means of entering into the redemption that comes to us through Christ is first to identify ourselves with the first Adam and then to make ourselves one with the sinful race to which we belong, whose burden our own transgressions increase. Until we adopt this attitude and so long as we throw upon others, particularly on the first man, the responsibility for our wretchedness, we only multiply the ruptures which crush every member of the human race, for not to recognize one's condition as a sinful creature is to cut oneself off from the Creator. On the contrary if, accepting the divisions which wound us and taking them upon ourselves, we consider them as normal in view of our acts—if, going further, we are surprised that the state of man is not worse and that all things have not irrevocably gone forward to death, we have the chance of discovering the positive significance of the evil that befalls us.

For sufferings and trials are not only the consequence of sin, they are the beginning of redemption—punishment can become the means of salvation. First, when we assume our share of responsibility we enter into communion with others and we forge those links which can unite companions in misfortune, not with a view to a greater crime to be committed together, but to the help we can bring each other. In a deeper sense, because God himself has become the friend of sinners, because he who was innocent has made himself one with our race, he has changed the meaning of our trials. They were the sign of a separation from God. For the future, through Christ Jesus who has borne them, they are a sign of the new covenant which God in person has established with man. A more radical reversal of roles it is not possible to imagine. Man had wandered far from his Creator and consequently suffered death, but now the Creator, so to speak, moves away from himself, places himself even lower than man, in the ranks of criminals and evildoers, of gluttons and drunkards, of prostitutes and adulteresses, and comes to take upon himself our nothingness.

Not only must we no longer seek to rid ourselves of our sinful condition under the pretext that it is not our fault if we have arrived at that point, but we must love and cherish it as the most valuable treasure at our disposal with which to attract him who wills to espouse our humanity therein. The only beauty which can attract the eyes of the Bridegroom is our ugliness and deformity. Because "I am black but beautiful, O ye daughters of Jerusalem" (*Cant.*, 1, 4), he does not ask me to give him anything other than this or to bring him a more valuable gift. This is a strange way of acting and we can understand that it scandalized the Jews and seems to us Christians one of those somewhat exaggerated Gospel truths which we must be careful not to put into practice. We cannot bring ourselves to believe that the first and last thing we have to put before God in prayer is our wretchedness and our sin, the sin we committed formerly, the sin we could commit and, in any case, the abject basis which makes us capable of all crimes. There is no return to God, no real salvation, and thus no cessation of our trials, without the continual passing through this point of wretchedness, where we meet these sufferings at their source, our sin, but equally in their end, the love of God.

Yet the more we approach God with our wounds, the more we shall desire to offer him something other than this countenance which does not even resemble a human face. We shall long to receive his purity and his beauty. He will gradually set us free, showing us what he is, so that we may become like him. For if he has made himself the friend of sinners it is so that for the future, through the strength he communicates to them, they may sin no longer and may become, in their turn, justified and friends of him who alone is just.

But, whereas this change is taking place in our hearts and bodies, another change which seems contrary to it appears before our eyes. In fact the more the light of the Lord penetrates into us, the more the darkness which until then has been hidden, becomes unveiled, causing the most acute suffering. When the sun shoots forth its rays, it tans our complexion. "The sun turns brown him whom it touches closely; so the Lord, when he comes, darkens him whom he most touches by his grace, for the closer we come to grace, the more we recognize that we are sinners."* It is not that our trials really increase, but since the demands of Christ become more precise and more exigent, it seems to us that our state is worse and we come to regret having begun to follow the Word made flesh. When the patient is offered his medicine, his sufferings which had subsided reawaken and sear him.

* Gregory the Great, *Super Cantica Canticorum expositio,* P.L. 79, col. 486.

It is doubtless for this reason that we take ingenious precautions to blind ourselves and not consider what is hindering God's progress in us, for his approach brings danger with it. Pharisees that we are, we want to silence our Lord and prevent him from advancing, lest under his eyes and the fire of his words our sin should come to superabound, making us enter upon sufferings ever deeper and more painful. The friends of God go through this temptation to give up the struggle. After having desired so much that the Saviour should come to save them, they begin to think that their previous circumstances were easier than the hell through which they must now pass. It is quite true, in fact, that grace cannot superabound in us unless sin has previously abounded (Rom. 5, 20), that is, so long as it has not been revealed to our eyes. One cannot be treated for a disease one is unaware of, and the physician can do nothing for the patient who considers himself in good health.

The man who really believes that the chastisement of sin has become in Christ the means of salvation, draws near to him continually or rather asks Christ to draw him near so that what is wrong with him may be revealed to him and that, once again, the same Lord may deliver him from it. We then understand this saying: "Persevere under discipline. God dealeth with you as with his sons. For what son is there, whom the father doth not correct? But if you be without chastisement, whereof all are made partakers, then are you bastards and not true sons" (Heb. 12, 7–8). It is not God who is the cause of our trials, it is sin; but that does not prevent us from being able to receive them from the hand of the Lord and thus as benefits, since through the passing sadness they cause, they are the indispensable byroad leading to peace, justice and joy. Since Christ "hath borne our infirmities and carried our sorrows" (Isa. 53, 4), in order to take them away and remove them (Matt. 8, 17), all the evils of the universe belong to him. He gives them to each one when it seems good to him, without ever trying anyone beyond his strength (I Cor. 10, 13). Man had separated himself from his

Creator and by his flight caused every wretchedness which then belonged to him alone. But Christ has come to take all this away from man, to take it into his human nature to change it into his love, so much so that for the future we no longer have even these sufferings as our own. We can no longer do what we like with them, but can only receive them as gifts, at the moment when the Lord sends them "for our profit, that we might receive his sanctification" (Heb. 12, 10).

Our vision must be enlarged still further. There is no common measure between our sufferings and our sins, for the only equivalence that exists is that between the sufferings of all mankind and man's denial of God. What should haunt us then is that all human sufferings must finally be brought back by all men even to Christ, in order that they may lose all contact with their origin and no longer appear as chastisements but as means of fulfillment. That is why we have not to ask ourselves if it is we or our parents who have sinned (Jn. 9, 2), since through our trials, as through those of Jesus Christ, the glory of God wills to manifest itself. The more I agree to bear the ills of men in Christ, the more also I shall say, thinking and willing it, "I now rejoice in my sufferings for you and fill up those things that are wanting of the sufferings of Christ, in my flesh, for his body, which is the Church" (Col. 1, 24), i.e., the new humanity.

To the extent that tribulations come upon me through the hand of Christ, to be transformed into me by his grace in order to hasten his coming, I shall desire to bear them with his strength and his courage. Pushing this interior movement even to the point of foolishness, and knowing that Christ was only able to save us from malediction by becoming "the accursed hanging from the tree" (Gal. 3, 13), I shall come to the point of wishing to be "anathema from Christ, for my brethren, who are my kinsmen according to the flesh" (Rom. 9, 3). For the man who undergoes the worst possible suffering in Christ—all suffering being for the future a revelation of his glory—avoids for men, his brothers, the endurance of this tribulation as a fruitless chastisement. St. Teresa of the Child Jesus and of the Holy Face willed to make herself one with sinners as long as God should will it and to bear the same penalty. She would thus give it positive value in order that even a presence in hell might be the supreme fruit of love.*

We ought then to receive all suffering as already transformed by Christ (since he has borne the evils of all mankind) and thus as able to bring salvation to all. It matters little whether or not it is in relation with our personal sins, it is much more necessary to consider it as the passage of man towards his end and his happiness. If it is in Christ that we suffer, it is he who allows us to share in his suffering humanity so that we may show forth his glorious humanity. In moving out of the infernal circle of sin and punishment we enter into Christ, we penetrate the heavenly movement of suffering and sanctification, of the love that dies and rises again. If we turn towards the past to groan over our sins and that of Adam, if we regret having advanced towards the Light of the World who makes our consciences blacker than they were, if we seek to give up the struggle and no longer to look upon that Light,

* This extraordinary page of the saint's writings, which links her up with so many holy souls before her, is worth quoting. "But, Lord, your child has understood your divine light, she asks pardon for her brothers, she is willing to eat the bread of suffering as long as you wish and will indeed not get up from this table filled with bitterness at which poor sinners eat, before the day you have marked. . . . But can she not also say in her name, in the name of her brothers, 'Have pity on us, Lord, for we are poor sinners. . . .' O Lord, send us away justified. . . . Let all those who are not lighted by the luminous torch of the Faith see it shine at last. . . . O Jesus, if the table sullied by them must be made clean by a soul who loves you, I am more than willing to eat the bread of suffering there alone until it shall please you to bring me into your Kingdom of Light. The only grace I ask of you is never to offend you." *Autobiography of a Saint,* pp. 254–255.

then our sufferings will become progressively more sterile and more numerous.

On the other hand, each time we welcome our sufferings as a share of those of the humanity of Christ, and accept their increase or diminution in us at the good pleasure of his desires, there is the fruitfulness of the grain which has fallen into the ground and will come forth and bear fruit a hundredfold. Suffering is inseparable from our condition as sinners, but it is of the utmost importance to know what meaning and significance we are going to give it. So long as we see in it nothing but a point at which things end, it remains in fact the term of all things, but if we place it at the beginning, in Christ Jesus, of itself it produces the contrary effect. "He that loveth his life shall lose it: and he that hateth his life in this world keepeth it unto life eternal" (Jn. 12, 25). We must thus not wilt under suffering and allow ourselves to be crushed by it; we must will it through Christ in order to attain to the fullness of Christ.

Accepted with a View to Liberty

A long time will pass, however, before we can share with all our being in the Cross of Christ. Before this comes about, it is necessary that God should make us pass through a series of trials which will strengthen our faith and give our liberty the possibility of responding to faith utterly. In one sense, here it is no longer sin that is in question, but conversion—as free creatures we have slowly to learn to dispose of our person under the eyes of God in order that he may lead us according to his good pleasure. The trial here is the one the just man must undergo, he who already obeys God sincerely and is scandalized that he still has deliberately to prefer God, that he does not discover him here and now and perfectly, that he must again go through a time of expectancy and dryness and find that he never succeeds in understanding as he should God's designs for him. It is true that this kind of trial can lead to sin, but sin is not what is at issue in the choice, for we have not to decide between good and evil, but between the best and the less good.

It seems at first as if God tests the just man by the attraction of the world. All things that the Lord puts before us are good, but he prevents us from using them according to our tastes. Fetters are placed on our appetite for enjoyment and on our desire for domination, and we feel a contradiction between our vitality which would seek to expand, and social and religious sanctions. What the Creator gives he also seems to take away from us, by restricting the use we can make of it or even by prohibiting it. Our liberty cannot unfold as it would like. It cannot understand that such narrow limits can be assigned to it. This is because, by this trial, God wants to force us to go beyond our instincts. If he did not allow his law to lay heavy upon us, if he did not point out to us a particular tree in paradise whose fruit we could in no circumstances eat, our spirit would dissolve into animality. Constraint is thus the first means the Divine Pedagogue has at his disposal to elicit our most personal forces. When he shuts our liberty within the enclosure of his precepts, he is protecting it and allowing it to take its first steps at ease.

But it may happen that God asks us to give up completely these riches of the world which he himself has taught us to appreciate and to make fruitful. There was no sin and even no disorder in living among created things. It was a duty for us to know and appreciate them, and to rejoice over them. What is now proposed to us is that we should leave all things to follow Christ. The rich young man to whom our Lord spoke had kept all the commandments, yet he was offered a greater perfection: "If thou wilt be perfect, go sell what thou hast and give to the poor and thou shalt have treasure in heaven. And come follow me" (Matt. 19, 21). No strict obligation was here imposed and no reproach was made to him who turned sadly away. The Creator never seeks to deprive us of the liberty he has given us, nor to constrain it by surprise. He wants it to be able to express itself in its own way and he is satisfied with putting the elements of choice at its disposal.

The stronger we have become through loyalty to the commandments, the more God gives us a power which we must use ourselves but which can become of itself alone a terrible trial in the using of it, for we are tempted to make use of it if not against God, at least outside him and without his continual control. In proportion as the Lord transmits his gifts to us, he enriches us with his superabundance. He does not lend his benefits, he bestows them so really that they make us capable of independence even in regard to him. When we have become free through submission to the commandments, we are asked if we are going to stay there or if we will take a step towards the foolishness of a love that has no other rule than itself. Mary of the Incarnation who had won access to spiritual liberty was thus tempted to use it to detach herself from her Lord, so true is it that God takes the creature, who is his image, seriously and that he indeed wants to attract us to himself, but not without our consent.

This trial no doubt Judas experienced and was not able to resist. Already, St. Teresa of Avila tells us,* he had known the grace of union, already he had become the friend of the Bridegroom, but under God's very eyes he had begun to steal the divine riches to appropriate them to himself. After this, he had only to swell his purse with the thirty silver pieces of Satan and to return as a traitor to the garden where his sin forbade him to remain as companion. Each of the apostles enjoyed this liberty in a very real sense and it remains astonishing and admirable that they should have preferred the attraction of the Master to this extraordinary power. Man, in fact, whom Jesus Christ establishes anew through contact with his

* *Obras Completas* (Madrid, BAC, 1954), II, p. 404. For Teresa the call to the apostolate was thus to bring men to the state of union, described in the fifth mansion. Cf. *op. cit.*, p. 259.

person, is not only delivered from sin, he is also freed from the law, i.e., from every social or religious pressure, from every automatic obedience. He no longer fears any force in this world, or any person, for he has at his disposal the power that sustains the universe, and this he knows. At this hour of solitude, which is an hour marvellously human, delirious with the total mastery over himself, in possession of his knowledge and his power, man knows that he must choose between a good or reasonable existence and the adoration of the Holy Face, gratuitous, absolute, decisive, of which it is impossible to say whether it will show itself yet, for it remains outside his grasp.

But if, like Peter, we weep with repentance at the idea of the folly we had imagined, or with tenderness because we were preparing to lose sight of the only countenance which was capable of giving us peace, a further trial awaits us. To follow Christ, in fact, does not provide the solution to every problem and every difficulty. Moreover loyalty to his person leads us, as he foretold, to persecutions and the cross. We do not succeed in entering into these perspectives, we do not understand why, since we place ourselves at the victor's side, he does not associate us with his victory from the first. Like the apostles, we ask, "Wilt thou at this time restore again the Kingdom to Israel?" (Acts 1, 6), that is, in our favor. Encountered by all the disciples, this scandal is still ours today, having due regard to the proportion of things, in the face of a Church founded on Jesus Christ, which delays the clear evidence that she belongs to him and which succeeds so little in uniting men that she seems to let them attack her.

This is the trial of the impatience referred to by Jeremias, which has staked everything on the word of God and is now disappointed: "Thou hast deceived me, O Lord, and I am deceived: thou hast been stronger than I, and thou hast prevailed. I am become a laughing-stock all the day: all scoff at me" (Jeremias 20, 7). We have abandoned all support in favor of trust in the Lord and now he has failed us. He delays the accomplishment of his promises towards us, and it even seems to us that the more we advance the less the expected realization is to be seen. But our impatience is precisely the proof that we have not trusted God and that our faith is not yet that which led Abraham "who against hope believed in hope" (Rom. 4, 18). We want to be paid for our obedience and we consider salvation or success as a reward which is due to us, not as a grace. If then God makes us be patient and asks us to keep watch without letting us know the day and hour of his coming, it is to show us that we are again seeking to take back the initiative of our destinies and that we are not yet totally dependent on him.

The prolonged wait saps at its root our will to build up our own lives and to use the nearness of Jesus Christ for our own ends, reverting in a more subtle but all the more harmful way to that will to power and appetite for pleasure which preceded the first trial our liberty had to undergo. Without this inexhaustible patience we should only transfer on to the spiritual plane the refusal of absolute dependence in regard to the Lord who is to come. We must not seize the gifts of God greedily as if they belonged to us, but enjoy them humbly, receiving them from his bounty, without asking what he will do tomorrow, without claiming anything from him, without asking of him anything more than the grace to receive his grace.

Thus by the resistance of things and of human beings to the plans, excellent though they be, created in us by God and conceived for his glory, our hearts are stripped until we come to find that constancy of the Gospel which gives true peace. The trial of patience forms in us that childlike soul which seeks to impose nothing but which stretches out its hands so that the manna on which it will be able to feed may be sent to it from heaven. We come to think, on the contrary, like the Hebrews in the desert—since Moses tarries and his God never comes to the end of dictating the law to him, let us set to work, give ourselves a god, make a golden calf so that the men who are waiting round us may immediately find someone to worship.

In actual fact God does not defer the accomplishment of his promises as if he were not mighty enough to give effect to them here and now, or as if he took pleasure in seeing us return, through the byroad of our impatience, even to idolatry; he only wants to prepare us to receive his gifts. It is our impatience that, wanting to fashion them to its own pleasure, pushes them back to him and refuses them entry. Even should God, who is essentially the gratuitous gift of love, wish it, he cannot let himself be taken or enclosed. He thus waits at our door until we too begin to love, that is to accept gratuitously, to be filled to overflowing for nothing, without hoping that in the following moment this may still be the case. When the Lord finds us established in this reverential constancy, which considers it incomprehensible that it should be given anything, he can no longer refrain from coming to us and filling us, not for an hour, but always and everlastingly, with the riches of his power, his light and his wisdom. It is then he gives us as our heritage the lasting possession of our hearts. "In your patience you shall possess your souls" (Lk. 21, 19).

To communicate himself to us, it would seem that to the trial of patience God adds that of impossibility. It is true that St. Paul declares that "God is faithful, who will not suffer you to be tempted above that which you are able" (I Cor. 10, 13). Yet in our eyes certain human sufferings exceed all measure—the death of a child whom we have surrounded with loving care, the entering into solitude which no affection can come to soften, the rupture of a love that meant more to us than life. Such troubles and many others, when they pour upon us, seem unbearable. The scandal is all the greater since they have no connection with our sin or with that of those around us. Job was right not to listen to the comforters who advised him to strike his breast and admit that he was guilty. He knew his innocence before God and that there was nothing in his life to account for his sufferings. At such moments it is always the same cry that is heard in man's heart: "Waters wear away the stones: and with inundation the ground by little—little is washed away. So in like manner thou shalt destroy man. Thou hast strengthened him for a little while, that he may pass away for ever: thou shalt change his face, and shalt send him away" (Job 14, 19–20).

But the impossible is to be found not only in the evils we undergo, it is in the orders we hear pronounced by God himself: "Take thy only begotten son Isaac, whom thou lovest, and go into the land of vision: and there thou shalt offer him for an holocaust upon one of the mountains which I shall show thee!" (Gen. 22, 2). At this hour we are not asked to wait for a posterity which cannot come, but to sacrifice that which has been born after long patience and after constancy that was calm but at the same time unreasonable. This fruit freely bestowed, humbly accepted and kept, on which we have never placed the sacrilegious hand of the possessor, and which precisely because of that was a hope founded on the divine goodness alone, this it is that, with our own hand, we have to cause to disappear and abolish for ever. We are not attached to it for ourselves, we love it with all our being, because to act otherwise would be not to love God and not to respect him. But as it is still visible, this purest of hopes must be taken away from us. It is no longer the "hope against all hope," but the total disappearance of all hope. It is the trial of despair in which God, according to all appearances, contradicts himself and undoes what he had taken so much care to form through manifold miracles. It is the anguish of Gethsemane during which the Father asks his son, the first-born of creation, the fairest of the children of men, the jewel beyond price, to move serenely into his own death, in such a way that he in whom the universe had seen its only hope, would not evade the issue if it were the Father's will. After him the Church who is the Bride and every soul who would be the spouse of Christ will share this agony, not through compassion, for it is he who came to suffer with us, but to learn what hope beyond the fruit of hope is, love beyond all its most transparent and perfect signs. When the Lord utters within us the contrary of what we had always heard him say, the gifts he has freely bestowed upon us are beyond the dimensions of reason and then it is his personal gratuitousness which emerges.

Nevertheless, instead of being our joy, this appearing of his becomes a supreme trial for we do not recognize the link it can have with earlier realities. When God effects the impossible thing he asks of us, how could we not believe ourselves to be the subjects of an illusion? That is the reason why in the eyes of the astonished apostles, the risen Christ at first seemed indistinguishable from the silhouette of a ghost. He had in fact a human form, but he was not subject to the conditions of our common humanity. The reaction of Thomas was thus natural. He refused to believe a contradiction—the Word made flesh could not have entered that room, since the doors were duly shut; a body cannot pass through walls. Recently God seemed to contradict himself by destroying the work of his hands, for the future the trial is doubled, for he presents himself under an appearance similar to ours. Daily life will begin again as before, we shall go fishing and he will come and eat with us, but this appearance is different from ours and from that we knew in him.

In the Passion God did the opposite of what we expected. In his Resurrection he disconcerts us more deeply, since he returns to the first appearance which he had rejected, to reject it as an appearance by not submitting to the laws of an appearance. If the death of Christ, as a contradiction of the fullness of his existence, was a trial for faith, how much more so his new life which in its resemblance to the one he led among us, was in opposition to it point by point. Now it is through that that our faith is definitively established, for we know now that through the impossible the reconciliation of the invisible God with the visible world is wrought. Faith alone can perceive the risen Christ, because it is the Resurrection which authorizes faith in a Lord who is all things, being no longer particularized and limited, and who is at the same time each one of us, for he is mankind.

Thus it is in our lives, when Christ rises again under the form of answered prayer. At the time when Jesus was walking along the road from Jerusalem to Emmaus, the disciples did not recognize him. He whom they were expecting to deliver Israel was quite close to them, after accomplishing this deliverance, but they were incapable of understanding that all they wished was accomplished, so far did the response to their question go beyond both the question itself and those who asked it. If, after we have been asking God for a long time to take us away from a path with no outlet, this impossible request comes to be realized, our eyes grasp nothing and we continue to lift our hands to heaven. The reason is that God has answered our prayer by setting our dialogue with him on an entirely different plane. The hundredfold promised he gives us today and that superabundantly, but penetrating it with life eternal (Matt. 19, 29). He enriches us in a way we could not have imagined, for he makes us poor by transforming us into his Spirit instead of providing us with wealth on which we could let our hearts rest. What he gives us we can only receive by giving it in turn and distributing it without thought of the morrow. A power then goes through us of which we know neither the source nor the outcome.

If the answers to our prayer become a trial to us, it is not that the Lord, like some necromancer, takes pleasure in disconcerting us. It is much more because in the request we made, error was still mingled with truth. In sending us his grace God dissolves the darkness to which our eyes are accustomed, so that things and the world are unrecognizable for us. We no longer see clearly because of the light of God which is shining in us. In begging him to grant us his benefits, we cannot know what they will be since we have not yet obtained them and since they infinitely exceed all we could wish for in our partial and shortsighted views. Since what the Creator and Redeemer grants is as vast and immense as himself, how could our customary small-mindedness be otherwise than dazzled and, in fact, blinded? Our expectation is thus disappointed not because what happens is less beautiful than we had foreseen, but because our desires are more than fulfilled on every side. It is thus an excellent thing that answered prayer should be an enigma to us, so that we cannot be complacent over our pretensions and God may ever appear to us outside our grasp.

Desired by Love

Suffering is not simply the consequence of sin and the means of salvation, it is not only necessary for the formation of our liberty and for the discovery of God's gratuitousness, it is also the privileged place of union with God. The Lord's disappearance, which for us is the ultimate suffering, stimulates us, in fact, to searching for him beyond our impressions and feelings. It also enables us to discover the bond of love which attaches us to him in the very heart of division and death. Finally it makes us the artisans of the reunion of all men in Christ.

At the hour which follows our decision to accept him it is his absence we chiefly feel. He had shown us his will and through our response to his call we had felt his action and his presence. Now, however, he effaces himself and abandons us to our own strength, whereas he promised to dwell with us in fidelity and goodness. But we soon understand that, far from crushing us, this remoteness stimulates in us the desire to find him again and that if he hides himself from our eyes, it is in order to see us seek him more eagerly. When we set out to find him again and, in prayer and action, we hasten along the paths by which he might have fled, he seems to us nearer than before. When he is there, we think we can sleep and let our heart alone keep watch to hear his voice (Cant. 5, 2), but if he should go away, our whole being awakens to follow the traces of his steps. In a continual presence the greatest love is in danger, whereas it is quickened by absence. If he is no longer quite close to me, I must seek him everywhere, because everywhere he may be dwelling and I risk not finding him. What he has given to me by his presence stimulates the vehemence of my quest, but his absence makes me lose my taste for all things other than him and invites me to cry out "Till the day break, and the shadows retire. Return" (Cant. 2, 17).

Thus begins a long journeying during which remoteness can also signify nearness for we perhaps know God more surely when we seem to have lost him. The presence is good because it nourishes and rests, because, without it, we should know nothing of him whom we desire, but there is also a danger of the drowsiness of satiety; whereas absence, which causes suffering, accentuates our hunger and thirst, and urges us continually forward. We no longer know whether we must wish more for the one or the other. Transposing this tension into the definite terms of the absence of God here on earth and of his complete presence in the hereafter, St. Paul wonders if he should remain "in the body," but "absent from the Lord," or if he must prefer "to be absent rather from the body and to be present with the Lord." That is why he concludes: "And therefore we labor, whether absent or present, to please him."* Thus the sentiments we feel and

* II Cor. 5, 6–9. St. Teresa of Avila in one of her poems (*Complete Works*, vol. III, p. 280) uses similar terms:

> Let me live or let me die;
> Give me sickness, give me health;
> Give me poverty or wealth;
> Let me strive or peaceful lie.
> Weakness give or strength supply—
> I accept it all of Thee:
> What wilt thou have done with me?

the situations in which we may move matter little, what counts is that all should serve to bring us near to him to whom we wish to attach ourselves, and that his love should become perfect in us. At the root of this alternation of contraries which are in danger of causing uneasiness and division, "by honor and dishonor," (II Cor. 6, 8) "both to abound and to suffer need," (Phil. 4, 12), the same tranquil union must be pursued. The wood which feeds the interior fire can be called suffering or joy, tribulation or success, frustration or consolation, it is always the same unalterable tenderness which in order to grow makes use of all it finds.

Yet the love of God which passes through the imitation of Christ crucified has always transmitted to his true disciples a leaning towards the Cross. We only go back to the Father, the source of the love of the Trinity, through identification with his Son who gives his life for men. The honor and abundance desired by every man seem not to ring true in the eyes of him who is seeking union. For him honor is humiliation for it is the proof that he is not judged worthy to walk where his Master has trod before him. In contempt, on the other hand, he sees a mark of esteem on the part of the Beloved. Plenty he finds more disturbing than deprivation because it makes the finding of him who came as a poor man less sure. For whosoever is joined to Christ crucified, the wisdom of men seems foolishness and the language of the Cross divine strength (I Cor. 1, 18). Suffering thus becomes the surest pledge of intimacy and familiar friendship with God, to such a point that we cannot but desire the cross and that, so much dreaded by men, appears as the supreme gain. "To me, to live is Christ: and to die is gain" (Phil. 1, 2).

Suffering alone, however, is not sufficient to unite us to Christ. If the Cross is to bring us near the Father, it must be his love alone that leads us to it. If man is not drawn to the Cross by God himself, it is impossible for him to imitate Jesus Christ. In actual fact, by the self-stripping it causes, suffering lays bare the hidden roots of our being and reveals the union which already existed in latent fashion. When St. Teresa of the Child Jesus underwent the supreme trial of her life, she admitted that God sent it to her at the moment she was capable of bearing it: "Earlier, I think it would have plunged me into discouragement. . . . Now it removes from me any natural satisfaction that might have been found in the desire I had of heaven. . . . Dearest mother, it seems to me now that nothing is preventing me from taking wing, for I have no longer any great desires except that of loving until I die of love."* It is for this reason that suffering is identified with happiness: "Is there a greater joy than to suffer for your love?"† she writes a little earlier in her prayer to our Lord.

Suffering then no longer appears as a means or condition of salvation, it becomes the effect of love. When God's tenderness floods the heart of man, it empties it of everything and gives him the impression that it is seeking to destroy him. It is simply that the tide of love sweeps away everything in its way, that it breaks the dikes of our limitations, that it overflows from a being that cannot contain it. As she consented to live a longer life St. Teresa noted: "The only grace that I desire is that my life may be broken by love."‡ In the face of this invasion the soul no longer formulates anything but a single wish, "martyrdom of the heart or of the body, or rather both,"§ because it is absolutely necessary for it to be wholly rent so that love may find the place that befits it, so that there may no longer be anything which is not consumed by its devouring fire. We cannot live perfectly by love so long as we have not died from love; so long as there still remains something foreign to this love, which has not been destroyed and refashioned in it. If we fear to die when we approach the face of Yahweh, it is not because he is an avenging

* *Autobiography of a Saint*, p. 257.

† *Ibid.*, p. 256.

‡ *Ibid.*, p. 258.

§ *Ibid.*, p. 259.

and terrible God, but because he loves us to the point of changing us into him and of making the old man disappear for ever.

To us who walk far from God and perhaps even farther from the Cross of Christ, this simplicity of vision which touches the term of the suffering directly, is forbidden. That is why the nearness of God makes us suffer so much and so acutely. We cannot perceive the result of the trials that are multiplied as we advance, or of this darkness which accumulates, shutting out the horizon and imprisoning our lives. We refuse to believe that the radiance of love is there in the suffering and the imprint of the Father's substance in the blood which flows. Woe to me for I have fallen into the hands of the living God! Yet this love is already inviting me to his table in making me share these torments. A holy woman, writing in the thirteenth century, ends a poem in which she explains the names of love with these phrases:

> The seventh name, just and sublime,
> Says that love is Gehenna,
> As it is, in fact, according to its nature.
> For it destroys the soul and the senses
> So that they never rise again:
> For the time to come Lovers will only be able to wander
> Amid the tempests of love,
> To wander body and soul, with heart and thought,
> Lovers lost in this Hell.
> If man wishes to face this, let him take care!
> For in the presence of love—there is nothing
> Which he who seeks to offer true love
> May retain, except
> At every hour to accept the blows and caresses
> Of the faithful heart right to the depths—
> Thus we shall win—if he should still
> Seem to us far off, we shall reach Love.*

* *Hadewijch d'Anvers* (Paris, Ed. du Seuil, 1954), pp. 128–129.

Just as no one can escape death, but it is important to know whether it is an end or a passage, so it would seem that no one can escape hell, because it is the necessary place of our metamorphosis.* If, despite the urge of love we refuse to go forward towards the supreme suffering in which our limbs are wrenched, in which our hearts experience a state of division close to death, the end of our life is in danger of coinciding with the entry into a pool of fire. It is again love which will burn us there, not to change us into itself, but because we are eternally strangers to it. Doubtless in both cases the words death and hell will take on different meanings; yet, if the greatest mystics have sought to employ them, it must be that this proximity in remoteness had a significance impossible to hide. When St. Teresa of Lisieux broke off the description of her interior sufferings for fear of blasphemy, it was because she was sharing in the infamy of the damned and was as it were overwhelmed by it. She no longer had any feeling of faith in God. It was no longer a veil that separated her from him, "it is a wall which rises up to the heavens and covers the starry firmament."† She knew that she believed only through the certainty that she willed to believe. However strange this experience may be, in which it seems we are the contrary of what we are in reality, it becomes clear if we compare it with the Cross of Christ, in which love no longer appears except under the form of the effects of sin.

But when the descent into hell is the result of superabundant love,

* Referring to the trial undergone by certain souls in the Night of the Spirit, St. John of the Cross explains: "It is these souls who in truth go down alive into hell (Ps. 54, 16) for they are purified here in the same manner as there. This purification is, in fact, that which should be undergone there. Thus the soul who passes through it, either does not enter that place or remains there a very short time, for here it makes more progress in an hour than there in many." Cf. E. A. Peers (ed.), *Complete Works of St. John of the Cross* (Westminster, Newman, 1953), Vol. I, *Dark Night of the Soul,* Bk. II, ch. VI, p. 387.

† *Autobiography of a Saint, op. cit.,* p. 257.

it is no longer our personal case that interests us; it is the redemption of sinners. If it were only ourselves in question, perhaps we should seek to withdraw from this tide which is crushing us, but if the salvation of others is concerned, if our suffering is for men, our brothers, the gate of happiness, it is changed into unalterable joy. St. Teresa of Avila tells how the sight of her place in hell was for her a choice apostolic grace;* and it was in a similar perspective that the crucial experience of Teresa of Lisieux developed. Traversing, but in an inverse direction, the path traced out by sinners, these mystics bring them light and peace, after the example of what was accomplished in Jesus Christ. In a vision in which he was evoking the building up of the heavenly Jerusalem, St. Isaac Jogues perceived the significance of his sufferings: "This tribunal and this judgment to which I was delivered and where I received blows, I thought was the divine judgment in which those are purified who are to be admitted to this holy city, or thanks to which, carved by the saving chisel and struck with repeated blows by the hammer which polishes, the stones which build it up are set in place."†

Through this trial it is no longer the individual alone, but already the whole human race that is united to God in suffering. What Jesus said of himself, "And I, if I be lifted up from the earth, will draw all things to myself" (Jn. 12, 32), applies to each one of the faithful. They know full well that amid these sufferings they are working for the reconciliation of the universe with God. "For we who live are always delivered unto death for Jesus' sake: that the life also of Jesus may be made manifest in our mortal flesh. So then death worketh in us: but life in you" (II Cor. 4, 11–12). All men feel vaguely in the depth of their suffering that in the serious crisis to which it is leading them they are together as they never were before, but they have no idea of the source of this union through suffering. They do not

* *Obras Completas* (Madrid, BAC, 1951), I, p. 798. Cf. *op. cit.,* I, p. 215.
† *Jésuites de la Nouvelle-France* (Paris, DDB, 1961), p. 102.

know that it flows from the Cross of Christ, who reunited all mankind in himself when he died and went down into the tomb. That is why the saints must come and reveal it to them, for "the stone which the builders rejected, the same is become the head of the corner" (Matt. 21, 42).

In all our sufferings, small and great, there is this hidden secret of a love which is not to be sought elsewhere or afterwards, but in the very heart of loneliness and dereliction. There are suffering countenances more open and more welcoming than any other; their features, on which are the traces of tears, show that they are no longer ready for anything but to love. Like poor men, they no longer cling to anything, for they no longer have anything. Far from despairing, their eyes light up at an encounter of which perhaps as yet they had no idea. But we who look at them understand. When the cords are broken, the ship puts out to sea, freed from its mooring ropes, and it no longer trusts in anything but the breath of the Spirit of love. Suffering has then consummated its work, to diffuse its radiance around; there is no longer question of our sins, but of God in us all. Because of the sin I had recognized before thy face, I returned to my nothingness. It was there I found thee waiting for me and waiting for us.

7 EXPANSION IN JOY

IN THE COURSE OF THE EARLIER STAGES, the end of the spiritual life was already perceptible. It can only be, in fact, the perfect expression of our meeting with God, of the action of the Spirit in us, of union born of the choice of God's will, or again of love which is revealed in the depths of suffering. To define this end in itself should, however, enable us to grasp the essence of the spiritual life more perfectly and thereby to discover and desire more fully the end we are pursuing in our search for God.

It is difficult, however, to speak of an expansion which is not yet attained. We remain like pilgrims far off from the place of blessing where we shall all be gathered and where we shall know as we are known. Even if some particular individual were to win access to the perfection of divine love, he would not be able to transmit his experience to us—the perfect achievement of our spiritual life is dependent on the spiritual life of every other human being. It is only when the whole universe is transfigured in the Spirit of love that each one, in soul and body, will perceive the goal towards which he is travelling, for union with God is inseparable from the relationship of men among themselves, and from their relations with the world.

We should have to take refuge in silence if we did not already possess in the risen Christ the first-fruits of our inheritance and if we were not identified in him here and now with mankind which is renewed in the Spirit. We shall have nothing to discover later, nothing to linger over and understand, other than the triumph of the Word made flesh in every creature. In Christ there is nothing that is outside the universal reconciliation with the God of love. Moreover, because he has given himself to us without return and without reserve, nothing of the fullness of his Spirit is unknown to us.

Here we should perhaps show that the expansion of the spiritual life begins by our becoming aware of the inaccessible character of the goal, which is pure grace. But in proportion as this end reveals itself as impossible of attainment, it becomes more necessary and indispensable to us. It is then that, firmly rooted in God's pure gift, our person acquires in regard to God, others and the world, the transparency of the Spirit who keeps nothing for himself, but who relates to God alone all he receives.

The Inaccessible Goal

It is in joy that the coming of the Kingdom of Christ finds expression in our hearts. It is thus through a more profound description of joy that we shall be able to comprehend the perfection of the spiritual life. In fact, when all things are submitted to the Lord, his love wells up in us to raise everything towards him, feed it with him, fill it with him. Now this quivering of our whole being, which thus attains its fullness and its overflowing fecundity, is nothing other than the gratuitous manifestation of the overflow of divine love. To describe the genesis of joy and its conditions is thus to understand that the expansion of the spiritual life is inseparable from an ever-increasing realization of the grace bestowed upon us, that is of the gratuitousness of God's action in our regard.

Joy will appear to us inaccessible, in its relationship with sin and suffering, both at the moment it is received, and finally when it becomes permanent in us.

That joy has nothing in common with our efforts and our virtues, our desires or our requests, is apparent when it is set over against sin. Sin is, in fact, a privileged occasion of joy. Is it not written that "there shall be joy in heaven upon one sinner that doth penance, more than upon ninety-nine just who need not penance" (Lk. 15, 7)? When the Paschal liturgy sings of the "happy fault that has earned us such a Redeemer," it is speaking with all seriousness, for it touches on the focal point of our salvation and our existences. If "Jesus, My Joy," to use the title of a well-known hymn, has revealed himself to my eyes of flesh, if he has come in a human body, if he has been Emmanuel, "God with us," it is doubtless because of love, but also—incomprehensible mystery—because of sin. Happy fault which, so to speak, has constrained Christ in his strength and tenderness to leave his Father and the courts of heaven, thus surpassing not only all human measure but the wildest of human desires, leaving his Father and his all.*

When Moses approached the burning bush, Yahweh revealed himself as he who is par excellence, "I am who am," (Ex. 3, 14), but later, after sin, after the making of the golden calf and after the rejection by his people, God seemed to abandon this distant majesty, this kind of lofty reserve, and to open to mankind the depths of his intimacy. He made himself vulnerable to men, in the tenderness of his love he allowed himself to be touched by them. "O the Lord, the Lord God, merciful and gracious, patient and of much compassion, and true, who keepest mercy unto thousands: who takest away

* It is normal that here we should again find the perspectives already described in regard to sin (cf. pp. 58–59). They are repeated here from the point of view of the goal of the spiritual life.

iniquity, and wickedness, and sin" (Ex. 34, 6–7). Sin would thus no longer be only an evil but a good, since its lack of due measure calls forth the measureless charity of our God. It is not that we should "contrive in sin that grace may abound" (Rom. 6, 1), but in our own lives we cannot fail to see that our sins and wretchedness bring us on the part of God a restoration to life which is each time more wonderful. Before he denied his Master, Peter could boast of his generosity, his attachment and his fiery impetuosity, but it was only after the death of him whom he had neither confessed nor defended that the Prince of Apostles dared to say because it had now become superabundantly clear and true for him, "Thou knowest all things: thou knowest that I love thee" (Jn. 21, 17).

If joy, the upsurging of love, is something beyond sin, a *fortiori* will it escape our grasp by contradicting the evidence to which we seek to cling. When the women told the Apostles that they had found the tomb empty and that Christ was waiting for them in Galilee, as sensible men who knew what things are, they could only take this announcement as "idle tales" (Lk. 24, 11). Death was death and no one would make them believe that he who was put into a shroud three days before was no longer to be found there. What contradicts certain facts can only come from a disordered imagination. Thus we act in our own lives when we want to leave the last word to suffering and evil and when we think we can put forward as proof of our assertions man's helplessness and inevitable dereliction. The individual who prides himself on his intelligence thinks that he knows beyond question that suffering is suffering and that evil is evil. It is, however, truisms like these that joy contradicts, for it believes that the sense of being crushed can well be what restores, "For my yoke is sweet and my burden light" (Matt. 11, 30); though it is also necessary that, through joy, it is he in person who shall place it on our shoulders. We do not understand that the power of God triumphs not only *over* weakness, but *in* weakness (II Cor. 12, 9) and that situations which are apparently definitive are never the final word of our own history, but a link which has mysteriously become indispensable.

The joy that pervades us—and in this it proves that it comes from God alone—is thus not forgetfulness of suffering and evil, as if from the suffering we could pass to an easy enthusiasm, to a euphoria of bliss. If that were the case, it would be conceivable that some should refuse joy, preferring pain to falsehood and the hard truth to flight into the unreal. Joy would then no longer be outside our grasp, for we should fabricate a caricature of it by shutting our eyes and closing our ears to the laments we might hear. True joy listens, looks, considers this poor humanity which moves slowly or swiftly to death passing through every form of decadence and deformity. It will hide nothing from itself nor will it hide anything from others. It strives on the contrary to open our wounds wide to see at what depths evil can indeed situate itself. Nevertheless, without ceasing to be clear-sighted, it transforms all things into the sweetness of the light it brings and the remedy it proposes. With the song of the joy which comes from God is always mingled a touch of gravity, for, when joy contemplates the body of the Risen Lord, it sees the traces of the nails in the pierced hands and in the side the opening made by the thrust of the lance. On this earth, the upsurging of divine love will never cause us to neglect anything of man, for this love could not misconstrue the depth of the distress amid which it appears. It may happen that even the superabundance of the Joy everlasting will fail to cause this after-taste of ashes, from which our universe cannot be freed, to disappear completely:

> O heart, living joy,
>   Set in ground of pain.
> O heart, shining silk,
>   Set in wool most plain.

When we have received it, joy reveals itself more fully as the goal that is inaccessible, for our desire to see it continue tends of itself to make it disappear. Here the paradox is only apparent. It corresponds to the very essence of divine grace. When God grants us a benefit, we seek to retain and conserve it. But that which at the beginning can be a mark of love, since to accept what comes from God is praiseworthy, quickly changes into the will to take for ourselves and in our own way that which is entrusted to us for the glory of God alone. The instinct for possession from which we shall never succeed in freeing ourselves entirely, spoils the quality of the gift, for it makes us neglect him who gives to seek our own pleasure in a selfish joy. Because we are not, in regard to the divine action, in a state of complete receptiveness, because a certain avarice is mingled with our acceptance, the grace transmitted is soon corrupted, like the manna which was kept longer than the prescribed day. If Jesus did not want to be touched by Mary Magdalene (Jn. 20, 17), it was not because of a want of love, it was because her tenderness was still possessive and she took the Lord for a man who was to be her joy here on earth, without seeing that he is the absolutely pure gift coming from the Father and that he must manifest this origin by returning to him who sent him. As soon as we want to encircle God's graces and enclose them so that they remain at our disposal, they disappear as graces, since they are the actual and gratuitous gift of the sovereign liberty of God. Of these graces we then keep only a residue according to our own measure.

That is one of the decisive aspects of every spiritual life. Until we are familiar with these perspectives, we shall doubtless be able to become virtuous people, but we shall quickly revert either to the pharasaical pride that believes that its heroic virtue in applying the law depends on its own strength, or to the pagan pretentiousness which judges everything by its own view of things and justifies its actions by principles which it has given itself.

There is nothing astonishing in the fact that joy should always seem precarious. It is not so in reality, since it is linked to eternal strength and divine solidity. In this sense, nothing is more certain than the gift given by our Lord. But, as the source of the riches of God is not in us, as we can never force them to well up and thus never foresee with certainty the time when they should begin to flow, their coming is, as it would seem, subject to chance. In actual fact this "chance" comes only from ignorance of the laws which preside over the birth and development of divine love. It is indeed desirable that it should be thus, for this helps us to remember that we are dependent on a God who gives himself freely and gratuitously. The more we advance in true joy, the more it becomes clear to us that our existence has its foundation in God alone, for this sentiment that he communicates to us when it seems good to him is the manifestation of our being—a being which is nothing of itself, but which exists wholly through God. Through joy it is given to us to perceive the love by which the Creator and Redeemer sets us in his presence and allows us to converse with him.

No sooner is joy established in us in a lasting fashion than we think it exists if not through us, at least as a reality that belongs to us. We forget that the creative relationship can only be actual, i.e., dependent on the present action of God. Hence the long slow work of education undertaken by the Lord, during which joy appears, but not continuously, under the form of unexpected visits.

The divine Word is not irrevocable like the human word. He comes and goes, at his good pleasure, he visits the soul at dawn and puts it to the test by suddenly withdrawing himself. If he goes away, that is again a way of giving himself; his return is always a free decision of his will; and the two movements are justified in a similar way, but he alone knows the reasons for them.*

If we are to realize that he is acting freely, his actions must assume the appearance of happening unexpectedly, like a fire which flares

* St. Bernard, *Oeuvres Mystiques* (Paris, Ed. du Seuil, 1953), p. 764.

up in different places without our being able to know the cause or duration of it. If we knew the day and the hour we should be in danger of thinking that this action was subject to our own dimensions since we had foreseen it. Gradually, however, through these marvellous and incomprehensible interventions, God teaches us to consider him as the Beloved who possesses in himself the source of all love. He invites us to turn our eyes to him, to keep vigil while we are waiting for his approach, not to be surprised that he tarries, to find it natural that he should leave us, because he cannot yet love himself in us. If he were to show himself before our eyes, we should rejoice in his presence without truly recognizing him for what he is. The time will perhaps come when he will be able to dwell in us and let us know that he is there in a lasting and continuous fashion. This will be the proof that we have wholly and completely left ourselves to find him and that we shall never again want to return to ourselves.

In acting thus God repeats for each individual what he has accomplished for mankind. He began by speaking to men in different ways and on different occasions by his patriarchs, his kings, his prophets, and then he communicated himself totally and finally "by his Son, whom he hath appointed heir of all things, by whom also he made the world" (Heb. 1, 2). For the Word to come and dwell among men, a preparation of several millennia was necessary. A long period of waiting will be necessary for us before we can see joy establishing itself in our hearts, before it can be continually found in us as a thing that in no way belongs to us of ourselves.

The Indispensable Foundation

Joy is inaccessible because it is the manifestation of a God who infinitely surpasses man, and with whom man cannot enter into relations unless God himself takes the initiative. However, as this gratuitous gift is at the same time that which established us in being long before we knew him and could respond to him, God must no longer be considered only as the term, but as the origin of our being, as our basis and foundation. Joy reveals this beginning of ourselves, which the dimness of our habitual vision prevents us from perceiving. To desire to feel joy in oneself is thus to want to correspond consciously, voluntarily and with the heart to this truth of our being—it is to become according to the spirit what we were in fact. Just as we cannot even exist without the action of God, so we can say that our person is still nothing without the actual recognition of this divine intervention which joy makes manifest. For a being saturated with and wholly turned towards love, not to remain constantly in the grasp of love is not to live. It will now be understood that every man, having truly experienced, even if only once, the upsurge of love which is his very foundation, cannot live without it. When joy is wanting, everything happens as if he were going to die. For his existence no longer moves in the fullness of the dialogue with God, which forms the only interest of his life.

After this, we see joy as necessary if our persons are to subsist, necessary to give them life, to enable them to make decisions according to God, finally to enable them to radiate his presence.

St. Ignatius, who preferred to judge a man by his degree of mortification rather than by the stage he had reached in prayer,* and who taught men to serve God whatever might be their interior feelings,† also said "that it seemed to him that he could not live if he did not feel in his soul a thing which was not his own, which could not be so, which was not a human thing, but depended solely on God."‡ He described on one occasion, for St. Francis Borgia, the most direct way of finding the Lord of all:

* MHSJ, *Fontes Narr.* II, p. 364.

† *Spiritual Exercises,* no. 318–322 (Rickaby, *op. cit.,* pp. 69–71).

‡ MHSJ, *Fontes Narr.* II, p. 338.

That in which God our Lord communicates himself more by his very holy gifts and his spiritual graces. He sees, he knows what is best and, as he knows all things, he shows the way to be followed. On our part it is a great help to us, aided by his divine grace, to search and experiment in numerous ways, in order to find and walk in the way which is the clearest, the happiest, the most blissful here on earth, wholly directed and ordained to eternal life, and in this way we find ourselves surrounded and penetrated by these very holy gifts. By these gifts I mean those that it is not in our power to have 'at our pleasure,' but which are granted solely by the mighty giver of all good gifts. Such are, when we place ourselves in the perspective of God's Majesty, faith, hope, very intense charity, 'joy and spiritual repose,' tears, intense consolation, elevation of spirit, divine impressions and illuminations, and all other spiritual tastes and sentiments relative to such gifts, such as humility and reverence towards our holy Mother the Church and those whose mission it is to govern her and teach in her. Any one at all of these very holy gifts should be preferred to all acts of bodily penance, which are good in so far as their purpose is to obtain these gifts or a part of them. I do not mean that we should only seek them to take pleasure in them or delight in them, but, convinced as we are in our deepest selves that without them our thoughts, words and works are impure, cold and restless, in order that they may become warm, clear and just for the greater service of God, we ought to desire these gifts, wholly or in part, and these spiritual graces, in so far as they can help us for the greater glory of God.*

St. Teresa of Avila was of a similar opinion when she wrote: "Our nature is so inert that we do not attend to what we see here and now. That is why these favors come to reawaken our faith and make it strong. Perhaps, since I have so little virtue, I judge others by myself. It can be that the virtue of faith alone is sufficient for certain souls to accomplish very perfect works. As to me, wretch that I am, I have need of all these helps."† As to St. Bernard, as we have seen,

* St. Ignatius, *Letters* (Paris, DDB, 1959), p. 171.

† *Complete Works* (Paris, Ed. du Seuil, 1948), p. 99. Cf. *op. cit.,* I, p. 68.

nothing had any taste for him in the absence of his Beloved: "I no longer take pleasure in anything, so long as he who is my only pleasure, is not here at hand."†

Such claims may seem exaggerated, for Christians who do not aspire to anything beyond our common faith continue to live and to lead good lives, just as, on another level, men who do not trouble about God pursue their existence with energy and even with passion. But to compare God's privileged friends with other men suggests the very reason for our surprise. If all the good things on which he feeds are withdrawn from a man who takes pleasure in the things of earth, his reason for living is taken away from him. Similarly, if we want to take away from a Christian his faith in Jesus Christ, his Saviour and his only Master, he prefers death to denial, for outside the Word made flesh life cannot have the slightest meaning. Now for him who has once seen the face of God, is it possible that existence can be anything else than an uninterrupted dialogue with him? The man who has had this experience may lack everything else, but he can no longer do without what is more than himself, this secret, hidden treasure, unknown until then, on which he has set his heart. When he loses sight of God and is no longer allowed to feel the presence of his Love, his situation becomes more painful than if life were torn away from him. That is why he no longer cares about anything but to cry out with the Bride, "Come back." In acting thus, he does not move out of the common condition, he only develops what was pre-contained in the act of faith posited by every Christian. Through the actual upsurging of love the grace of baptism is unveiled; and the divine presence allows itself to be grasped as if the opaqueness of the world of others and of oneself had been removed to allow the pure light to pass through. What he has perceived and glimpsed for a moment man begins to desire, despising all the rest. For him, not to live without the constant radiance of this Face is not

† Cf. St. Bernard, *Oeuvres Mystiques* (Paris, Ed. du Seuil, 1953), p. 768.

to live. When it has been experienced for a single day, this inaccessible joy becomes something indispensable.

We need it to detach ourselves from creatures and advance towards God. How can we turn aside, in fact, from the good things that we see and enjoy, if we do not already have a foretaste of heavenly things? As the well-known adage says, *trahit sua quemque voluptas,* and there can be no exception to this rule. When the mystics speak of the nights they pass through, they perhaps do not tell us sufficiently that it is the favors received, the interior certainty infused into them by grace, the deep-rooted attachment to Jesus Christ, which enable them to progress in this way, seeing and feeling nothing. At another level they are already tasting the first-fruits of a higher vision and feeling.

St. Teresa of Avila often reverts to this fact—if God does not attract us, to the point of making us know that our greatest happiness is in him, we shall never attain to true detachment. Without a joy that communicates to us a sweetness and an expansion of our whole being that surpass the pleasures we could find on this earth, a certain Christian life is perhaps possible, but not the total conversion of our being, which presupposes that we no longer set our rest in the things of this world. Teachers well know that one may never take away from a pupil anything except what has already been replaced by something else. How could God who is our pedagogue, act otherwise? He detaches us from ourselves after he has attached us to him, he withdraws all support because he has become our one and only rock. Thus, until we know joy, until joy revealing the action of God has become, and continuously so, our sole strength and our sole pleasure, our hearts will not be fixed on God alone. There is no one who can cease to seek and enjoy the things of earth if he is not able to seek and taste the things from on high. The Spirit who, by the Father's will, seeks to be our sole support and the very breath of our life must pervade our being in a perceptible manner, if he wishes us to belong wholly, according to the spirit, to our Creator.

Joy is necessary to vivify our person. The more we advance, in fact, the clearer it becomes that without the consolation that the Risen Lord brings us, we "can do nothing" (Jn. 15, 5). What comes from us is death; and we know that of ourselves we can produce nothing but wretchedness and degradation. We have no need to be in extreme distress to utter the prayer of the Psalmist; we can truly say throughout the length of the happiest days: "Save me, O God: for the waters are come in even unto my soul. I stick fast in the mire of the deep: and there is no sure standing" (Ps. 68, 2–3). For when the face of God is removed, all happens as if the abyss were opening before us. All we can do then is to wear ourselves away with expectation and entreat the Lord "to attend to my soul" (Ps. 68, 19) so that he may set it free. For us to have the courage to pursue our way, he has to show us here and now that he is mighty and capable of triumphing over all obstacles.

If his Spirit does not come into us to make us glad, we remain stiff and withered like paralytics. The water which once flowed from the side of Christ and into which we were plunged at our baptism must water our soul each day and quench its thirst every moment. In calling down the Spirit, on the day of Pentecost, we are not formulating a vague request, we are enunciating a truth of experience from which we know we cannot escape:

Sine tuo numine,
Nihil est in homine,
Nihil est innoxium.

Riga quod est aridum,
Sana quod est saucium,
Fove quod est frigidum.

Our wretchedness and helplessness must be constantly re-animated by the breath of joy, like the dry bones of which Ezechiel speaks; and it is doubtless because we are easily contented with the pale shadow of an atrophied existence, because we do not cry out more to God when we see our wounds, our aridity, our deformities, that the Spirit of consolation does not come to us. Otherwise that food par excellence, the bread of the Eucharist, the bread of thanksgiving and joy, would have greater effects in us. This bread would change our very substance and make living beings of us.

It is again when we have to make decisions that are imperative that consolation is necessary. It then comes as the word proffered by the Father to his sons who are advancing in darkness and uncertainty. The dialogue with God leads us to receive his counsels and his orders, to follow or abandon them, but without joy we are incapable of connecting together what he says to us and what we must accomplish. Without this source of nourishment in which our decisions are rooted, we should either seek to entertain ourselves with the Lord in intimate dialogue, forgetful of the world, or we should strive to solve the problems of our daily life by ourselves. Traditional image of the true contemplative, Moses never entered the tent of union except to consult God (Ex. 33, 11) on what he was to do; and Yahweh then spoke to him "as a man is wont to speak to his friend" (Ex. 33, 11) in the tenderness of intimacy. Through the joy in which God reveals himself, our lives are illuminated in such a way that we can see clearly the paths we must take and those we must avoid.

When joy has presided over our decisions for a long time past, it permeates us, like the oil of the Spirit, and enables us to act with ease and flexibility. In joy we direct our steps towards the places and labors where Christ our Lord awaits us. Since the Spirit has penetrated our heart with his unction, we no longer need, in one sense, to deliberate, for a spiritual instinct guides us amid the tempest of this world and, without apparent effort, we find the surest and most direct path. There where the joy of the Spirit is, there also is the liberty that works without ceasing, which no longer waits for explanations in order to understand, for instruction in order to know, for reasons in order to begin a certain course of action, for it possesses all that within itself. Since he now accomplishes all things in God, it is no longer necessary for man to reconcile himself with things and beings, for by a secret affinity he finds himself attuned to them.

But as a result of being attracted by the perfume of the breath of God and of the spiritual ointment with which he has anointed us, we spread "the good odor of Christ" (II Cor. 2, 15), which is the ministry of consolation and joy. At this stage, we no longer have to concern ourselves with what we are going to do for others, with what we should be capable of giving them to show our love for them, or again with what we should build up together with them so that Christ may become the Lord of all. We simply exist and, like the light, the best of ourselves is diffused without our thinking of it. The aroma of true sanctity penetrates all things and purifies the air around from the corruption of death, as the mandrakes exhale their perfume (*Cant.* 7, 13). Until we are flooded with the Spirit, our charity in regard to others can never be that inestimable benefit to them that nourishes, refashions, heals and enlarges the heart.

The pouring out of the Spirit of love is thus necessary at each phase of our existence, to detach us from creatures, to vivify us, to enable us to make the decisions that are necessary. There is thus nothing surprising in the fact that the saints declare that they cannot live without consolation and joy, that is, without the actual knowledge of God's initiative. What is true of the body, for which food is necessary, is equally true of the soul which could not subsist without this food of joy. If it is so easy for us to do without it, it is because we are not yet really awake to the spiritual life and because sleep protects us from the hunger and thirst that can become excruciating. "If thou thyself dost not go before," exclaimed Moses addressing Yahweh, "bring us not out of this place" (Ex. 33, 15). It is useless to show me another area within myself if you do not come continually to sow your word there, to water it and make it bear fruit. For if you abandon me my state will become worse and the fire of desire will burn me without anything coming to assuage it.

In proportion as God communicates himself to us, our eagerness increases to such an extent that it subordinates everything to itself and is ready for any extravagant foolishness in order to satisfy itself. To love God is no longer to be able to exist if he does not love us, indeed, if he does not reveal his love to us and make it perceptible to our hearts. This is rashness, no doubt, but surely the Lord encourages such audacity. Moreover in acting thus, we do no wrong to the Divine Majesty for to tell God that we need him and cannot bear that he should give himself to us only partially, is to respect his Majesty to the highest degree. Lack of spiritual ambition is no respect towards God for his view is that he ought not to have to put before us the necessity of love. This sort of moderation thinks it is linked with Christian humility, whereas it merely traces out a derisory caricature of it. On the contrary, when the passion for God dwells in us and we have lost the taste for all things save him, we thereby emphasize that he is the principle of our being and that we wish to subordinate all things to discovering him. We desire to take or snatch nothing from him, we want him to communicate himself to us, remaining himself in the gratuitousness of his love.

It does not suffice for us, moreover, that he should grant us today what is strictly necessary. We are not content or satisfied until he has shown himself in his entirety, as he is in himself. To fix a limit to love, to assign to it a prudent measure, is to despise it, for it is to assert that it is neither eternal nor total nor absolute. Moses who found grace in the eyes of Yahweh still insisted on having something more. Not that he needed a confirmation of the mission entrusted to him, but he wanted everything, and without cost, simply because love was consuming him: "Show me thy glory" (Ex. 33, 18) show thyself in thy divine radiance, in the transparency of thy sweetness and thy tenderness, and I shall then know that I enjoy thy favor and that thou knowest me by my name (Ex. 33, 17). Hence is explained, in all God's faithful followers, "that longing for paradise," that desire to enter at last into the promised land of eternity, where their passion for him will find rest, and where God will no longer have to show himself jealous in their regard, for he will be able to take pleasure in them.

Transparency

Joy is thus inaccessible and at the same time indispensable. Our God is out of our reach and communicates himself to us if he pleases; yet we could not live without receiving him. At the term of the spiritual life, these two elements which constitute joy, far from neutralizing each other, strengthen each other, for the more necessary love becomes to us, the more we wish that it be freely given to us. Already in the sphere of human relationships, if we need the esteem and affection of others, we scarcely appreciate the flatteries or pity of which we are the object, for these gestures and sentiments are elicited either by a false picture of ourselves or by our wretchedness. They do not touch our person in its truth or its depth. The condescendence or "charity" that comes from the outside of people could not fill the expectation of our hearts, which are wounded and not healed by such adulterated offerings. In our relations with God we desire even more to obtain his benefits without constraining him by fraudulent means. We should not like it finally if he were to pay us in return for our merits or our efforts and if it were not through a pure motive of love that he opened his hands to us. Are not the true poor proud and, in the very heart of their poverty, do they not care more for the generosity of the donor than for the shower of riches bestowed?

We know that it is impossible to rob God of his gifts. But even were they within our reach, we should carefully refrain from touching them. We do not want to snatch anything or take anything from him and still less to *demand* that he should grant us that for which, however, we are hungering and thirsting. The nearer we draw to God, the more we desire to meet him in person, beyond even this joy which floods us for we wish to respect the gratuitousness of his love. Because his tenderness has become for us a matter of life and death, we want it to come to us without our having to make the least sign or say the least word. He who loves fears that the marks of love given to him may arise from a passion which has a natural tendency to manifest itself. He dreads hearing words pronounced which do not come from the heart and stimulating others to acts which would not come from an overflow of interior feeling. That is why if, *per impossibile,* God were accessible to us, we should drive him back to the inaccessible in order to be certain that he was coming down to us by the very movement of his love. If the Lord were at our disposal, he would no longer interest us and he could not satisfy us, for we want to encounter an initiative that is gratuitous.

Such is already the case with human love. We are tempted to obtain it by the exercise of charm, by presents or by tears, but we soon realize that we have stolen love rather than been given it. Just when the need of tenderness has been assuaged and we are in possession of the beloved face, it becomes disfigured, it has lost the personal beauty which attracted us towards it. It is no longer he whom we had seen opposite us and whom we longed to discover, for the lack of respect of desire has consumed the secret treasure which could have satisfied us. The other, so long as he remains other, can alone quench our thirst; and he could no longer slake it if, in filling us with his presence, he did not take refuge in what is beyond our grasp. Genuine love is a paradox and withdraws the beloved in proportion as he comes close—the more intimate and familiar you are with me, the more I want you far away and above me as an incomprehensible mystery which I shall always be able to respect and venerate.

It is often thought that adoration is an attitude linked to the fear of a God whom we have not yet touched, and that it becomes blurred when the Lord communicates himself with intensity. In fact, the Master before whom the slave prostrates himself is for him an unreal being; he is remote like a reality which is imposed from outside, soon forgotten when the trembling caused by his passage has ceased. If, on the other hand, the source of my life and of all life reveals himself to me, what I will with all my being is that he shall identify himself with me and yet remain something utterly other than my nothingness and completely outside the limited possibility of welcome that I feel I possess. Because God has become indispensable to me, I desire that he remain inaccessible. Because of myself I can have no access to him, I know he will be able to dispense his gifts and his love to me.

On this point man is indeed the image of what takes place in God himself. For the Son the only life and the only joy is to belong to his Father and receive everything from him. Nothing is more necessary than this gift of the Father, since the Word is nothing and does nothing of himself but only what he sees the Father do. Nevertheless God who gives everything to his Son and who gives himself, cannot transmit his Paternity, that is, he cannot make the Son the source of the gift. He communicates to him his power of giving, since the Son gives himself wholly in the Spirit, but the Father cannot cease to be the first origin. The Word is filled to overflowing. He exists eternally without having need of anything.

But it is because his Father who bestows all things upon him, remains his Father that "He respects him as his Principle."* The power to engender is for ever outside the grasp of the Beloved Son; and, with all his infinite love, the latter wills that what constitutes the Person of his Father shall be for ever denied him. Otherwise, love would vanish, the Word no longer having one from whom to receive. Yet he has been granted the power to give love, to give to him from whom he holds all things, the Spirit who is all himself and all his love. He diffuses himself totally, but without ceasing to be the one who receives all and returns all to its Origin. The Son who has nothing of himself is indispensable to the Father; and this power of acceptance which the Father has engendered is only accessible to him if it gives everything back to him. They are in some sort present one to the other while remaining absent one from the other in a third element which is their reciprocal presence. Their intimacy is all the more total since they are not absorbed one

* St. John Damascene, *De Fide Orthodoxa,* P.G. 94, 1092.

in the other, but both move out of themselves into another, and that, even, is their return one into the other. It is in the Spirit that they are transparent one to the other without confusion and without separation.

The union of the inaccessible and the indispensable, perfectly realized in the love of the Trinity, is made manifest by the Resurrection of Christ. That is why it is the cause of our joy. Christ was never more necessary to the Apostles than when he appeared to them in Galilee, for then they had no longer any hope. Yet never more than at that moment did his appearances and disappearances give them that impression of gratuitousness which pervaded his Person throughout his public life. He was present without his own being able to say whence he came and when he would go away. He showed them his wounds and ate with them, flooding them with peace and joy, but at the same time the Lord was more fundamentally elusive than before. Before the very eyes of the disciples of Emmaus, when they recognized him, he vanished—his presence had become so intense that at the instant when it appeared in this world of ours it was hidden from their sight. It can only be an absent presence, an absence which makes itself present everywhere, a presence which can thus no longer be there in the way to which we are accustomed, for it is equally everywhere. If he appears here, it is to disappear from everything, in order that we may seek him everywhere and that, finding him in everything, he may be present under a mode that escapes us. To give himself to us at all times and in all places, he must not be dependent on this time and this place.

In hiding himself from our eyes, the risen Christ does not go away from us. He wants, on the contrary, to become the sole desire of our hearts, minds and bodies. Thus he cannot allow us to approach him at one unique and privileged moment or in *one* particular place where we could be certain of finding him. To make himself continually indispensable, he must remain ever inaccessible. But, on the other hand, we must have access to him at every moment, otherwise we could no longer live. If he did not give himself to us at all times and in all places, if we were not certain of slaking our thirst in him everywhere and always, we should never find him again. The Risen Lord thus submits himself to the laws of time and space, whether he comes or goes, whether he is present or absent, whether he appears or disappears, for otherwise he could never have a relationship with us.

But, on the contrary, because he is accessible to him who seeks him and space and time no longer form an obstacle to his presence, he submits himself to them totally, so much so that they are in him more than he is in them. He fills time and space for he is the life of the believer and he wills to communicate himself to him continually. This forbids him to be enclosed not only by our all too narrow hearts, but by the moment and the place. The more he seems to us truly near, as the Master who holds all things in himself, the more we wish him to be remote and to surpass what we are and what we can become infinitely. The God whom we need and whom our person calls out for with all its might, must be the principle of all life and reconcile the whole universe in himself. If we could grasp him, we should no longer seek him everywhere. If he could continually appear before our fleshly eyes, we should be in danger of losing him by turning our gaze away. For his presence to be universal it is thus essential that it should always present itself as absent from the particular, from which we are incapable of freeing ourselves completely.

What manifests the Resurrection is the omnipresence of the Creator in whom all things have been made and in whom everything dwells. He cannot be in one place more than in another, but he is wholly here and wholly there. Created in the Word, the universe has returned to its origin. How then, henceforward, could the world fix bounds beyond which the Redeemer should not pass?

He has reconciled the world to himself by his death, in such a way that that world is no longer anything but the revelation of his presence. Although no addition has been made to creation by the coming of the Son and his resurrection, something radically new has taken place, since the Being who sustains all things for the future has a human countenance. The Christ who appears in the light of Easter morning (Jn. 21, 4) is not indistinguishable from that light. He is not a phantom who takes shape in our eyes still heavy with sleep—he speaks our language and calls us his children so that we may eat with him. The infinite Being does not lose himself in a universal presence without shape or form, he is for ever someone who possesses an individual body, and the eyes of the spirit can ceaselessly discover the beauty of it. "Predestinated the Son of God in power, by the resurrection of our Lord Jesus Christ from the dead" (Rom. 1, 4) he is everywhere because, having returned to his Father, he is again, and exclusively, that filial power of acceptance that receives all and gives all, so much so that his transparency is not an impalpable mist but a full intensity which shines limitlessly and absorbs all obstacles into itself. His body which formerly, to reveal him to men, had equally to hide and veil him, has become a pure means of manifestation and communication. Having again become what he was at the beginning and has always been, he can be at the same time with each one and with all of us, with God and with the world.

The expansion of the spiritual life is thus situated in the perspective of a share in the resurrection of Christ. If he is our joy it is because, for all mankind, he is the one who has united us to his Father and the one through whom henceforward love springs up in our hearts and is diffused throughout the world. Like joy which is his image, Christ the consoler is at the same time the distant goal towards which we are marching and the sole foundation of our destinies. But it is not only the existence of individuals which must be considered here. The consolation brought by our Lord is the end and the beginning of each person, because Christ risen has already identified himself with the whole of mankind now perfectly in tune with God, with itself and with the cosmos. The spiritual transparency of the Word incarnate, dead and risen again, which expresses the transparency of the dialogue maintained with his Father in the Spirit, from now onwards is communicated to all men. In Christ the humanity of the future grows, so that each man will no longer see in his own body a barrier but a way of communication enabling him to spread, to the uttermost ends of the earth, the love that comes to him from God in order that all may return to the Father. Far from being a rejection of the world and of persons, the final resurrection which is in preparation will be the accomplishment of them beyond death. Like Christ himself, each man will be all in all and will recognize in each one the other he needs and who freely grants him his love. The final fruit of the joy that overflows from the heart of the risen Christ will be expressed by the distribution of the divine riches in all and in each one, in such a way that man will be, in Christ, present to all the others, everywhere, always and totally, in freedom and gratitude.

Here and now we have the first-fruits of this goal of history, not only through a faith which asserts itself but at the root of an experience still, it is true, not wholly pure. Are there not faces that are transparent, are there not human bodies which a long life of renunciation and fidelity, of contemplation or of suffering has gradually spiritualized? They have no longer anything to preserve or to hide, because they have kept nothing for themselves. At a chance meeting we find ourselves completely at home in their company, as if we had met our dearest friend. Even their limitations and their peculiarities are lovable and do not make them impenetrable to the light. A look which no longer seeks to subjugate but which penetrates the soul without effort; hands which have ceased to snatch and constrain, but which now open to give everything they have. Age counts for little. What matters is the deep peace to which certain men attain. Such men are in harmony with things and with beings, they find their way into men's hearts, because they abandon themselves without reserve, but with respect and discretion. St. Francis spoke to the birds and calmed the hungry beasts, bringing about, in gentleness, the promise of old: "The wolf shall dwell with the lamb: and the leopard shall lie down with the kid. The calf and the lion and the sheep shall abide together: and a little child shall lead them. . . . They shall not hurt, nor shall they kill in all my holy mountain for the earth is filled with the knowledge of the Lord" (Isa. 11, 6–9).

An idyllic vision? Perhaps, but more simply the realization already begun before our eyes of the paradise where there will be no place except for understanding and harmony. For the saints, even here on earth every meeting is a happy circumstance and every thing a friend, because in them all, even suffering, is received in the risen Christ as a gift of the Father's bounty and because the world already appears with the transparency of grace. When the soul has gone out of itself to enter into its Creator, the Redeemer restores all things to it in his Spirit, gathering up for it not only the interior powers, but the forces of the universe. God is then found and experienced in men and in the world as much as in our inmost heart. Joy is not only feeling and climate, it becomes the song of all creation and the effect of this first harmony rediscovered in the heart of the Beloved.

He who, acknowledging himself the worst of sinners, bears the wretchedness and sufferings of all mankind, slowly becomes, by the joy that transforms and submerges him, the happiest man on earth. No one will ever be more completely filled than he, for no one will be able to deprive him of the joy that the Only-begotten Son has transmitted to him, by sending to him the overflowing consolation of the Spirit.

8 SPIRITUAL PROGRESS

IT IS ONLY IN PARADISE that the spiritual life will find its full development, when the love that breaks forth, perceived here on earth from time to time through joy, will never cease renewing itself in us to overflowing. To approach this haven of tenderness and wonder, we have to enter more deeply into suffering day by day in order that, thus purified, we may be transformed by the power of the Resurrection.

On this earth it is impossible to taste final repose or to enjoy that blissful tranquillity which would demand no further effort, would avoid suffering and dispense us from further search. Liberty always remains in danger; it has to correct itself every hour to direct its steps anew towards God who is drawing near to and soliciting it. The more it advances, the more its only happiness is on the side of acceptance, welcome and responsiveness, but it remains tempted to escape and to give up the dialogue with God.

Spiritual progress must not, however, be considered only under this negative aspect, as the proof of an insufficiency and a lack which it is necessary to fill gradually in the course of time. For, in this world where God has come to live, progress defined as walking at our Lord's side is also the clearest sign of the perfection attained by the spiritual man. Our fulfillment at a given moment does not consist, in fact, in the accomplishment of an abstract ideal, but in our present opening to the action of the Spirit. In the measure in which, at a given moment, we accept the call of God, such as it presents itself to us, without temporizing with it and without rejecting anything of it, we are already perfect. Perfection is not to be seen only in the accomplishment of redemption at the term of history, it is equally to be found today in obedience to the will of him who saves us, in terms of the concrete possibilities of the day that is in our hands.

But, to understand that progress is our perfection, we ought first of all to inquire of what it is made and what are the principal stages through which it must pass. Its purpose is to assemble together the elements of our becoming and our being in order that liberty may dispose of them and submit them to God. To walk in spiritual ways is to unify, ever more perfectly and extensively, all the factors which make up the human person, together with those elements which it comes across in its action. Thus spiritual perfection is both in the present act which surmounts divisions and in the result of this act and of all acts which, accomplished under the impulse of God, gradually bring about the unity of the forces of this world.

Progress and Totality

The progress of our union with God is inseparable from the fulfillment of the human person, for the aim of Christ's taking hold of us is not to reduce man to slavery, but to communicate to him ever more numerous benefits. Far from inducing us to escape from our condition, intimacy with the Creator brings us constantly back to it, to improve it, enlarge it and bring it to its fullness. Thus, what our Lord and Master seeks is not to absorb us into himself, but to bind together all our forces, to restore our past and to build with us a better future.

The consequence of our contact with God is to reveal to us the sinner we really are. But, in a second phase, the divine light bids us free ourselves from sin and receive the grace which will heal us, in order that, re-established in our dignity, we may run more swiftly towards him who is inviting us to love him. Of ourselves, we are incapable of giving ourselves to God, but when he comes to us, he intimates to us his strong desire that we should reform our person so that it may become his dwelling-place. The more he becomes our friend, the more we find that certain regions of our being escape him or that they are in such disorder that he could not dwell there. St. John of the Cross compares the soul to the glass panes of a window.* In the darkness the dust that covers the glass is not visible; in daylight we perceive it better but if the full midday sun flashes on the windowpanes, the slightest speck catches the eye. The growth of our union with God thus obliges us to an ever greater purification.

Moreover, what our Lord wants is not only to free us from sin, but to liberate the living forces of our being in order to set us up before him as true sons filled with light and strength. Not only does he wash us from our impurities, he communicates to us his strength and his light and patiently brings into being that stature of man of which St. Paul speaks. Without God, our personality lacks the center it needs, and we remain divided, like puppets with maladjusted limbs. With him, on the contrary, all the elements of our person are related to the whole. For, revealing his presence in

* E. A. Peers (ed.), *Complete Works of St. John of the Cross, op. cit., Ascent of Mt Carmel,* Bk. II, ch. V, p. 77. St. John of the Cross uses this comparison to show that the specks on the window form an obstacle to the light.

spheres unknown until then to our liberty, which is founded on him, he allows us to bring this new element into relation with the center and thus to lead it to its fullness.

Again, spiritual growth develops in another direction—that of time. To encounter God we must, it has been said, live in the present moment. In fact, the divine presence, revealed "today," projects us towards a future where we shall be able to recognize it better. It is not a question of a better future, but of knowing that God will reveal himself more in the days and years to come, until it is time to see him face to face. Attracted by the knowledge of this final manifestation, the spiritual man sees the veils that have covered the face of God fall one by one. It is in fact from this end of time that Christ returns to visit his children and prevent them from looking back. They hasten towards the promised land where they will enjoy the total presence of their Master and Lord.

But, in thus directing us towards the future, he continually sends us back to the distant past where we did not recognize him at work. The more the future appears in the divine light, the more God demands that the past from which we have come be filled with him alone. Otherwise our tending towards the future will gradually weaken our living strength which is rooted in what was. The tissue of our personality, all our relations with others and with the world, must be transformed, in order that, behind as before us, there is only Christ. The more a tree shoots upwards towards the sky, the more deeply must it penetrate into the earth, there to find its basis and be able to defy the storm. If our past were to escape God, we should escape him ourselves, for we can neither act nor understand unless it is in terms of what we have already perceived and accomplished. Hence this backward-looking glance in order to see better the providential action of the Lord and the way in which he has changed everything into grace, even sin. If Jesus Christ is the alpha and omega, all that was must be mastered by him and renewed in him.

According to modern psychology,* mental illnesses come from the fact that the personality is incapable of assimilating certain situations or certain events. It is fettered by them so long as it has not been possible for it to become aware of and accept them. This is because man's liberty is founded on the acceptance of a destiny of which he is not the creator. When he wants to give himself a universe of relationships in accordance with his dreams, instead of his recognizing and desiring the setting in which he is placed, the reality he ignores continues to impose itself upon him, crushing him and making him suffer. The personality expands when it has been able to integrate and arrange in their order of values the facts of its existence.

A spiritual life in process of growth should bring these truths to their ultimate point of development. Even if we are free from any malformation, a part of ourselves always remains enslaved because it has not yet been taken stock of, exposed to the light and re-assumed. Over and above the conscious sins which disfigure me there exists a "disorder of my actions,"† that is to say of the more or less deep zones which escape the control of my liberty and that of God. If there is no question for us, with a view to becoming aware of them, of making use of the processes employed in the case of nervous disorders, it remains true that a prayer which strives after truth and an action intelligently conducted, will gradually show us these elements of our personality, still paralyzed and withered, because

* In this passage we understand by psychology the science that enables man to have access to liberty by the conscious and voluntary integration of all the relationships constituting his personality. As a science and as a therapeutic, it can only lead to the restoration of the exercise of free will; it does not set before this power of choice a content or orientations capable of determining it. When it is successful, it restores health, but it is incapable of suggesting to the patient when cured what he should do and why he should do it.

† *Spiritual Exercises,* no. 63 (Rickaby, *op. cit.,* p. 38).

the grace which passes through our liberty has not yet given them life.

Often it seems as if all that spiritual direction proposes to us is to tend towards the future with all our strength, to give ourselves up to contemplation or zeal until we have exhausted ourselves. We are invited to practice virtue, to ask God for his grace so that we may become new men identified with Christ. Forgetting the past we must put everything into operation so that we may come to a perfect charity and a complete gift of ourselves. Yet if we do not take care, if we consider this aspect of things only, we are in danger of building a lofty edifice on sand. Certainly spiritual direction is not to be confused with a psychological cure, it should adopt neither the means nor the ends of such a science, but good desires and good will will not be able to advance very far, if someone does not suggest to us that we must go back, to the existential foundations of our person which are the bases of liberty in order to throw light on them, make them healthy and fortify them.

The impossibility of putting our sinful past between parentheses has already been stressed several times. If we refuse to return to it, the God to whom we reach out can only be a more or less attractive image, formed according to our desires, and not at all the living and true God, for one can never know the Lord without knowing oneself. One can never meet the truth of God without being compelled to live the truth oneself. But what is said of sin is also true of all that makes our past: the acceptance of grace and access to the intimacy of God pass through the recognition of the lowliness of our condition, through clear-sightedness in regard to our wretchedness and failures, through the wish to see the secret folds of our being transformed in the divine presence. To return to our past life is simply to consider the natural bases of our person in order to unravel there all that is not yet assumed by our liberty, all that has not yet been thrown open to the presence of the new Adam who must supplant the old. We cannot welcome God or know him more until we have reformed our power of acceptance. But how are we to effect this reform if we do not visualize on what points it must focus, if the light is not pouring into us at every moment? Until then God can no longer grow in the soul or infuse new life into it.

A certain intelligence is indispensable to spiritual progress. Not that the progress of our union with God is bound up with the intellectual capacities and the gifts of abstraction, still less with scholastic success or with culture. True intelligence is a power of attention to the real, a respect for the facts that impose themselves upon us, an absence of obstinacy and a keen desire to penetrate to the heart of things, beings or events. It thus links up with humility, for it rejects ready-made theories, never thinks it knows enough, doubts whether it has understood, is capable of setting out again for the conquest of the true, without ever esteeming itself satisfied. If we want to understand what this intelligence necessary to progress is, we must compare it to the awakening of knowledge at the moment when it is identified with that surprise that leads to discovery. There are individuals who succeed without difficulty in examinations or tests simply because they have a well-equipped mental mechanism and have acquired by their labor a certain store of knowledge. But an intelligent being is a being capable of opening to a new truth. To be intelligent is thus in the first place not to know, not to experience, not to be sure of oneself, to call in question what one has learned and above all to call oneself in question, in order that what has already been seen and understood may be contemplated anew in the act of knowing. Intelligence is finally a certain youthfulness of mind which lives because it consents to receive life from its object.

If the spiritual life is a dialogue between the Spirit of God and the spirit of man, this intelligence, which is the recognition of what one is and transparency in regard to God, has a special role to play in the growth of the union of all things with God. It must not be satisfied with throwing light on the past, it must change things by directing them in a new way towards a future that liberty visualizes only with difficulty. Psychological therapeutics may perhaps succeed in restoring a correct relationship of the personality with the real, they have no power to give it a positive content and a meaning. At best they allow us to posit true questions and they prepare the ego for a lucid option. This, however, being granted, we necessarily arrive at the following question: "Liberty, yes, but what for?" It is then that the answer put forward by Christ comes in. This makes us move towards the truth of our future and, by that very fact, unifies, in terms of the end of time, all we have been until then. Once discovered, the meaning of our existence flows back over our whole being, reveals to it the ultimate significance of all reality and allows it to conform to reality freely. To react as one should to one's surroundings and the world is still only a preliminary step towards determination and choice. Without the giving of the power from on high, which alone creates our history, we remain like an empty vessel. But, on the other hand, to turn solely towards the wealth to come, without taking account of the one who is going to receive wealth and without purifying it by reform, is practically to refuse to integrate man in the divine movement which seeks to fill history and is thus to deny the power of the resurrection which changes all things into itself. Constituted as it is by our previous situations, events, relationships, acts and thoughts, nature must thus ceaselessly be corrected by grace to develop itself to its measure. Our past has no value apart from the future that God is preparing for us and which eludes us always. The future, however, is only a dangerous myth if in its desire to advance and accept what comes, it does not base itself on the past.

Without claiming to resolve the difficult problem of the relationship between psychiatry and the spiritual life, let us add a few remarks. What matters to the Christian is not to be this or that any more than to accomplish such and such a thing, but to accept what he is as a gift and a grace. Just as no miracle will be able to restore a limb that has been amputated, so there are incurable nervous disorders. Yet the fact of orientating ourselves as we are, knowingly and willingly, in the direction Christ imprints upon our lives, transforms our wounds or our deficiencies. A face which certain features disfigure to the point of ugliness is capable of remaining harmonious and even of attaining to beauty if it is bathed in the sweetness of love and abandonment. What is important is to leave nothing outside liberty, to accept all things, to organize them into a hierarchy where our being receives, under the eye of God, and through him, order, cohesion and a certain equilibrium. Spiritual progress can then be defined as the growing union of the factors composing the human being, without forgetting that, the more they are recognized by liberty and assimilated by it, the more capable they will be of receiving grace and letting themselves be transformed into its image. So long as we remain on the level of psychology, we can speak of health, as a doctor would do in relation to one's body; we could not put forward an orientation worthy of the spirit. God alone can transmit the power finally to ordain human nature so as to make it transparent to the Spirit.

Ribadeneira says of St. Ignatius:

> The Father was so much master of his affective nature, as Mâitre André des Freux said, that in him the grace of God seemed to be as it were innate and connatural. In fact in him the passions were so controlled and dominated, the movements of his heart were so rooted and, so to speak, so steeped in virtue, that they served for no other use than that of virtue and sanctity; and they were as it were born from him into God. This does not mean that we attribute to nature what belongs to grace, but that we magnify and exalt grace itself which strengthens man to the point of making him victorious over nature and capable of submitting to God. Thus at last one can say, "I live, yet not I, for Christ liveth in me."*

* MHSJ, *Fontes Narr.*, II, pp. 364–365.

The attempt made to unify the forces at the disposal of liberty is thus nothing if it does not lead to the submission of everything to grace, in order that our being may be its domain and that God may thus express himself freely at all levels of the personality to manifest his glory there. Thus we must not oppose psychology and spiritual life, as if they could be independent. They must be situated one in relation to the other, as two facets of our being which must ceaselessly strengthen each other, like the past and the future which, in the present, condition and cause each other. Far from becoming confused, these two spheres will acquire a cohesion that is all the stronger if we refuse to separate them.

Psychology considers man and his liberty more especially from the point of view of observation. Besides our relationship with ourselves, it studies our relationship with others and with the world, the perfection of which becomes more perceptible in proportion to progress. Conversely, the spiritual life lays stress on the subject's acts in his relation to God. But it is inseparable from the other orientations of the human person, since to obey the Spirit of God is to submit ourselves to his suggestions here and now, in the context, wide but at the same time precisely defined, which is ours. Thus these two points of view do not exclude each other, since the social integration of which the psychologists speak is already the spiritual accomplishment of the universe in Jesus Christ with him guiding us, in his love, to authentic charity, which is order, peace and justice in this universe. The more we enter into ourselves to find God and the foundation of all things, the more also we go out into the world in order to meet him who is all and more than all. Attentive as it is to the dialogue with God, the spiritual life does not reject other dialogues, it rather gives them their true focus and enables them to develop in plenitude. Thus spiritual progress has no other end than the introduction of every bond into this bond that unites the Spirit of God and every spirit to our own spirit.

The Stages of Progress

The perspective which has just been described does not allow us to conceive spiritual progress in terms of the spatial route of an itinerary. Even if he does not yet know or visualize it, the totality of the spiritual life must be ceaselessly present to man. No object of the interior or external worlds could disappear during the journey, for each one of these worlds must be known in a more precise way, in itself and in its relationship with the universe as a whole. Spiritual growth may rather be compared to an ascent revealing an ever vaster horizon which gives greater relief to forms and colors and shows us in clearer fashion the harmony created and re-created by God.

It is classic to distinguish the purgative, illuminative and unitive ways, or again to speak of beginners, progressives and perfect. In regard to these different stages, each writer insists on the characteristics which seem to him more important. Without denying the value of these schemes, it would seem preferable to adopt a more general point of view and to stress, first of all, that the principal movements of the spiritual life correspond to the perception of phases of our interior life hitherto unsuspected. At the beginning liberty moves in a restricted sphere. Gradually it enlarges its field of action, so that its knowledge of God becomes transformed and, without forgetting its previous acquisitions, its view of others and of the world finds itself renewed and becomes capable of unifying ends hitherto set against each other. A law often met with is here verified once more—the discovery of oneself sends one continually back to the discovery of God and this brings about the reform of our vision of the world. "I know that if I knew myself according to the truth, I should know all creatures perfectly."*

Before describing each of the stages of the spiritual life, it is thus desirable to indicate briefly to what phases of man's being we can

* Master Eckhart, *Telle était Soeur Katrei* (Cahiers du Sud, 1954), p. 51.

relate them. The personality first of all lives its relationship to God on the level of the explicit consciousness, where distinct acts are posited according to the different faculties. Next a phase is revealed in which our affective nature as a whole assumes a greater importance than the succession of thoughts, desires or sentiments which concern intelligence, will or sensitivity. Finally in the third stage, the personality expresses itself according to its origin, its center or its foundation.†

In the early stages of the spiritual life experience develops in clear consciousness. When we pray, for instance, we have the impression of being in touch with our Lord in so far as we think of him, so much so that our almost exclusive effort is aimed at rejecting distractions which, in hiding him from our view, seem to remove his existence. People may try to explain to us that our fundamental attitude is more important than numerous analyses, but we do not grasp the meaning of these words and we again begin to formulate phrases expressing our demands and desires. In our daily lives our efforts tend to the mastery over ourselves, to the control of our instincts, to the ordering of our activity according to a plan traced by us. What matters is to make everything depend on our intelligence and our will, in order that nothing may be left to whim or chance.

The spiritual life thus appears in the form of practices which cover, as far as possible, the whole of our activities. Even if the latter arrange themselves in a sort of group, we do not perceive the internal unity of it. Moreover, when these acts of thought or will

† These three levels of the person refer us back in inverse order to the "three times or occasions of the election," such as we have tried to understand them in connection with the spiritual choice. The first "time" is that in which God acts directly at the center of the soul, to indicate to us the action to be undertaken. The second is the privileged place of the discernment of spirits. The third is characterized by the activity of the conscious reason itself, enlightened by faith.

are lacking, it seems to us we are failing God. Hence the desire to make such acts more numerous, to make them more conscious and more determined, without our being able to succeed in joining together the complex elements of our existence. We then suffer at one moment because we are not spending all our time in prayer and penance, at another because we are not spending it wholly in the service of our neighbor. The preoccupation which we give to one of these elements, it seems to us we take away from the others; and we are more uneasy still when a great part of our days is devoted to a world from which Christ seems absent. Hence a tension which we hope to slacken by imposing other tasks upon ourselves. It becomes strengthened, however, by this new yoke.

Because at this stage the spiritual life consists in what we think, will and do, everything seems to us as if it depended on us. However much we hear our Lord repeat to us, "Without me, you can do nothing" (Jn. 15, 5), we can only admit this in the most obscure faith, we are convinced that it is sufficient to make an effort for God to give us his grace, and that he always gives it to us if we dispose ourselves to receive it by our prayers and penances. Moreover we presuppose the reality of this grace, for it is not perceptible to us in any way, so much so that, in practice, the action of God in our lives has no other existence than that we choose to attribute to it. We are willing to affirm that God has given us everything, that he is our Creator and Redeemer, that he loved us first and that he alone is capable of leading us to him. These truths, however, remain abstractions. We have to believe them because the faith says so, but since they are inaccessible to us, we have no means of verifying their authenticity.

Thus in its first stage the spiritual life appears at grips with insoluble contradictions and with affirmations whose content it fails to grasp. These tensions, however, oblige the personality to seek at a deeper level the unity which is invariably lacking to it in the orbit in which it moves. Not finding any stability in its own clear conscience or in the apparent universe which surrounds it, it moves forward and slowly penetrates a zone which was but recently closed to it. Blindly asserted up till now, for the future the world of faith takes on a consistency of its own. The decisive step in the knowledge of God is taken the day when we perceive that cohabitation is possible between a secret certainty and a visible evidence that is contrary to it, between lasting peace and external suffering, between a joy that rises from the depths and superficial trouble. This is an experience that is commonplace, perhaps, but which, if taken seriously, at first recognized fleetingly, soon grasped as a law of our being, serves us as introduction to the spiritual sphere properly so-called.

Beyond our acts and feelings a more total and deeper equilibrium of the personality takes shape and expresses itself no longer in sensitivity, but in an interior affectivity. At first we shall merely treat with suspicion the bases of our being or the threats of instability and destruction. Soon, working back from effects to causes, on the one hand we shall see our generous acts issuing from an interior order, linked with obedience to God, and on the other we shall realize that our sins come from the disorder that dwells in us, because of our present revolt in regard to our Lord's particular desire for us.

This access to the domain of interior peace renews the form of the dialogue with God. In the course of the first stage, faith remained an assertion the content of which we did not perceive; but when we came to distinguish clearly the sentiments elicited on the surface of our being by pleasure or displeasure, by interior tastes and distastes, we realized that the latter were due to the presence or absence of God. Certainly, we do not see him face to face. Nevertheless, through what happens, i.e., through the intermediary of the fruits that his action produces, or through those which his departure prevents from ripening, we glimpse what he is—the superabundant life that seeks to lead us to joy, the Master mighty in work and in word.

We then enter into the mystery of Christ in a new way. Instead of lingering over the contemplation of his gestures and his words, we perceive how each of them transmits to us his unique love. Such an assertion is no longer merely a beautiful idea heard and repeated, it corresponds to our experience of the relationship that our Lord entertains with us. The Gospel seems to have been written for us that very day. Before, we were reduced to imagining the inner life of Christ, and according to all appearances, to make it live for us by the effort of our thought. For the future, it is he who will take the initiative in us, he who will make himself known by the movements he brings about in our soul, by the healing of our wounds, by the strength he gives us, by the light with which he surrounds us. We sense that beyond the effects produced, he exists as he did yesterday, more powerful and more mighty. Thus because we have entered into ourselves, there to discover new regions, we have come out of ourselves and have entered the unfathomable mystery of the Word.

This stage is equally marked by a transformation of our way of conducting ourselves in the world. At this stage, our intelligence looks for the means to obey God in all things and asceticism rejects every fetter imposed on this concrete and present submission. It is in the action itself that the dialogue with God is established, for since his will is ever manifesting itself, since his demands are always unforeseen and unpredictable, we have never finished interpreting the signs he gives us which must direct our words, our gestures and our acts.

When our interior affectivity has been sufficiently developed for its own sake and is no longer concerned with the backwash of sensible feeling, we trouble less and less about our peace and happiness. We only want to know whether we are in truth responding to God. The second stage of the spiritual life is thus more marked by the desire of personal stability than by the search for God. But, as we advance along this road, God ceases to be the means of our joy to become the term who interests us in himself. Our affectivity disengages itself from the alternation of contentment and anxiety, to focus its attention only on the Person to whom we wish to give ourselves freely not for the benefits he can grant, but solely for himself. It is then that a third stage is traversed in which we find that a deeper, more stable and more final happiness consists in the fact of being always with him. If we can leave him by moving away from his will, he never abandons us, for he sustains us by his creative and redeeming act. In spite of all we can say or do, the tender and compassionate God can never fail us.

He does not need our acts as at the beginning of our meeting, he no longer reminds us of his presence; he cannot separate himself from us. It was of this state that our Lord explained to St. Catherine of Siena:

> These souls, thrown into the furnace of my charity, without anything of them being outside me, wholly aflame in me, no one can take or snatch away from my grace, because they have become one single thing with me and I with them. I never withdraw from them the sentiment of my presence, their spirit always perceives me in itself, unlike that of the others in whom I go and return—not that I withdraw my grace from them, but the feeling of my presence. If I acted in that way, it was precisely to lead them to great perfection. When they have reached this perfection, I deprive them of this interplay of love—the coming and the going away that I call interplay of love because it is through love that I go away and return to them—not myself properly speaking since I am your unchangeable God who does not move, but this sentiment that my charity communicates to the soul and which goes away and returns.*

Thus beyond the succession of sentiments aroused by the action of the different spirits, the very origin of our being is now in God's

* *Le livre des Dialogues* (Paris, Ed. du Seuil, 1953), p. 253. Cf. Thorold, *op. cit.*, p. 149.

firm grasp and the basis of the person is recognized as established in God.

But if we wish to arrive at this end, we must pass through suffering. If the attachment to God is to appear in us, former tastes must disappear. It is true we could only die or despair if this essential union with God were not our supreme and sufficient good. But before we recognize him we must pass through the night of agony, after the pattern of that of Christ. So long as the will of God is linked to the fruits we receive in accepting it, our tendency is to take our submission for a means. This veils his presence and his action from us. Nevertheless, after the alternation of peace and disturbance, of joy and suffering, has purified our hearts, our desire to find God himself, over and above his gifts, increases. We wish to reach his will in itself, for the sole reason that it is his will. Now the crucible in which this discovery is tested is the decisive anguish in which we really lose everything, even the peace that gave us the proof that we were with him. All the supports we had at our disposal must be rejected to leave room for the foundation which does not come from us, so that the experience of nothingness, the total absence of certainty, is identified with the absolute knowledge that we hold our stability from another. Yet this night is already day, this death is already life, for if we accept our disappearance and are willing to see our sufficiency vanish, it is so that our essential link with God, who is our very being, may come to the fore.

At the second stage of the spiritual life, there is still a distance between our willing acceptance of God and the peace which is the affective resonance of this acceptance; thus our repose is still threatened. Here, for the future, it is not only pleasure which will be surpassed, but all happiness and even all joy, since we shall then be what we should be, and in the Spirit our origin will manifest itself as origin. Established beyond sensitivity and even beyond affectivity, it is God whom we can consider in himself as Creator and Redeemer. We certainly do not forget that he has drawn us out of sin and of ourselves. But, because we have left ourselves, we remain totally free to say and do all things in God.

Here now is the goal of the struggle of the solitary. Here is his end, his reward, the repose of his labors, and, at the same time, the consolation of his sufferings. Here is perfection itself and man's true wisdom—when the soul embraces and is clothed with all the virtues, not as elements borrowed from elsewhere, but as almost natural productions of its being, after the resemblance of God who is himself all his being. Then, as God is what he is, so the dispositions of a good will in regard to good and virtue appear sure and strengthened in the good spirit; the soul itself adheres to the unchangeable good with such vehemence, that in no way, it seems, can it ever be moved from what it is at that moment.*

If we know ourselves, it is no longer through God and in God, to such an extent that our person no longer interests us for its own sake, but because God is interested in it and takes pleasure in it. All creatures and all mankind come towards us in the Son so completely that we in our turn, in the Son, can be at the inmost heart of all creation and of the multitude of men. We may have had the impression of going down into ourselves and certainly it was such a movement that attracted our attention, for we were then making ourselves our starting-point. But this descent to the lowest possible or this rise to the highest has become so complete that it is not only ourselves we have found, but the Other towards whom we were going, without at first knowing it; and through him we have attained to all things. Neither pleasure nor peace are important, because, like their opposites, they are received from the hand of God with the conviction that he gives us each day what is best and most useful. Thus, as in him we welcome everything, everything becomes pleasant to us.

These three stages of the spiritual life resemble those passed

* William of St. Thierry, *Golden Epistle* (London, 1930), ch. 16, pp. 112–113.

through by the apostles. In the course of our Lord's public life, they only knew Christ according to the flesh, and he reproached them for being slow to believe and for having a closed mind. Their Master's death made them pass through the night of the senses and they were able to be trained to love after the resurrection by the interplay of coming and going that our Lord used at the time of his appearances. The apostles then experienced the alternation of joy, when Christ was found among them, and of sadness when he disappeared. Then came the Ascension which brought them into the night of the spirit, and it was only after Pentecost that they were confirmed in their apostolic vocation, that they spread throughout the world and that they welcomed persecutions or success with equal serenity.

Progress as Perfection

Here on earth no man can claim to have arrived at the term of the spiritual life. There is no rest for him until he has passed through death, for his liberty is always in danger of being perverted. Even if this danger of retracing his steps were excluded, there is still the necessity of opening day by day to unforeseen grace which can only be actual. Yesterday's faithfulness can never be acceptable as a response to God in the present moment and all remains to be done over again, because the Lord is not primarily he whom we have found, but he whom we find moment by moment in the act of submission to his will. We can thus never stop, unlike him who, after a long trek, sits down to contemplate the end of his journey.

Certainly, our successive meetings with God weave a pattern of increasingly firm texture; but it would break if it were not continued. We can advance towards perfection, that is, towards the progressive integration of all the elements of our personality in a stronger and wider relationship with God, others or the world. Yet this perfection always remains relative, on the one hand to the previous perfection we have experienced and, on the other, to the perfection of Christ which stimulates our growth. If, then, we must leave behind us what we have been and draw near to Christ, it will be without the power ever to identify ourselves totally with him. Man cannot be perfect here on earth, he can only be in process of becoming.

Spiritual tradition repeats over and over that he who does not advance, loses ground. This surprises us, for we imagine a neutral state which, without improving the present, would yet not compromise the future. Such a conception would be justified if the Christian life consisted in fulfilling certain obligations. To avoid falling back, it would be sufficient to confine oneself to a certain degree of practice. But if religion is to be defined by our relationship to God in Jesus Christ, when the Christian no longer receives true life by his submission to the divine will, he wilts. The love of God which is distributed in the creature who is obedient draws us upwards towards a growing intimacy with the Creator. Should this ascent come to be interrupted, the downward trend begins at once, by the weight of sin which imposes its law. When the breath of the Spirit leaves us, it is impossible to resist the forces from below.

It is doubtless legitimate to distinguish the perfect from progressives and beginners. At the same time the meaning of these expressions must be understood. The perfect is not he who has arrived at the place of his repose, but he whose ascent towards God is constant. He is not and cannot be totally identified with the only-begotten Son, but, day after day, he responds to what God expects of and enjoins upon him, so much so that, filled with increasing joy, he is borne aloft towards the heavenly dwelling. Hence a certain stability even in movement. The perfect Christian formulates, in an uninterrupted manner, the act by which he welcomes his God, so much so that he seems to have acquired a second nature and it is practically impossible for him not to give everything to the Lord and Master of his life. In the course of the first stages, he was so weak that he had constantly to pull himself up, to go out of himself and advance towards God, but when he has lived for a long time in search of the Beloved, he has lost the taste and desire to shut himself up in himself and he no longer has the impression of having to do violence to himself to abandon himself to God's will. Thus the Christian's perfection only assumes the appearance of a state in as much as it is assimilated to an act that is permanent.

But it is the act alone which makes the perfection of the state. The love which defines Christianity is not a rigid thing but a living, free relationship of eternal youth which, like all true love, is always in process of being born. Spiritual perfection is thus the actuality of an authentic relationship to the Creator and Redeemer. When this is given, nothing else is to be wished for or indeed is desirable. We forget this truth, to clutch with our greedy hands at the gift that our opening to God has made possible, to make ourselves masters of what has no existence outside the act of the donor and the act of him who receives. He is perfect who, such as he is, perseveres in his colloquy with God and who, in the present instance, accepts and gives thanks, recognizing that all things in his past were good and that the future can only be filled with benefits, since the same Lord will shower his bounty on us in the future as it seems to him good. Every Christian who, in the present which is at his disposal, spreads out his arms in prayer so that the task necessary to the Kingdom in the particular situation that is his may be entrusted to him, does not need to expect any other completion, any other revelation, or any higher understanding of the divine mystery and the depths hidden from his vision.

It is not easy to get rid of the idea of a perfection which, like the justice of the Pharisees, would consist in putting a program into operation, whereas perfection consists in the accomplishment of the possible that God asks of us here and now and for which he gives us his strength. He is perfect who, at the very heart of his sin and wretchedness, sincerely responds to God without setting limits to his demands, for the divine perfection is communicated to him, even if it cannot yet pervade his whole being. Supposing he should die at this moment when he has allowed his Master to act in him, the destiny of this man will be truly achieved and he will enter into the joy of God. On the other hand, if the sinful man contented himself with desiring an abstract perfection, in itself better than the wretched life he leads, he would not find God, whose goodness never stoops towards the possible but to the existing. It descends to what we are, to change us gradually into itself. The perfection of the Christian is accomplished in the very point at which he finds himself because here and now God gives himself to him and makes him share in the movement of his love. Thus we must not seek perfection elsewhere than in real and concrete progress—with all its limitations and difficulties our present situation will serve as fulcrum for the divine lever that will set our hearts in movement.

This means that perfection is to be identified with humility. It can be total each day like that of the Blessed Virgin who ceaselessly acquired greater perfection throughout the course of her existence. But humility only subsists in the measure in which the recognition of our present weaknesses and helplessness is joined with the will to overcome them by God's help and to cry out without respite for the salvation which is still to come. The closer we come to God the more we see that we can do nothing without him and that if we are to continue to advance he must draw us after him. Perfection then becomes in us the progress of humility, that is the acceptance, ever more lucid and peaceful, of a disciplining of ourselves and an indefinite growth. If we stop, thinking our state already comprises sufficient perfection, we fall into pride and our being will become perverted. Being the contrary of progress, sufficiency is also the inversion of spiritual perfection and of union with God.

It might be concluded that there is no need to consider the stages of progress since the only thing that counts finally is the act of submission to the present will of God. But to judge the genuineness of our opening to God, it is important to advert to the phases through which we must pass and to the orientations which characterize every spiritual life. To know if a particular way of praying is good, if some particular apostolic work is willed by God, we must ask ourselves whether they make our spiritual being grow in unity and in transparency to the action of God. Verified by the help of recognized spiritual stages, progress is a guarantee of our attitude here and now in regard to God, others and the world. We must not then set a perfection which would consist in the act of obedience of creature to Creator over against a succession of states, since free acts transform the state of the person.

If indeed the dialogue with God makes us ascend to him then and there, it is normal that the succession of instants should trace a movement of ascent which is manifested externally. Here we again find what was pointed out on the subject of the discernment of spirits: the criterion of the spiritual authenticity of a choice consists in the positive orientation of the sentiments which go with it—an orientation which can only be perceived in the course of a fairly long lapse of time. But what was said of affectivity must also be verified for all the factors of the spiritual life. Between the act which creates a new state and the state that engenders the present act, there exists an interaction—it is in moving continually from the one to the other that, under the divine impulse, liberty constructs the new man, image of the perfection of the heavenly Father.

If many Christians realized the extraordinary adventure that is offered them, they would throw all their living strength into it. To know that everything is possible, that we so far know nothing of God, but that he is ready to lift from his face the veil that hides him from us and that his mystery will become both more obscure in its depth and more intimate in its light. To cross this ocean, our justice and our virtue are of no help to us; what is essential is the desire the Eternal Friend puts in our hearts, to prevent us from satisfying ourselves with the glitter of this world, or with the marvels that he unfolds there. It is not to the sound of the magic flute that we shall advance, but amid the noise of the storm. Who would not, however, set out? In the very death that surrounds us, in the danger which, with tenacity and courage, demands an understanding of unaccustomed paths, the breath coming from so far and from such remote heights draws us above ourselves. What have we to give to those who are dear to us, that is to all men, if it is not this mighty aspiration, this incoercible movement the force of which is capable of carrying the universe with it?

9 THE MEANS OF PROGRESS

IF PERFECTION CONSISTS IN PROGRESS, we must now inquire what means are to be used if we are to let God promote our advance towards him. To prayer and penance, the importance of which it has become classic to emphasize, must be joined action undertaken for God. We must set down precisely in what sense this must be understood if it is to form an aid to the deepening of the spiritual life.

The means of progress can be considered in three different ways. Since each has its share of truth, none can be neglected without leaving aside fundamental aspects of the Christian life. We have first of all to act and to dispose ourselves to receive the divine gifts. If God does not make himself heard, if the word by which he addresses us does not bear fruit, it is because on our side we do not do the minimum to put ourselves on the road where we have the chance of meeting him. The Lord is always ready to intervene. It thus depends on us whether or not we open our dwelling to him and let him work there at his pleasure. In this case our attention is concentrated on the effort we have to make, since that is a preliminary both necessary and sufficient.

But in proportion as we advance, it seems to us increasingly doubtful if we shall be capable of using the traditional means as we should. Instead of making us receptive, putting them into operation is liable to enclose us within ourselves or to lead us astray into voluntarism. The only thing that matters is what comes from God, what he grants us and even what he imposes on us. How could means whose initiative is in our own hands bring us near to God who infinitely exceeds our aspirations and desires? Passivity in regard to God is indeed the only attitude that respects him, since he is the sole source and author of all good, whereas "sin and lying"* alone can come from us. Our attachment to our own actions is merely a lingering over self and is indeed to build on sand.

Finally there exists a third way of considering the means of spiritual progress. The divine action, which reaches the heart of man, brings to us renewed personal strength and demands an ever more perfect response. If he himself who has created and redeemed us transmits his strength and light to us, it is so that we may be capable of seeking for and finding him more quickly, more easily and more truly. It is so that we may speak to him as sons and act accordingly. Then the means share in God's work and cooperate with grace. To do what depends on us is no longer action set in a sphere apart where man would be an autonomous master, but action set in this Kingdom where we shall be truly called to sit at God's right hand and where man will appear in his full glory because he will be made totally divine. To speak of the means of the spiritual life is doubtless to go back to its beginning, but if these means are understood in their depth and their progressive unity, to do so is also already to reach the goal, for the person who is subordinated to God and filled with his presence is at the same time the one who can find him when he wishes and who in a certain sense is capable of giving God to himself.

* *Nemo habet de suo nisi mendacium et peccatum.* Council of Orange, Denz. 195.

Prayer

Even if we give them other names, it is usual to distinquish three forms of prayer:* *meditation, affective prayer* and *contemplation*.† Let us try to describe them briefly, to show their significance and to suggest how they remain present in every spiritual life.

In meditation, we strive to extract all the riches possible from a text, some scene in the Gospel or some religious truth. We reflect, we analyse, we try to discover the link that exists between the different aspects of a subject, in order that we may penetrate the mystery of God and of Jesus Christ more deeply. For meditation is not merely a working of the mind on some given fact; it tends gradually to assimilate God into itself by working from some particular point of departure. Moreover in this method memory plays as important a part as intelligence, not only because it is often necessary to remember in order to understand, but in a deeper way because the mind, which turns towards the past to draw memories from it, puts itself in a state of receptivity. We cannot draw just any conclusions from a subject presented for reflection, for we do not invent the Divine Persons, or the deeds and acts of Jesus Christ. We have to rediscover them as they have been revealed. It is impossible today to appreciate a particular page of the Gospel without referring to the

* Here we are confining ourselves to considering the forms of what is known as ordinary or active prayer (in contrast to infused or passive prayer). We are moreover giving it the widest meaning possible, for it seems to us desirable to emphasize the passive aspects of the prayer that is called active.

† As an example of this classic distinction we should like to quote this extract from Surin: "Those who meditate can be compared to men who travel on foot. They advance only slowly and with much fatigue. Those who practice the prayer of affection may be compared to men who travel on horseback. They advance much more quickly without making so much effort. Those who are raised to contemplation may be compared to men who travel in a comfortable carriage, who make much progress in little time, and without taking any trouble." *Catéchisme Spirituel* (Lyons, 1836), I, pp. 11–12.

whole of Scripture and without recalling what God has done for us all and for each one of us. To meditate is thus to understand what God wants to do here and now through the knowledge of his ways of acting in history.

This reference to the past makes of memory a power which welcomes the text and allows it to give its message instead of imposing its own law on it. But meditation equally stretches out towards the future, for the effort to understand cannot be satisfied with taking the truth and allowing it to penetrate us, it has to find its completion in action and in work to transform the person and his behavior. The mind that has received the mystery soon perceives that it is not in accord with it, that a distance exists between the man I am and the Christian I ought to be in Jesus Christ. Then we experience the desire for identification and for the love that tends to rejoin him from whom we are still separated. The work of mind and memory thus finds itself naturally directed towards that of the will which seeks to change itself and change the world in function of what has been understood, taking what has been received as its starting-point.

Meditation thus allows the human mind to exercise its affective powers to the full. To penetrate into the present, it insists that it base itself on the past, the consequence of which is to turn it towards the future. Because it wants to enter into the mystery it is meditating, to grasp and comprehend it, the mind is obliged to adopt an attitude of acceptance and dependence in regard to a fact which escapes it, which it must not reconstruct but merely accept, or await in desire. Properly understood, meditation thus already sums up all the riches of the spiritual life—it begins by the activity of the mind which changes into the receptivity of the memory; this, in its turn, sends us back through the will to the search for the gift and for love. In other words, the mind, in quest of God in *prayer,* must do *penance* and renounce itself by moving into the memory in order that the spirit as a whole may enter into *action* in accordance with the love it experiences.

The depths contained in meditation, however, are not perceived by the beginner, for he is preoccupied with the consideration of his activity. Yet God is at work at a level so far unsuspected, but which will gradually be recognized through affective prayer. The soul refuses to analyze the mystery in order to draw distinct inspirations from it, it gives itself in acts which engage the whole of its being. Through or beyond the acts and deeds of Christ, the soul wants to reach his Person. It is not so much what Christ says that interests me, it is himself, it is to be near him, to enjoy his presence, to experience what he is, much more than to know what he formulates. That he should give himself to me under such and such a form matters little, provided he communicates himself.

Like Mary I refuse to run and undertake a whole host of actions, but I sit near him and, without listening to his words or seeking to understand his actions, I am satisfied with hearing him and letting him take hold of and envelope me. He is there and that is sufficient for me.

This attitude of simple presence is, however, at this stage much more a desire than a reality, so much so that to advance to where it wants to get, the soul begins to multiply acts of attachment and submission to God our Lord. Gradually it realizes that it is not Jesus Christ who is evading it but that it is the soul itself that is not ready to receive him. It would indeed like to be able to take hold of him, but to enjoy him in its own manner and while remaining what it is. It does not mind about his coming to accomplish what he will and as seems to him good. The result of its graspingness is that God disappears continually and even seems to hide himself more deeply in proportion as the soul would like to see him reveal himself. But as it has already found him partially, its own wretchedness, from this contact, becomes acute and unbearable to it. In this form of prayer, the contradictions of the human soul in its relations with God stand out more strongly. If it seeks to take hold of him, he goes away because he can only give himself freely. If it welcomes him, it is revealed to itself in such a sort that it soon rejects this light that shows it its darkness. But if it rejects God, it is still more unhappy, for already it has understood that the Lord is good, that he is very good, and that nothing could replace him. The more God seems to remove himself, the more, then, the soul seeks for him, because it can no longer find rest in any other.

This interplay of love is necessary to make us aware of the obstacles to our Lord's lasting presence. But we also perceive the distance between the acts we produce and all he is doing in us. We thus begin to experience the passive aspect of prayer which is no longer now, as in meditation, a simple effort of acceptance in regard to a long-standing revelation that is transmitted to us, but an actual coming of the Lord. In regard to the prayer of quiet, but the remark is equally true for affective prayer properly understood, St. Teresa of Avila distinguishes the satisfactions we can procure for ourselves by our own efforts or which arise from certain happy events and which end in God, from those "pleasures which, on the contrary, begin in God and which our nature feels afterwards."* This experience is decisive, for it teaches us in a new way in what the action of God and his Spirit consists in our souls.

If affective prayer appears first of all as a simple method, it thus reveals also fundamental aspects of the spiritual life: the necessity of reforming our lives to the extent that we wish to allow God to come to us, the absence of common measure between our acts, our efforts, our attempts and the initiative that comes from God to work in us what seems to him best.

It still remains to be discovered, through contemplation, how much the presence of God is active in our lives and to allow him to do what he will in bringing us to his Son. For this, we have to cast our eyes on the scenes of the Gospel, to listen to Christ and those who

* *Oeuvres Complètes* (Paris, Ed. du Seuil, 1949), p. 865. Cf. *op. cit.,* II, pp. 277 ff.

addressed him, to sense the climate in which the episode took place. It is equally possible to identify ourselves with each of the persons involved, not to reflect on how they act, as in meditation, any more than to exercise ourselves by interior acts in changing our lives, as in affective prayer, but more simply to embrace the Gospel in which we are the actors. I am Simon the Pharisee who receives Jesus inhospitably and who despises others in their way of seeking God (Lk. 7, 36–50). I am the sinful woman who does not dare to say anything but who only waits for forgiveness from him whom she would like to love. Finally, I am Christ since, immersed in his death by baptism, I am risen with him.

The Christian mystery and the mystery of man are summed up on each page of the Gospel. To reach the end of the spiritual life, it would be sufficient to feed on and assimilate a single one of them. In former times Christ Jesus made himself the contemporary of the apostles and for the future each one of us is a contemporary of Jesus Christ, the Eternal Word who has come in the flesh. Nothing can be added to the Gospel and human history already has its laws and its development contained therein. To put on Christ is thus to identify oneself with those who followed him, it is to live each day the eternal present of Jesus of Nazareth, the alpha and omega, the beginning and the end. The disciples did not understand with their minds him who had come among them and we do not need to understand either. They rarely made acts of adherence to his Person, and perhaps we too have not to multiply words to prove to him a love that is still so weak and so disloyal. With them, let us be satisfied with contemplating him in wonder, in letting ourselves be attracted and caught up by him like the dead leaves by the wind.

It is possible that our contemplation may assume yet another form. The presence alone is sufficient to fill us, without the mind attaching itself to particular attitudes and adopting them in turn. What at first approach seems like an impoverishment because we have no longer any distinct light at our disposal, reveals itself in reality as great riches and as a light which contains in itself all others. To explain this difficult point, Father de Caussade quotes St. Augustine:

How far removed is this school where peace and silence reign, from the senses and the flesh. It is the school where God makes himself heard, where there is the counsel of the heart. . . . The astonished senses see nothing there and the soul that eludes them seems to them as if reduced to nothing: *ad nihilum redactus sum et nescivi;* I am reduced to nothing, said David. And this nothingness even that I find in myself in an abyss to which God leads me back is impenetrable to me, *et nescivi.* This made him add: I am become as a beast before thee, *ut jumentum,* without reasoning power, without speech; and all I can say in this state is that I am always with you and that I find only you in the darkness of faith into which you have plunged me: *Et ego semper tecum.**

Many spiritual writers stress the depth of this form of prayer. It is not to be confused with a prayer that is vague and without object, for it would be just as much to the point to say that the mystery of God, which is incomprehensible to us and which remains beyond our grasp, is itself indeterminate and fluid. It is indeed, on the contrary, because it is infinitely clear, of the utmost fullness, of unutterable concentration, that it eludes us and leaves us as it were baffled when we fix our attention on it. Cassian relates this saying of St. Antony, "The prayer in which the monk is aware of himself or is aware that he is praying is not perfect,"† and spiritual tradition asserts with him that what we can understand of God is nothing in comparison with what we do not understand, so much so that, in faith, "not-knowing" is as worthy of the mystery as knowledge.

Moreover it is not right to speak of contemplation in terms of knowledge and non-knowledge, for the essential consists in the transformation of our being and in the participation in the life of

* P. de Caussade, *Bossuet, Maître d'Oraison* (Paris, Bloud et Gay, 1931), pp. 42–43.

† Cassian, *Collatio* IX, 31. P.L. 49, 808.

the Trinity. The benefit of the darkness which surrounds our mind, when it focuses its attention on God, is precisely to remind us that it is not a question of having more light on the divine Persons but of letting ourselves be worked on by them. Moreover the darkness is necessary for us, to force us to abandon, in regard to the divine gifts, the possessive attitude which is an obstacle to God's intervention. Like the blind, if we place our confidence in ourselves we cannot move. Moreover, at the very heart of this blindness we obtain a more exact and more peaceful vision of what must be left aside and what must be undertaken; for the darkness that surrounds us is not caused by an absence of sun but by the superabundance of the brightness of its rays.

Contemplation thus makes us discover that "God is greater than our heart" (I Jn. 3, 20), that he is the source whose waters can slake our thirst, but the welling up of which is out of our grasp. We experience that he is the one who must accomplish in us both the willing and the doing, if we are to be restored to ourselves. If we have the impression that it is we alone who are active, this can only be so through a lack of penetration and because we are incapable of recognizing that our activity must be confined to allowing God to act in us. This third way of praying reminds us then of certain fundamental traits of the spiritual life—everything comes from God; if he blinds us, it is so that we may accept the putting of ourselves aside and give ourselves up to his goodness. Nothing should exist for us except through the recognition that it is a grace.

Having first of all considered meditation, affective prayer and contemplation as methods of prayer, we have been led to disentangle the constant factors which define the relations of man with God. Not only does meditation teach us to make all the dimensions and all the activity of the human mind enter into our prayer, but it teaches us in a general way that all Catholic prayer must include an unfolding of the whole being in its relationship to God. Affective prayer in its turn, which trains us in practice to a more simple adherence and to an attention to the word of the Lord, makes us realize that every Christian life is a response to God's call. Lastly contemplation which initiates us gradually into passivity in regard to him whom we wish to love, makes us learn by experience that there is nothing except through God, for God and in God. In each case the method, which is a means of access for the discovery of Jesus Christ, is at the same time an end, since it causes us to adopt a permanent attitude, considered as an indispensable factor of the spiritual life.

Here we touch on a specific aspect of Christianity. To reach the end of their path, pagan mystics make use of a certain number of means, but when they have arrived at the supreme stage, they rid themselves of all intermediaries and even assert the artificial, illusory and unreal character of the path they have travelled. The reality when discovered dissolves the mere appearance they had before. For a Christian, on the contrary, there are no means that can one day be rejected, for, although it is possible for him to misunderstand, abuse or misuse them, in each of these practices that mark his route, there is a real and permanent presence of God. For the Christian mystics, the contemplation of the earthly image of Jesus Christ is never a hindrance to union with God. But since the Word made flesh gathers up in himself the whole of the universe and the whole of history, must we not extend to all things and at least, here, to all the traditional forms of prayer, what is said of Jesus of Nazareth, for, whatever may be the particular aspects it assumes, there is no real prayer except in Jesus Christ?

We must never cease our efforts to stir our mind in order that it may pass into God, we must never forget the abyss that separates our will from God's will, finally we should always remember that the activity of God alone counts. Methods serve to place us before God in a posture that is increasingly spontaneous. Thus what disappears in the course of spiritual progress is the painful effort, the distance between the processes and the attitude that results from them, or again the utilization of a single form of prayer to the exclusion of the others. In fact, if each of us discovers an essential aspect of prayer, our relationship to God is true in the measure in which we pass from one to the other until we finally adopt all together. Meditation first sent us back from the activity of the mind to the receptivity of the memory so that we could undertake an activity of love. At the other extreme, contemplation, which makes us perceive God's initiative better and develops the strength and clearness of our response, shows us also, as in affective prayer, to what extent we resist grace and how necessary it is for the Lord to be mighty in us in word and in work to make us more open to him and to make us act in him alone.

These ways of prayer are often regarded as following one another along the line of spiritual progress, the earlier method having to be abandoned when we move on to the following one. This point of view doubtless has its value, for our prayer is really transformed in proportion as the relationship to Jesus Christ becomes more personal and more determining. The dialogue becomes more simple and can begin apropos of anything, can continue without embracing rigid laws and go straight to what is essential to it, namely attention to the Person himself. Nevertheless these methods reach the different levels of the personality in such a way that each form of prayer brings into play one of the factors that compose our being. It is necessary for us in fact, whatever be our degree of intimacy with God, to feed our faculties by meditation on the Scripture and on Christian literature, to attune our affections to the inspirations of the Spirit in obeying the divine will, and to open the center of our person to him who is its source. Starting from the pure consideration of these methods, we thus now come to envisage them as indispensable and constant factors of spiritual progress. Doubtless it would be possible to describe them in a different way and each writer lays the emphasis on aspects which seem to him more important, but if we go beneath the surface we perceive that all the different points of view meet, and that meditation, affective prayer and contemplation which are the means of the spiritual life, equally symbolize the principal stages of progress and moreover suggest the levels at which the soul enters into direct contact with its Creator and Lord.

Penance

The second means for us to advance towards God is penance. It will be sufficient to describe its different forms and to indicate its meaning to show us that these forms are necessary for the union with God. Like his prayer, the spiritual man's penance must gradually become more interior and from being a sheer means must become a permanent and indispensable element of Christian behavior.

To do penance is to impose on the body abstinence from food or drink, to contradict on particular points our need of enjoyment or comfort, or again to demand prolonged and painful efforts from our body. The purpose of penance is to prevent our slipping into the pleasures of the senses, to release us from the forces that drag us down and which would otherwise soon succeed in enchaining the spirit. It is scarcely necessary to say that these practices are not followed out of contempt for the body and the senses, but out of a refusal to let ourselves be guided, like superior animals, by the seduction of the things of earth. We are threatened with disorder and disequilibrium, because reason does not dispose of the sensitive powers of our personality but is dominated by them. Even were it through pain, we must then counteract their upsurging, in order to master them and make them play the part for which they were created.

Thus understood, the purpose of penance is a certain training. We must not see in it an effort to destroy or strangle the lower forces of flesh and blood, but the will to re-establish the harmony that was compromised by sin. Until we have integrated under the control of our liberty the physical and sensitive factors of our being, we must do penance to avoid the slavery of what is imposed upon us unchecked. If asceticism enables us to resist the pressure of instinct, it is so that we may judge and situate it in function of an order that comes from on high.

But when that which is of the senses in us has been subjected to reason, only half the way has been travelled, for penance must obtain the obedience of the reason to the spirit which receives its inspiration from God. In so far as our different acts of abstinence remain only the fruit of a personal decision without reference to God, they are in danger of developing in a climate of pagan heroism or of pharisaical self-sufficiency. In this case, instead of setting the soul free, they make it carry a burden that is all the more harmful *because* it is accompanied by zeal and good will. If we bring our body into subjection, it must be to die to ourselves, to go down into the tomb with Christ and to experience anew the plunge into death that our baptism was. Time will of course be necessary for these truths to be perceptible to our inward vision. In the meantime we shall have to fluctuate between the acceptance of a courageous asceticism which seems to come from us and the conviction, still obscure, that we should undertake nothing except under the impulse of God.

This state corresponds to that which is ours when we begin to pray—we scarcely perceive the action of God and we are absorbed by the acts we make to meditate on the divine mysteries. We are still on the surface of ourselves and our faith has blindly to affirm the presence and initiative of God without having the experience of them. This is, moreover, normal. It is essential for us during a long period to run the risk of mistakes and false steps, to have the impression of accomplishing something by ourselves in prayer and penance, in order gradually to obtain access to other depths and really to go forth to meet our Master. It is not a catastrophe, however, at these early stages, that our illusions should be shattered. The more we have at our disposal a firm will and a vigorous mind, the more we shall be inclined to do without God and to fail to ask him humbly for the strength to dominate the lower powers and the light to enter further into his mysteries.

We shall have overcome a considerable obstacle when prayer and penance condition each other, for their unity will be able to become the guarantee of their orientation. If it is necessary to deprive oneself of food and sleep, it is not to establish a performance or glorify oneself over an exploit, but to allow the spirit to give itself freely to prayer, since, if it is less strongly captivated by the things of earth, it will be able to give attention to what is above it. The refusal to savor the things of earth must thus be continually accompanied by the aspiration to taste the things from on high, and to eat the food of the divine Word. Much more, this impossibility of satisfying our covetous desires should urge us to seek peace, quiet and even enjoyment beyond; otherwise we shall soon be condemned to aridity of heart. On the other hand penance must be a preparation for prayer. To find God and to hear more clearly what he wants to say to us, we shall want to free ourselves from immediate desires, turn ourselves aside from these waters that are incapable of quenching our thirst. If meditation quickens our eagerness for the essential meeting, we shall be prepared to rid ourselves of everything that slows down our steps, as we should of glue which makes us stick to the ground.

But, if we did not go further than this in death to ourselves, our personal efforts would be in danger of being perverted. Mastery over self and liberty of spirit, to which penance gives us access, are not to be confused with sanctity. It cannot even be said that they are Christian virtues, still less that the presence of them conditions the discovery of God. Christ finds us, in fact, when he wills to do so, in the midst of disorder and even of sin, whereas he cannot cross the barrier that complacency in our self-sacrifice has erected before him. If we place our confidence in the steps we take ourselves, even in those which should, according to our estimation, bring us closer to God, we hamper our spiritual progress instead of favoring it. Outside obedience to God, mortification is not only vain, but harmful. "For I desired mercy and not sacrifice" (Osee 6, 6). Penance will thus have to assume another form and detach us from our certainties, from our own views and even from our good intentions.

A search for God that is in any way sincere will not fail to reveal to us the opposition that exists between our desires and God's will, so much so that mortification must bear first of all on the giving up of our own will—penance that is more deeply rooted, more painful too, into which we so often refuse to enter and the very threshold of which makes us afraid. Slowly we grasp the fact that in the course of our first attempt at doing penance, it is ourselves we want to assert and not God. We shall also discover that the practices chosen by us sometimes remain the subtle means of guarding ourselves from God's intervention; just as, through meditation on the mysteries of faith, we secretly strive to veil from our eyes the particular truth that Jesus Christ would have us know, but which would upset too many things in our lives for us to be able to accept it with cheerfulness of heart. What penance must thus do away with for the future is the mirage of our good conscience, in order to make us understand that the perfection that depends on us, of which we seek to retain control, is the greatest enemy of the true holiness that comes from God.

We must then mortify ourselves, that is, share in the death of Christ, so that he may establish his will in us. In identifying the spiritual life with the acts we posit, or with good and holy thoughts, we short-circuit matters confusing the term willed by God with our beginning. It is not sufficient sincerely to will to serve God for our thoughts and acts to correspond to what the Lord expects of us. Penance must begin by the calling in question of our own plans so that the design of salvation may be revealed to us, and that it may become possible for us to accomplish it under the special form foreseen for us. If we succeed in effecting this detachment in regard to our personal views, and in this case only, God will come to us and manifest his desires, for he is in truth a Father who comes down to our help as soon as he sees us return to him and expect everything from him. To crush the flesh does not necessarily draw down grace, but to strip oneself of one's own will and have no other care but to put on Christ and his will—this immediately opens the way for the strength from on high. It is here, moreover, that external penance resumes its true meaning—to present to God our visible acts as the sign of interior renunciation, if not effective, at least desired. It will be sufficient to add humbly that these efforts are infinitesimal, but that our Lord will know how to read in them the expression of our most essential wish, that of being delivered from ourselves to belong to him.

For the future, then, penance must be defined as the means of moving towards submission to the divine will. This obliges us to consider the relations between prayer and penance under a new light. We have seen that the second form of prayer, affective prayer, led to the revelation of the distance between the light of God and our darkness. More precisely, the love of our Lord which grows in the soul and which, at least intermittently, is recognized as such, unveils what St. Ignatius calls "disordered attachments." The harmony that God wishes to establish in the human person brings to light the points of resistance which must be suppressed. Without prayer, penance remains blind and does not know on what to focus its effort and struggle. When these "disorderly affections," these attachments of the will which ordinarily escape our eyes, are revealed, asceticism is no longer in danger of going astray through attempts that are ineffective, it removes the present concrete obstacles to the action of God, the intentions of which are shown to us in prayer.

By adopting this form of penance, we conversely make the contact with God easier, for it is always our disobedience to his will that prevents us from having access to him. To favor prayer in its beginnings, penance had to remove the external difficulties and facilitate recollection. But of itself alone, the deepest silence is incapable of opening the divine secrets to us. It can even become a danger in the measure in which it is not changed into receptiveness, for the void we can provoke can never engender anything but emptiness. If penance is a help to prayer, it is because it removes from us that on which we lean externally to constrain us to throw ourselves upon God alone. When penance conforms us with God's will by death to our own desires, prayer can surge up in the calm thus created and God can show himself through the injunction he formulates.

Penance must be taken further still, for it is not enough that we should make an end of the interior disorder and that we should submit our liberty to that of God today, the detachment must reach to every form of affection, even the most legitimate and most sacred. If it is true that we must pass through the death of Christ in order to rise again in him, it is indispensable to mortify, to put to death, the whole of our being. Doubtless this is the logical development of the form of penance just described, but a development which must reach to both root and summit. If it has been in the past a matter of conforming our actions to the orders and suggestions of God, for the future we must only exist by his will and his love alone. More often than not it seems to us that we have at our disposal a certain number of possibilities and capacities and that we must strive to put them to our Lord's service by becoming the servants of others. This, however, is an optical illusion. In reality nothing is at our disposal; everything is precarious, all is gratuitous and depends on the unpredictable will of God alone. To attain this new vision of things, the only true one, we have to practice a final form of penance, as radical as it is beneficial.

If constantly we desire to see, in prayer and in the course of our life, him who is the sole source of all things and who is the author of all good, we must, according to the words of St. Ignatius, "seek in our Lord a greater abnegation and a continual mortification in all things possible."* It is impossible to evade such a strong recommendation if we seriously admit that God is in everything and everywhere the sole end, the sole beginning, and that he is equally all that comes between. To contemplate the creative act, it is necessary to go back to the nothingness from which the universe is formed by God at each eternal instant. Consequently, the only legitimate movement that remains for us to adopt is that that leads us to the denial of ourselves. All the bases of our actions, of our enterprises, of our thoughts, all that upholds our enthusiasm and our courage, all that serves us to get going again and to find rest, all this we must reject as capable of keeping us if not in error, at least in illusion. Spontaneously we rely on our successes to give us the strength to continue and to make our hopes legitimate. In failure we seek to justify ourselves and to throw the causes of our misfortunes back on others or on forces impossible to control. We are seized with panic at the mere idea of being called to account or at having nothing to reply to the accusations that our conscience, that of others and the unfortunate situations we have more or less provoked bring against us. Penance must leave us alone, helpless and guilty.

But if we had penetrated right to the depths of this perpetual contradiction of our desires, we should soon be led to despair and brought to the edge of the abyss. Until God has strengthened a soul and filled it in a special way, it is dangerous for it to perceive the wrong foundations on which its existence rests, for it does not yet possess anything with which to replace them and its liberty is still too weak to receive the grace which, like a rock, will be the basis of the new edifice. It is thread by thread that the Lord re-makes the canvas of which we are woven. He alone can know the amount of uprooting that we can bear today without harm and without the danger of collapse. Christ was able to take the initiative of death because he had the power to take up his life again after giving it.

* *Constitutiones Societatis Jesu,* no. 103.

We can only humbly let ourselves be carried away and transported day after day to the depths of this abyss. Whoever has experience of this form of penance which God uses in our regard will take good care not to plunge wildly into it, for no human suffering can account for the strange dislocation it causes in us. The saints are there to tell us this and it is better to take their word for it.

Yet it is essential that we should advance along this road. God's tenderness for us is jealous to the extent that he will never cease finding himself and himself alone in us, making of our liberty the pure mirror of his presence. To do penance is thus now to allow God to effect in us the total disappearance of the old creation, in order to identify with us his Son, who "emptied himself, taking the form of a servant . . . even to the death of the cross" (Phil. 2, 7–8). It is important to enter upon this way and that the Lord should not be constrained to force our resistance. If he gives us the grace, we shall even be able to ask him to come to us as the vintager who will tread us in the wine press (Isa. 63, 3), and at the same time beg him to consider our weakness and fill us with his sweetness.

On this level prayer and penance are equated. As we have seen, in contemplation God himself takes the initiative and allows us to see him at work. Now, although under a negative mode, it is to the same end that "continual mortification in all things" should lead. Its purpose is not, indeed, to destroy us and still less to make us disappear, but to re-create us in such a way that we may become similar to the filial outpouring of love which has nothing, is nothing, can do nothing of itself, but at the very heart of this nothing receives what the Other possesses, what he is and what he does. Nevertheless before they are equated, contemplative prayer and spiritual poverty mutually condition each other. Without a courageous and prolonged entry into the aridity of prayer, there will perhaps not be for us any desert and biting of serpents, but neither shall we see the promised land of union with God. For its part the light of contemplation does not spread without burning the objects it touches; for the fullness to which our hearts aspire presupposes an equal nudity if the wind of the Spirit is to pass into us freely.

Action

The Gospel often comes back to the fact that our acts show the state of our soul: "Either make the tree good and its fruit good: or make the tree evil and its fruit evil. For by the fruit the tree is known" (Matt. 12, 33). It is from within that good and bad actions spring, it is thus within that we must make healthy and transform our nature, comporting ourselves in the world according to the desires of God in order that his glory may be made manifest. It would not be possible to reverse these statements and think that action of itself can unite us to God, for a human enterprise must take its source from God if it wants to develop in him and perfect itself for his service.

This does not mean that the interior life can suffice unto itself. "Faith also, if it have not works, is dead" (James 2, 17). Just as the love of God made itself visible for us and has shown us his goodness in revealing his power in his Son, so no Christian can content himself with saying, "Lord, Lord," but must accomplish the will of God in the universe. Action is thus not only the sign that enables us to recognize of what spirit we are, it forms an integral part of faith, which dies if it does not spread itself. Taking the example of Abraham, St. James gives this lesson: "Seest thou that faith did cooperate with his works and by works faith was made perfect" (James 2, 22). If action must spring from the interior life as from a seed, the latter, to attain its perfection, needs action. Works are thus a condition of the development of faith, an indispensable means of spiritual growth.

Action appears primarily under the form of an exercise necessary to the expansion of the Christian life. At any age we need to act to get out of ourselves, to know ourselves, to experience what we should otherwise only sense; and reflexion on language teaches us that expression is the condition of knowledge. Now action is itself a word and a document which enable us to discover in a new way what might remain vague or unreal. Valid in the natural and human spheres, these laws are equally so for the spiritual life. Until our love for God is translated into charity and service, it remains inconsistent; it is in danger of withering and disappearing.

From the outset of the spiritual life, it is thus necessary to train ourselves to action even if, at this stage, we are still the principle of our own enterprises, even if prayer does not intervene to guide our steps. To wait for our works to spring forth from divine love in order to begin them, would be to fail to understand that the Lord who acts in our souls equally acts in the world and that he will bring us to meet him there. It would be to condemn oneself at the same time to both inward and outward sterility. Action can doubtless for long be an obstacle to spiritual poverty, because we have a tendency to rely on it and to put our glory in it, forgetting its impurity, its weakness, its total infirmity. But if at the same time as these works we practice prayer and penance, a compenetration is brought about between the different means of the spiritual life. Moreover, their remoteness from each other will make itself felt and will oblige us, by that very fact, to bring them together.

For in this beginning there is no question of action for the sake of action, we must put ourselves at the service of others so that they may discover God more. We must become apostles in everything, that is, bear witness to the charity of Christ, manifest outwardly his power and his love, make him recognized by others as the one and only Lord. Now, once the first enthusiasm has gone, difficulties in continuing our action will not fail to arise. It will not be possible always to give ourselves through the simple need or the simple desire of doing something. It will be necessary to have recourse to prayer again in order that God may give us his strength and his courage, in order that he may enable us to accept the numerous sacrifices which are involved in any serious enterprise. Certainly in this field we can deceive ourselves for a time—the manifold and harassing activities, accepted in the first place with a view to God's service, can lead to the abandonment of prayer. But sooner or later we have to come back to the reason for our action; then the self-deception we discover leads to an inward renewal.

One certain criterion of the positive orientation of our works will consist in the will to make prayer and penance coincide with them. We shall be able to oscillate for a long time between one and the other of these practices and we shall even frequently have the impression that we are leading at the same time several lives which do not fit in with one another. What we give to prayer, we shall think we are withdrawing from action and, conversely, because of the latter, we shall regret not spending a sufficient time with God. Similarly in the abstinences to which we force ourselves, we shall be tempted to see a diminution of our living strength which could be placed at the service of others. These difficulties are normal. What would be serious would be to be surprised at them or even to seek for an artificial unity to our own measure by suppressing one of the factors of our spiritual existence; neglecting to pray, for instance, in order to give ourselves wholly to action, refusing to undertake new works in order to take refuge in the dialogue with God.

In this first stage, the driving power of progress is precisely the increasingly penetrating and increasingly unbearable sentiment of the divisions which exist in us. Gradually we come to recognize that if we pray it is more to clutch at God than to give ourselves to him. If we do penance it is through a secret desire of surpassing a certain standard or because of the evidence of the benefits of asceticism. Finally, if we act, it is through a desire for domination, for success, or in order to obtain from others, in exchange for our services, at least esteem and consideration. At this point it is scarcely any longer possible to go back or to hide from ourselves these distortions of our spiritual effort even though we feel incapable of extricating ourselves from this false situation. It seems to us, indeed, that if God himself does not take the initiative of unifying our forces, we shall be able to use, indefinitely, first one means, then another, and pass on to the third without ever succeeding in making of our existence a single reality with manifold facets.

The conflicts from which we suffer do not consist in the fact that we have to make use of different means in turn. They arise from our incapacity to live each one fully. The problem is not to pray always, without ceasing. It comes from the fact that we cannot really reach God in prayer. It is not perpetually and in all things going against ourselves, but really stripping ourselves of ourselves to put on Christ. Similarly, we must not think of solving our difficulties by adding to some particular undertaking others more extensive or more attractive, but by giving ourselves wholly to the particular task willed by God. The sole cause, then, of our personal dividedness, is our desire to obtain a result by our own strength. In action, in particular, we can indeed sacrifice and spend ourselves, but we feel incapable of giving to others what they expect and of finding him whom we have sought by other ways. If it is not he who is at the root of our acts, if he does not manifest himself through us when he wishes, if he does not reveal himself to our hearts, we must indeed despair of advancing in spiritual ways.

The important thing is not to remain with our eyes fixed on these obstacles but to go forward courageously. Action can then become a means of our going out from ourselves. In prayer we are subject to illusion because we have the leisure to confuse our desires with the divine inspirations. But when, in daily life, our wishes meet with resistance, it is easy to discover if our projects are based on ourselves or on God's will. So long as the cockle remains beneath the ground we are incapable of recognizing it. When it has grown it is no longer possible to deny its existence and then it must be cut down and burned. Even if it is not undertaken purely for God, the service of others also makes us forget our trifling personal worries. It then becomes easier to situate the genuine problems and to keep them in the exact proportions that God wishes them to have for us. Action, which has freed us from the products of our imagination, then sends us back to a more genuine prayer.

To the extent that we have wearied ourselves in what we thought was the service of the Kingdom and we find ourselves with empty hands, we shall be more inclined to ask ourselves if we are acting according to the intentions of the King. Our work has been lost in the sand, has shown itself incapable of quenching our thirst, perhaps because we have not sufficiently questioned the Master and have rushed to the labor without realizing what was asked of us, without knowing how this action, willed by Providence, was inscribed in his plan. Here again action leads us afresh towards a more authentic prayer and penance, in which, putting aside our own desires, we listen more to those of our Lord. Thus instead of entering into conflict, the means of the spiritual life call out for each other. They are even identified with each other in Jesus Christ, who is ever with his Father, who is nourished with the will of him who sent him and who radiates on his countenance the glory of God.

At the term of the life of union, there is no longer any distance between the gaze we direct towards God, spiritual poverty and apostolic work. St. Teresa of Avila who, in the Seventh Mansion, describes the state of the soul at the summit of the mystical life, asserts that, far from restricting action, the habitual presence of the three divine Persons favors it: "It will seem to you from that that the soul is wholly beyond itself and so absorbed that it can no longer occupy itself in anything. This is a mistake. It is much more apt than before for everything that concerns the service of God."* Returning further on to the effects of this continual union, she writes:

> The first is such a forgetfulness of self that the soul seems truly no longer to have any being as I have said. It is so transformed that it no longer recognizes itself. She no longer thinks whether there is to be for

* *Oeuvres complètes* (Paris, Ed. du Seuil, 1949), p. 1031. Cf. *op. cit.,* p.359.

her heaven, a life, an honor of her own, because she is wholly occupied with the glory of God. It seems to her that the word our Lord said to her—"That she should have care of his interests and that he would watch over hers"—has brought about what it signified. Thus not only does she not concern herself with what may happen, but in this respect she is in such a strange forgetfulness that, I repeat, it seems that she is not and that she would be nothing in nothing, except when she understands that she can continue to increase, were it only by one degree, the honor and glory of God; for then she would willingly give her life. . . . There is little to say of her external works. If she has any suffering in regard to them, it is to see that what her strength allows is nothing. That is why no human consideration would make her neglect the least thing that might be in her power if she thought she would procure the glory of our Lord thereby.*

Here the Carmelite links up with St. Ignatius whose vocation was not one of contemplation but of service:

We know, wrote Nadal, that Father Ignatius had received from God the exceptional grace to be able, without effort, to pray and rest himself in the contemplation of the most Holy Trinity . . . contemplation which was often given to him, but above all, and then almost continually, in the last years of his pilgrimage. This way of praying Father Ignatius by a great privilege experienced to an eminent degree. To this was added that in all things, actions or conversations, he felt and contemplated the presence of God and the attraction of spiritual things. He was contemplative in action—a thing he usually expressed by these words—one must find God in all things.†

* *Ibid.*, pp. 1042–1043. Cf. *op. cit.*, pp. 339 ff.

† *Epistolae P. Nadal,* IV, p. 651. The mystics meet at the terminal point. As an example this saying of the most famous of the Rhineland theologians may be quoted: "He who possesses God entirely, in truth possesses him in all places, both in the street and with everybody, as much at church as in solitude or in a cell. Provided he possesses him as he should, provided he possesses him always, no one can distract him from him." Master Eckhart, *Traités et Sermons* (Paris, Aubier, 1942), p. 32.

Thus continual forgetfulness of self goes hand in hand with the continual contemplation of the divine Persons and the discovery of God in all things. All the means have disappeared to leave room only for the manifestation of God's glory, adored and served at each moment by the whole being transformed in Jesus Christ. Thus understood the end of action is no longer only the revelation of God, it is itself an end, because, coming from God, it develops and is completed in God and through God.

If the means of spiritual progress can be changed into permanent spiritual attitudes, it is simply because they are an image of the presence of the Trinity in us. When the Father fills us in prayer, we must empty ourselves until death like the Son, in order that, based on the will of him who is sending us, our action may not cease to move in the Spirit and to radiate his light. Methods of prayer are nothing, any more than our abstinences and our enterprises, if they do not result in our becoming mirrors of the love of the Trinity. We only pray in truth if we adopt the attitude of the Son who at every moment welcomes the power that engenders him. Penance is only suitably orientated in the measure in which it seeks to conform itself to the Christ of the Agony and of Calvary. Finally, if it is to be Christian, action must begin, continue and end in a climate of justice, peace and joy, that is, it must manifest the signs of the presence of the Holy Spirit.

Moreover there exists, among the means of spiritual progress, a hierarchical order similar to the order of the Blessed Trinity. Whatever may be the chronology of the manifestation of these various means to our conscience, it is finally from prayer that penance must issue, in order that, stripped of himself, man may be born again as son. As to action, it only assumes the fullness of its meaning if it is constantly developed against a background of spiritual poverty and union with the divine source.

CONCLUSION

IF CONTEMPLATION OF CHRIST'S HUMANITY is wonderfully suited to supporting our first steps along the way of the Spirit, the greatest Christian mystics have said over and over again that it equally helps those who have already entered into the intimacy of the Word. The Gospel adapts itself to the weakness of our intellect which, in order to rise, needs the help of sense objects, but it in no way restricts our final ascent, for the images it sets before us contain in themselves the whole of the message and the perfection of the Godhead. It will never become necessary to go beyond them. It is our eyes that have to be continually purified to enable them to see how the divine Word is wholly present in each of the scenes and each of the sayings by which he reveals to us the mystery of his love. Instead of turning aside from the Testament he has entrusted to us, we must rather make ourselves attentive to it, linger over all its tones, penetrate it until we realize that the fullness of the Word shines forth on every page. In Christ who comes in scarlet robes, and who advances magnificent in his human vesture, it is really all that God is in our regard that we discover.

In the first place he is the Lord, from whom Peter wanted to go away, well knowing that he was a sinner. How would this man of Galilee dare to touch the holy mountain where Yahweh becomes present, without incurring, as his fathers had taught him, the danger of death? The sin-stained creature trembles at meeting Christ, because it dreads the strength with which it sees he is invested, even when he is silent, even when he remains there without a gesture and without the slightest movement of his eyes. But Christ is again the one by whom we can kneel like Mary Magdalene, the one whose feet it is possible to wash with our tears in order to obtain pardon. We must say nothing, not only because he knows the secrets of our heart, but because the Word is the only one who can break the silence which his approach has reduced us to.

If we remain taken aback at his coming, it is not so much at the sight of our wretchedness, for it causes no scorn in his soul but only attentive compassion. Neither is it because of our wounds. He asks us, in fact, to show them to him, so that he may heal them with his strong hand and his outstretched arm. It is rather because of the incomprehensible majesty which flows from his countenance and his bearing. The Gospel is full of religious fear, of awe and even of dread. In it we breathe the heavy perfume of glory which surrounded Sinai. Similar to the men of his time and his country in all things, Christ retains in the eyes of him who contemplates him, a character of strangeness which derives from another world. No human being has spoken as he did, none has worked such miracles. Despite the intimacy to which he invited them, despite the explanations he continually gave them, the apostles were continually disconcerted by the sayings and deeds of their Master. They were afraid when they saw him walk, like Yahweh, on the mighty waters. The reason is that the carpenter's son is identified with the Word whom we adore and whose sovereign liberty resembles that of the Spirit who bloweth where he listeth. When we watch him speak and move, the unspeakable majesty of the Father is revealed to us.

Christ Jesus is also the pedagogue who guides us along the road towards total understanding of his mystery and at the same time towards participation in his own life. His Kingdom in us is like the grain of mustard seed which, tiny at first, grows until it becomes a tree capable of sheltering the birds of the air. The Lord, in fact, does not stop at sowing. He turns the earth over and over, waters and weeds at the proper seasons. He is exacting and severe, he accuses us, through his disciples, of having our ears closed. He rejects us, as he did St. Peter, when it happens that we obstruct his way. Yet he does not spare himself and never tires of explaining to us the reasons for his coming, the aim he is pursuing, the way in which we must behave when he has gone away and the time for contemplating him in his Gospel has passed.

With those who have the soul of a child and follow him without asking for explanations and without troubling about receiving a reward, he shows himself gentle and full of peace, for he knows quite well that they will abandon themselves to his action day by day. It is in accordance with the possibilities of each one of us that Jesus makes his words heard, to make all of us pass on to some further stage and in order that no one may cease his efforts even for a moment. Before each Christian the whole of the teaching of the Gospel is set, but, according to whether it is winter or spring for him, whether he is still in the time of youth or already in the prime of life, he understands certain passages of it better, he can read them at degrees of depth that are ever new.

Always adapted to the circumstances through which we are passing, the strength of Christ which leads us ever further, the power which attracts us and which, in drawing us towards him, makes us progress uninterruptedly, is nothing else but the face of the Father, the Origin from which he proceeds and to which he returns. Like the Apostles, we want to know where he is going, not to deduce therefrom whether this desired place suits us, but because we are certain that there only we shall find the secret of his love and the reason for his strangeness. Until we have seen where you were dwelling and whence you come, we shall follow you everywhere you lead us, we shall walk at your side and try to interpret the words which come from your lips. Where do you dwell, where is the house where you rest from your toil and labor? But, even more, who shares your intimacy in this retired place, who is he towards whom you step forward with gladness and with whom you hold converse openly? Who then is within your mystery, with whom do you dwell? Show us your Principle and the source of your wisdom. We ask nothing else of you, for you know well that it is for that alone that we have come to you.

Christ becomes the friend and brother who bears upon his shoulders our wretchedness and our sufferings, who is not indifferent to any of our cares. Far from seeking to lull to sleep the evil that has come upon us, he opens our wounds wide to let us know whence they have arisen. The interchange to which he invites us cannot stand the presence of a lie tacitly accepted. He never encourages us to feed on our sorrows and linger over the wounds we may have received, whereas all human friendship more or less stoops over itself to enclose misfortune in darkness. Christ comes and asks us to let the dead bury their dead, not to look back, since we have already put our hand to the plough, to draw straight the furrow which, with the help of his power, will lead us into the close presence of his Father. When, like the good Samaritan, he has poured over our troubles the oil of the Spirit, he invites us to rise and walk with him to Jerusalem. It is there that he wills to establish between him and us a relationship similar to the one he has with him who sent him.

If we experience a friendship with Christ open and pure to this extent, the reason is that he gives us nothing else but the eternal goodness he receives from his Father. You who were my servants, I make my friends, because I bestow on you the love with which I was loved from before the world began. More than this, the Father himself gathers you around me after having drawn you to him through me. He puts you with his Son, so that henceforward you form only one with me, as he himself is one with his Image. You are the companions who will never be able to separate from me for, having lived in the midst of you throughout the centuries, I shall assemble you together, I shall make you eat at my table, and together we shall share the same food and the same bread of tenderness.

Christ then becomes the Bridegroom, if it is possible to use this incredible word that he himself uttered. Each one of us must prepare for his coming like the virgin who awaits her affianced lover. An echo of the prophets who had already sung the espousals of Yahweh with Israel, John the Baptist presents himself as the friend who goes before the Beloved. The Kingdom is like a wedding-feast to which all men are invited, even—and above all—the halt, the lame and the blind. As to the end of time it will be marked by the definitive union of the Lamb and his Bride. This marriage, however, is not like ours, for it is from death that joy is spread over it. If the wedding of Cana is that of Christ and his Church, the unceasing flow of wine we drink at it is that of the blood shed on Calvary. Each Christian as he approaches the hour when there will no longer be any distance between the Word and the soul his bride, knows that he will have to be trodden down in the wine press of the Cross. But he also understands that Christ Jesus wishes to be followed right to Golgotha and to press us against his open heart, only to remain with us in the outpouring of love, as he himself remains eternally with his Father.

In the death of consummated love, there is no longer on the one hand the Word, its Principle and the bond between them, and on the other mankind. There are no longer on the one side the souls who in solitude tend to perfect union and on the other the Church without spot or wrinkle, adorned like a bride, for Christ who ascends anew to the summit of the Father's mercy, embraces every man and the whole universe in the Spirit of love. Already in the Gospel we can see Jesus on close terms with all things, like the Spirit who plays over the face of the earth. In every place and in all circumstances, he is he without whom nothing was made, he who knows things and beings, because he has formed them with his creative hands and maintains them in the sovereignty of his grace. Through individuals, however numerous and however close to God they may be, union cannot be attained. For this it is necessary that the love of Christ, at each moment, should appear in fullness on the Cross and that, his arms extended to the uttermost parts of the earth, Jesus should take hold of mankind and their history, to renew their youth with his gentleness and charity. Then each one can seek and find him in all things, since Lord, Pedagogue, Friend, Bridegroom, he is everywhere the new Man and the only-begotten Son.

Yet as long as we live the Gospel will remain an obscure book for us. The images which so profusely declare the power and glory of Christ to us continually veil him from our blind eyes. If they allow us to know and seek him, they do not give him to us as we should wish to find him. The nearer he makes himself, the more inaccessible he appears in his majesty. Lighting up our steps, his presence remains the impenetrable cloud which always seems to become thicker. This is doubtless good and we must desire no other torch than the very darkness of the night. When we finish the final page of the narrative in which Christ Jesus reveals himself, how are we to refrain from uttering this confession—God of light, thou art truly a hidden God.